Download Worksheets on Nolo.com

You can download the worksheets in this book at:

 www.nolo.com/back-of-book/EFFN.html

We'll also post updates whenever there's an important change to the law affecting this book—as well as articles and other related materials.

More Resources from Nolo.com

 Legal Forms, Books, & Software
Hundreds of do-it-yourself products—all written in plain English, approved, and updated by our in-house legal editors.

 Legal Articles
Get informed with thousands of free articles on everyday legal topics. Our articles are accurate, up to date, and reader friendly.

 Find a Lawyer
Want to talk to a lawyer? Use Nolo to find a lawyer who can help you with your case.

NOLO
LAW for ALL

5th Edition

Effective Fundraising for Nonprofits

Real-World Strategies That Work

Ilona Bray, J.D.

SIXTH EDITION	AUGUST 2019
Cover Design	SUSAN PUTNEY
Book Design	TERRI HEARSH
Proofreading	ROBERT WELLS
Index	UNGER INDEXING
Printing	BANG PRINTING

Names: Bray, Ilona M., 1962- author.
Title: Effective fundraising for nonprofits : real-world strategies that work / Ilona Bray, J.D.
Description: Sixth Edition. | Berkeley, CA : Nolo, [2019] | Revised edition of the author's Effective fundraising for nonprofits, [2016] | Includes index.
Identifiers: LCCN 2019006322 (print) | LCCN 2019007812 (ebook) | ISBN 9781413326642 (ebook) | ISBN 9781413326635 (pbk.)
Subjects: LCSH: Fund raising--United States. | Nonprofit organizations--United States--Finance.
Classification: LCC HG177.5.U6 (ebook) | LCC HG177.5.U6 B73 2019 (print) | DDC 658.15/224--dc23
LC record available at https://lccn.loc.gov/2019006322

This book covers only United States law, unless it specifically states otherwise.

Please note

We believe accurate, plain-English legal information should help you solve many of your own legal problems. But this text is not a substitute for personalized advice from a knowledgeable lawyer. If you want the help of a trained professional—and we'll always point out situations in which we think that's a good idea—consult an attorney licensed to practice in your state.

Dedication

To my mother, who showed me how commitment to a cause can help you accomplish things you never thought possible; and my father, who knows how to greet each new day with entrepreneurial optimism.

Acknowledgments

This book was envisioned as a collaborative effort, in which the voices of many nonprofit staff and experienced fundraising experts would be heard. Still, I was overwhelmed by the generosity with which the people named below offered their time, knowledge, and stories of successes as well as frustrations. You'll see many of their names and stories within the book—others preferred to play a more behind-the-scenes role. My deepest thanks to all of them for their contributions, and for keeping me inspired during the many months of pulling this book together. In addition, I'd like to thank the various organizations whose sample letters and printed materials you'll see throughout the book (not listed below).

Lauren Brown Adams, nonprofit fundraising/advancement consultant

Sophie Lei Aldrich, Global Development Centre at World Wildlife Fund

Bob Baldock, KPFA Radio

Randolph Belle, formerly of the East Bay Nonprofit Center

Linda Solow Bouwer, J.D., CFRE, CSU Maritime Academy

Robert Brenneman, Project Open Hand

Jennifer Castner, the Altai Project

Sarah Clark, formerly of San Francisco Girls Chorus

M. Eliza Dexter, formerly of Save The Bay (Oakland)

Grant Din, formerly of Angel Island Immigration Station Foundation

Laurie J. Earp, Earp Events and Fundraising

Lisa Ruth Elliott, formerly of Zen Hospice Project

Jan Etre, KPFA Radio

Judy Frankel, formerly of Project Open Hand

Lupe Gallegos-Diaz, Chicana Latino Student Development Office at UC Berkeley

Karen Garrison, formerly of Bernal Heights Neighborhood Center

Jennifer Gennari, consultant, formerly with Greenbelt Alliance

Leanne Grossman, writer, formerly of Global Fund for Women

Christine Grumm, consultant, formerly of the Women's Funding Network

Keven Guillory, KQED Radio

Sue Hall, Library Strategies

Pat Joseph, formerly of Sierra Club

Don Kiser, formerly of the Human Rights Campaign

Lynn Eve Komaromi, Berkeley Repertory Theatre

Greg Lassonde, Legacy Program Specialists

Marisa Lianggamphai, formerly of the World Institute on Disability

Harry Lin, formerly of KQED Radio

Jim Lynch, TechSoup Global

Sonja Mackenzie, former board co-president of WORLD

Marie-Noelle Marquis, formerly of Wildcare

Mike Maxwell, nonprofit professional

John M. McArdle, formerly of Project Open Hand, recently with Domino Effect Consulting

Kate McNulty, Asian Art Museum

Susan Messina, Iona Senior Services

Leemarie Mosca, Rosie's Place

Nick Parker, formerly of the California School Age Consortium

Peter Pearson, retired from The Friends of the Saint Paul Public Library

Ligia Peña, Greenpeace International

Sharon Rabichow, Save the Redwoods League

Angelina Ramsay, marketing professional

Peggy Rose, formerly of the San Francisco Mime Troupe

Ron Rowell, formerly of Common Counsel Foundation

Jim Schorr, formerly of Juma Ventures

Duane Silverstein, Seacology

Joseph Smooke, formerly of Bernal Heights Neighborhood Center

Anna Speck, Project Bread

Elizabeth Stampe, NRDC

Eric Talbert, MedShare

JoLynn Taylor, retired from Audubon California

David Thorpe, formerly of Housing Works

Jean Tom, Davis Wright Tremaine LLP, San Francisco

Krista Tuomi, American University

Anthony Tusler, Disability Resource Center, Sonoma State University

Amanda Vender, formerly of DAMAYAN

Mona Lisa Wallace, formerly of the East Bay Nonprofit Center

Anita Wetzel, Women's Studio Workshop

Debra and Rich Whitall

Lauren Williams

Jason Wilson, Share Our Strength

J.R. Yeager, CompassPoint

Audrey Yee, Esq., Golden Gate National Parks Conservancy

Many of my colleagues at Nolo also helped with the current and earlier editions of this book in important ways: **Marcia Stewart**, with early conceptualization and advice; **Stan Jacobsen**, with research; **Jake Warner**, whose first-draft edits incorporated his own extensive nonprofit as well as business experience; final editor **Lisa Guerin**, who took the manuscript up a notch with her wit and practical instincts; **Tomek Pilch**, for SEO tips; **Wendy Copley**, with technical advice on blogging; and the production folks, with all-important design and graphics help, including **Jaleh Doane, Emily Dunn, Susan Putney,** and **Toni Ihara**.

A final special "thank you" to **C.S.** and other friends, for ongoing support, and for apparently remembering my name even after many months of self-imposed hermitage.

About the Author

Ilona Bray has worked and volunteered with various nonprofit agencies in numerous capacities, including development director, staff attorney, department manager, advisory council member, and even dog walker. Bray is now a legal editor at Nolo and the author of other Nolo books, including *Becoming a U.S. Citizen* and *Nolo's Essential Guide to Buying Your First Home.*

Table of Contents

Appendix

Your Fundraising Companion

If you think you don't have time to read a book on fundraising, you're not alone. I've worked in some of the hardest-to-fund nonprofits around and fully appreciate that you may be reading this while simultaneously gulping down lunch and checking your email. But you probably know in your heart that when a person is too harried to learn to do fundraising right, mistakes and inefficiency are the inevitable result.

With all this in mind, I'm going to skip the traditional lectures on personal philosophy and fundraising history and get right to the heart of the matter: how this book will help you succeed as a fundraiser. It's an attempt to distill and assemble, in plain English, the most important things you need to know in order to do your fundraising job well (most likely as a development director or staff person, executive director, or board member). I won't be expounding new theories of nonprofit philosophy, or giving you touchy-feely ways of using Jungian symbols to contemplate your mission. (I've sat through too many meetings and retreats that did such things.)

Instead, I'll discuss how fundraising is being done, at its best, today. Gone are the days when a nonprofit could charm people with its desperation and grassroots inefficiencies. You'll learn how current technology, business savvy, and public attitudes toward nonprofits are shaping the fundraising environment. You'll get right into the nuts and bolts of how to plan your fundraising strategy, assemble the right people, technology, and other tools you'll need in order to maximize your returns, attract supporters, ask for gifts from individuals, businesses, and foundations, and much more.

Though this book will teach you the basics, it will also help you to think creatively. By understanding how other nonprofits are raising funds, you'll be better able to think up ways to outdo them or to see where you might bend the rules a bit. Throughout the chapters, you'll find stories from experienced development professionals—many of them at small, struggling nonprofits whose constraints may be similar to yours—who've employed interesting strategies to gain fundraising success.

The question is, how much of this book do you really need to read? Everyone should start with **Chapter 2**, which lays out all the tools you'll need for effective fundraising, including staffing, personal skills, and technology. Also take a look at **Chapter 11**, which explains how to bring visibility to your organization—and therefore potentially higher donations from all possible sources—through printed materials, the media, and your website.

After these, you can decide which additional chapters to refer to based on the types of fundraising your organization plans to engage in—choices you can make after reading **Chapter 3**, where you'll find instructions and worksheets that will help you create a fundraising plan that strategically uses your organization's existing strengths and assets.

Other chapters cover fundraising methods. I'll preview those chapters here, especially for those readers who may be new to the fundraising field or whose organizations are considering branching into new types of fundraising. Even if you don't use these methods now, many of the first-edition readers of this book report keeping it on their shelves for ongoing reference.

Chapter 4, Attracting Individual Supporters. The real, everyday people who believe in your organization should probably be its bread and butter. Their donations are a sign of community relevance and support and (conveniently for your organization) come with few strings attached. Yet many new fundraisers, as well as established organizations, come to rely too much on foundation grants, at the expense of paying attention to individual supporters. Read this chapter to learn how to reverse that trend and gain or expand your community support.

Chapter 5, How to Keep the Givers Giving. Your new supporters probably won't give very large gifts, and they're statistically likely to leave in a couple of years unless you take active steps to increase their interest in, and connection to, your organization. Read this chapter to learn how to analyze your donor base and further engage donors through personal contacts, appeal/renewal letters or emails and other communications, and invitations to volunteer at or attend other activities sponsored by your organization. Sample letters are included.

Chapter 6, Midscale and Major Donors. This chapter explains how to identify your most committed supporters and encourage them to give more. New fundraisers who have some anxiety about asking for major gifts will especially appreciate this chapter's gradual approach to building relationships between their organization and their potential major donors before popping the money question. It includes an extensive list of websites to help you do background research on prospective major donors.

Chapter 7, Funds From the Great Beyond: Bequests and Legacy Gifts. This final chapter on working with individual donors focuses on offering them alternative ways to give, namely through wills and living trusts. This chapter isn't appropriate for an organization whose existence is temporary or tenuous, because it involves planning around events that may take place far in the future (usually, a donor's death). However, the chapter will show how smaller, grassroots organizations can start programs to attract inheritance gifts without worrying about the more financially complex arrangements that some larger organizations are able to offer (such as charitable annuities). The chapter also provides plain-English explanations of these more complex arrangements, so you can plan your transition toward offering them.

Chapter 8, Special Events. There's almost no organization that won't put on a special event at some point in its existence, both because it's fun and because the simpler events, such as bake sales and garage sales, offer a quick way to raise money without much advance planning or experience. However, the bigger the party, the greater the chance that it will be a flop, financially and otherwise. This chapter explains how to choose an event that's most likely to be a success for your organization and how to maximize the fundraising potential of virtually every kind of special event, from auctions to walkathons. It includes budget worksheets that will help you make sure your event will bring in money.

Chapter 9, Raising Money Through Business or Sales Activities. If your bake sale went well, why not open a bakery? Thinking along these lines, many nonprofits have explored ways to make money through business activities, thereby reducing their reliance on foundations and the more limited donor—as opposed to consumer—pool. Unfortunately, enthusiasm has exceeded planning in many cases, and all too many nonprofit-run businesses have failed. Read this chapter to learn where others went wrong, how IRS requirements affect your business possibilities, and how to develop your own viable business idea, assess the competition and set appropriate prices, and launch your business in a gradual, low-risk way. Or, learn how to enter business at a less ambitious scale, such as through partnerships with existing businesses. This chapter includes a checklist that will help you identify a winning business idea.

Chapter 10, Seeking Grants From Foundations, Corporations, and Government. Nonprofits cannot live on grants alone, though many try. Nevertheless, grant funding, from foundations, corporations, and local or federal government sources, continues to have an important place in almost every nonprofit organization's budget. Such funding is especially good for jump-starting a new project or initiative. Read this chapter for tips on how to excite a foundation's interest in your organization before you start writing; how to fully address every important component of a grant proposal; and how to write in a voice whose clarity and passion wake up the overburdened reader at the other end. It includes worksheets for breaking down and comparing different grant possibilities and a sample query letter.

So, enough preliminaries. It's time to learn how you can raise more money for your group—and create the long-term relationships with your community, supporters, and foundations that lead to sustained fundraising success.

TIP
Look on the Nolo website for handy worksheets. Various worksheets and checklists are presented throughout this book. You'll find online versions at www.nolo.com; see the appendix for the exact link.

Fundraising Tools

An organization's fundraising office is often expected to perform feats of magic, sometimes with few more resources than the legendary pile of straw. But until your leader understands that success will depend, in large part, on investing in the people, resources, and technology necessary to do the job right, you'll be spinning your wheels. This means more than investing only in activities that will produce immediate results: A successful fundraising program must also budget for the long term, with plans for such things as donor recruitment, cultivation, stewardship, and acknowledgment. These will provide a solid foundation for the rest of your fundraising structure.

This chapter introduces the tools you'll need to create and execute a successful fundraising effort. The way you use these resources will depend on your group's size and experience, but most groups use some combination of them to raise money.

This chapter covers:

- how the position of each person in your organization—including volunteers and paid staff—can play a role in fundraising
- personal skills that any development professional will need to have or develop, and
- equipment and technology for fundraising, including computer and Web tools.

RESOURCE

Need help with legal tasks like incorporating your nonprofit? This book assumes that your organization has already taken care of some legal and tax basics—namely, forming a nonprofit corporation and successfully applying for 501(c)(3) tax-exempt status and any required state tax permits. In addition, most states require you to register with their attorney generals before soliciting funds within those states (even via the Internet!), and many states also require you to report on your fundraising expenditures and revenues. For step-by-step instructions on incorporating your nonprofit and applying for tax-exempt status, see *How to Form a Nonprofit Corporation* (national and California versions), by Anthony Mancuso (Nolo). Then check out *Nonprofit Fundraising Registration: Nolo's 50-State Digital Guide*, by Ronald J. Barrett and Stephen Fishman, J.D. (Nolo).

Fundraising People

In an ideal situation, your well-recognized and highly successful nonprofit would have a bustling staff of paid fundraising professionals, each with separate responsibilities and areas of expertise. More likely, however, you'll need to cobble together a mix of as many board members and other committed volunteers as you can recruit to the fundraising cause, hopefully with the assistance of one or more paid fundraising staffers.

The roles and functions of various fundraising positions are covered below, including how to involve and motivate your fundraising team. Especially during a nonprofit's early years, it's common for several people to wear two or more hats—your best fundraiser may also serve as your volunteer coordinator, your executive director, or even the president of your board of directors.

Those who might participate in your fundraising efforts include:

- the executive director
- the development director
- the board of directors
- an advisory council
- other paid development staff
- paid staff in nondevelopment roles
- other volunteers, and
- outside consultants.

> TIP
>
> **Track your own hours to find out your staffing needs.** If you have the chance to expand your development staff, you'll need to figure out what type of help will give you the most bang for your buck. The answer may be no further away than your own workday. Try keeping track of where each hour goes. Even quickly scribbling entries such as "9:30 to 11:00 planning meeting, 11:00 to 12:30 research" can reveal that you spend hours in ways you wouldn't have guessed. If, for example, you find that most of your time is spent on events planning, it might be worth contracting with an outside events planner rather than putting a new person on salary. Or, if most of your hours go toward clerical tasks, you might save some money by hiring a support staffer.

The Executive Director

Fundraising is, or should be, part of every executive director's (ED's) job description. This includes getting to know the organization's supporters, meeting individuals to solicit major gifts, interacting with staff at foundations, reviewing grant proposals, helping oversee special events, speaking at events, and more. Sounds like a lot of hours, doesn't it? And most EDs already have plenty on their plates concerning their organizations' missions, programs, and personnel. But any ED who doesn't somehow make the time for fundraising activities isn't fulfilling the job requirements, period.

 TIP

Former development directors can become great EDs. According to J.R. Yeager, a Bay Area nonprofit executive search consultant, "Many skilled, well-organized development directors are ready and well positioned to step into the role of ED, particularly with smaller nonprofits. Most smaller organizations truly need their ED to do much of the fundraising. As for the other parts of the ED's job, these can be supported (for example, the board treasurer and outside auditor can help with budgeting and financial matters) and ultimately learned as the new ED grows into the job."

The smaller your organization's staff, the more time your ED will need to spend on fundraising. But if your organization can afford to hire a development director, the ED might be tempted to delegate as many activities as possible to that person. This can be a mistake. To the outside world, the ED is the face of your organization, the person who (rightly or wrongly) is seen as having the fullest sense of how your organization's need for money intersects with its mission, goals, and day-to-day work. Whether you are pursuing a large grant or trying to coax a major donor to increase support, the ED is usually the best staff person to close the deal.

Fortunately, the ED won't be solely responsible for all or even most parts of the fundraising process. The ED should help solicit major gifts, for example, but need not be present for every gift request. Nor will the ED have to be involved in the day-to-day work of staying in close contact with donors. Your board and staff members may also participate, depending on who is being approached. And when it comes to grant applications, the

ED's role should be limited to reviewing proposals, not writing them. If you can afford a development director, grant writing and other behind-the-scenes tasks will be done by that person. If not, your organization may use board members and other volunteers, as well as paid consultants and freelance contractors, to do this day-to-day work.

On the other side of the coin, an ED must be willing and able to share fundraising tasks with other board and staff members, especially the development director. An ED who can't bear to part with these tasks, or won't trust others with them, can spell trouble for an organization's long-term survival. Over and over, one hears stories of a charismatic, successful ED who successfully grows a small nonprofit—but then continues to attempt to single-handedly raise all the money and lead the organization. Such EDs tend eventually to either burn out from overwork, neglect important tasks while trying to cope with too many others, or move on to another job, leaving the nonprofit with a huge leadership and fundraising void. J.R. Yeager of CompassPoint notes that, "The wise organization (no matter its size) engages in 'succession planning.' This means having an internal structure in place where a formal and clear line of succession, cross-training, and information sharing is planned in advance, so that a 'void' will not happen—or will at least be minimized if an organization's ED departs."

The Development Director

Perhaps you are the development director at your nonprofit, or perhaps you are a board member or an ED of a smaller organization that hasn't yet mustered up the funds to hire for this position. Although some small nonprofits that plan to stay small—let's say, Friends of the Rose Garden—find it practical to delegate fundraising to volunteers, most growing organizations need to hire a part- or full-time development director. (What salary can development directors command? Sources disagree, listing a median of anywhere between $48,000 and $107,000.)

Ideally, a full-time development director's role is to oversee all aspects of the fundraising process, including planning the fundraising strategy, gathering input from the board and ED, identifying potential funding sources, and ensuring smooth operation of fundraising activities. Typically, however, the development director's role also includes carrying out practically every other aspect of the fundraising program: writing appeals, acknowledgment and stewardship correspondence, and grant proposals; meeting with donors to solicit gifts; posting on social media sites; coordinating events; and more.

When this turns into busywork, it can prevent the development director from concentrating on important fundraising tasks. It will, therefore, be key to your group's long-term success to identify other people who can help take care of discrete or routine tasks.

A successful development director brings certain skills and abilities to your organization. Among the most important is good communication—in writing as well in person. You need a "people person"—someone who not only can express him- or herself, but also genuinely enjoys interacting with others. Remember, asking for money is just a small part of the greater —and often more fulfilling—process of building the nonprofit's relationship with donors.

Unfortunately, experienced and personable development directors are hard to find. There are more organizations seeking them than people up to the challenge. Those with an ounce of savvy won't hitch their wagons to organizations that are teetering on the edge of financial collapse, dealing with internal dissension, or experiencing other serious problems. Less-established organizations often have to compromise by, for example, sharing a development director with another (noncompetitive) organization, hiring someone who isn't fully qualified for the job, or hiring a part-time or assistant development director. Such a group usually gives the ED primary responsibility for fundraising.

TIP

A little recognition goes a long way. Smart EDs and board leaders know that a dedicated and effective development director may easily burn out. One way to prevent this is to make fundraising a high priority and encourage all key people to participate without whining. Another is to recognize the development director's hard work by thanking him or her, sincerely and in front of others, for jobs well done. Too often, recognition goes primarily to board members and volunteers, as if receiving a salary diminishes the value of the passion and energy the development director throws into a project. Don't make this mistake!

Board of Trustees

By law, every nonprofit must have a board of trustees (sometimes called a board of directors, a board of governors, or another similar term). This is usually a volunteer group of about 12 to 15 people, whose responsibilities include overseeing the organization and being accountable for its compliance with legal and other requirements.

Board members are not mere figureheads: If they neglect their duties and your organization is sued or collapses as a result, they can be held financially accountable. (Many boards buy insurance to guard against this type of liability.)

As a practical matter, a good board not only sets the direction of your programs, but will also help make fundraising an organizational priority and participate in it personally. To this end, it's a big help to have someone on the board with a thorough understanding of nonprofit budgeting and finance. There's little point in working hard to raise money if the board can't make sure that the organization is meeting its financial obligations and spending wisely.

Find Board Members Who Are Willing— And Able—To Raise Money

Unfortunately, there's often a wide gap between what nonprofits hope board members will do for them and how prospective board members envision their roles. In my earlier life as a corporate law associate, for example, my law firm employer encouraged me and my fellow associates to join nonprofit boards. The firm wanted us to get involved with the "community"—that is, with people whose incomes were high enough to hire lawyers—by any means necessary, and offered to help us get onto the board of just about any organization we wanted—the opera, the symphony, whatever. That sounded good to me: I envisioned myself sitting around a meeting table, mulling over a group's mission and giving sage advice. In short, like most novice board members, I was clueless. I not only had no idea about the depths of a board's responsibilities, I hadn't even considered that it might include plenty of time spent fundraising. Worse yet, I was only a few years out of law school, with little life experience beyond minimum wage summer jobs, so I was spectacularly ill-equipped for this role. (Luckily, I quit corporate law before inflicting myself on any boards.)

What lessons can be gleaned from my experience? Willing board members may be easier to find than you think, but:

- You must be selective to find the ones with the knowledge and experience you need.
- You need to be up front about your fundraising expectations.

Most board members serve terms of only three years, with one or more renewals allowed. Check your bylaws—and think about amending them if your board members can serve "life terms," and you've got a few who are running low on energy and ideas. (Or think about enforcing your bylaws if people are overstaying their prescribed welcome!) If your board members serve limited terms, you must build a process to incorporate new board members into the ongoing work of your organization.

Why would anyone voluntarily commit many hours per month to a demanding position, usually on top of work, family, and other responsibilities? A few board members are truly selfless—they live to help others. Some are newly retired, with an adequate income and time on their hands. Most are hard-working people genuinely interested in the cause, who hope that they'll be able to fit board responsibilities into their already-stretched schedules. Unfortunately, too many busy people turn out to be unrealistic in their hopes and end up unable to do much more than attend meetings (if that). Finally, there are the staff of corporate law and accounting firms and other companies that have a material interest in encouraging their employees to join boards. Even this category isn't all bad, especially if you can make use of their professional skills (but realize that nonprofit finance and law are specialty areas that your average accountant or lawyer will know nothing about).

No matter people's motivations, many of them will have trouble making the kind of long-term commitment that active board membership entails. Some nonprofits are thus rethinking how their boards are structured, perhaps paring them down to ten or fewer members, but asking these members to farm out work—including some fundraising—to committees. The committees may be composed of nonboard volunteers who can commit to the occasional sprint of activity—say, a donor campaign or a special event—but not to the marathon of full board membership.

Recruiting board members is a topic well covered in other places, so this book won't go into detail.

No matter what else they bring to the table, however, you must make sure that potential new board members have an interest in fundraising—and understand that this will be a substantial part of their role. Because there are so many ways to raise money, there's a role for any willing board member to play. You can help by preparing materials that excite potential board members' interest, such as a packet of items highlighting your organization's mission, fundraising activities, and accomplishments. Assemble a more extensive selection of such materials for purposes of training new board members.

Board Donations

Some organizations give prospective board members a very clear up-front understanding of their fundraising responsibilities, by asking them to commit to making a major financial contribution every year. You might require board members to contribute a set amount or base contributions on a sliding scale.

Asking board members for donations may seem odd—after all, they are already asked to give generously of their time, and now they're being told they have to pay dearly for the privilege. One reason for this practice is that board members will be much better at soliciting large gifts from others if they can say that they've given themselves. It demonstrates their commitment to the cause and their confidence that the donation will be well spent. Perhaps more importantly by now, potential donors—individuals as well as foundations—have learned to ask, "How much have board members given?" You might literally lose out on a grant opportunity because the foundation was unimpressed by your level of board giving.

For example, one environmental organization I know of not only specifically requires each board member to make a $10,000 donation as a condition of service, but also makes clear that each member's primary role will be fundraising. When the organization needs advice concerning the technical parts of its mission or activities, it turns to a separate advisory council, made up of scientists and other experts. This organization believes that policymaking and fundraising are the major roles of the board. Their experienced staff and advisers, they feel, are in the best position to know how the organization should be run. While there's merit to this approach, it also has a downside: If key staff members leave, or the organization faces another crisis or turning point, the board will not be well equipped to step in and provide continuity or plot a new course.

Of course, your organization will need to decide for itself—based in part on what kind of work you're doing and what community you serve—whether to solicit mostly affluent board members, or to ask for a particular monetary commitment. (For less-well-off board members, an alternative to the up-front donation might be to ask them to bring in an equivalent amount of money from a new donor or business.) For many community-based organizations or small advocacy groups, creating a financial requirement for entry could be just plain misguided. You might be lucky to have even a few affluent members. And the last thing you want is for representatives of a low-income community or dedicated former clients to be shut out. However, that doesn't mean you can't still ask a financially able board member to make a major gift.

Board Involvement in Fundraising Activities

Board members can help plan your fundraising program, spearhead or help carry out a special event, represent your organization in public, provide names of likely supporters, approach supporters for gifts, host house parties or other events, institute giving programs within their own workplaces, coordinate a new member drive, write personal letters, make phone calls thanking people for gifts, and much more. All of this will help take some weight off the shoulders of your in-house development staff. The wide variety of possible fundraising roles also allows board members who are reluctant to ask for major gifts to find a role behind the scenes.

Once board members become genuinely committed to your organization, they are more likely to stay interested and involved if you call on them for help on a regular basis. Performing minimal board activities—attending meetings and the occasional workshop, for example—can be less than soul satisfying.

Properly orchestrated, fundraising gets people out from behind the meeting table and into the community, where they can share what excites them about your organization. It also gives them a chance to enjoy the company of their fellow board members on a less formal basis, thus helping them form enduring friendships.

What If the Board Just Won't Fundraise?

Coping with board members who won't take the fundraising ball and run with it is a common concern. If you're a development staffer, it shouldn't be your responsibility to talk balky board members into helping raise money—this is the job of the board president or the chair of the development committee. However, because you're being judged by how much money you raise, you may find yourself with a vested interest in getting board participation. Here are some potential remedies:

- **Identify the board's strongest leaders.** Often, all it takes is one committed person on the board to inspire the others to put their shoulders to the wheel. For example, Grant Din, former executive director of San Francisco–based Asian Neighborhood Design (www.andnet.org), recalls, "We had one board member who was a development director at another nonprofit, which was perfect, because he could emphasize the importance of fundraising—and not have others tune him out the way they might if a staff member said the same thing. We also had another board member who really pushed for full participation by the board, and the two of them tried to create more of a giving-and-getting environment. As a board member for other nonprofits, I try to support the development staff by talking up the importance of board involvement in fundraising."

- **Make sure your board members understand and care about your organization's mission.** Some board members feel distant from the organization they serve. They may have joined the board for personal or career reasons rather than commitment to your cause. Will attending board meetings cure this? Not likely, if they consist of a superficial report by the ED and hours spent worrying about financial issues. But you can jazz up board meetings—for example, by bringing staff members to talk about what they're currently doing. Do some "show and tell"—sample projects, art works by clients, videos, testimonials by local activists, or anything else that might rev up the board and get them to do something more than just sitting back and voting. Also try moving fundraising higher on the meeting agenda (it's often left until the end). And serve food!

- **Enlist an outside voice.** Consultants are available to address a board meeting, lead a board retreat, and more. (Ask colleagues at other nonprofits to recommend a good one.) Or, you might arrange a webinar through the Grassroots Institute for Fundraising Training; see www.grassrootsfundraising.org.

RESOURCE

Need more information? For more on recruiting, structuring, and developing a strong, dynamic board, see:

- *Boards on Fire! Inspiring Leaders to Raise Money Joyfully*, by Susan Howlett (Perfect Paperback)
- *BoardSource*, a membership-based group that offers consulting, training, and various publications, at www.BoardSource.org, and
- *The Truth About What Nonprofit Boards Want*, by June J. Bradham (Wiley).

Advisory Council

A nonprofit isn't required to have an advisory council (or board or committee), but there are many good reasons to establish one. Such a group's responsibilities include little more than—as the name suggests—offering advice and input on what the nonprofit is or should be doing. Members might be experts in a certain field, represent a community you'd like information from, be well known, or be past staff or board members whose experience you don't want to lose—but who aren't able to commit to board membership.

For fundraising purposes, your advisory council can be a source of additional friends. At a minimum, members' names should be added to your mailing lists.

Their quasi-ceremonial role makes them particularly well suited to special events—you might call on them to buy seats, sell tickets to friends, greet arriving guests, make speeches, and more.

As the advisory council members develop an increased sense of connection to your organization, you may be able to solicit them for major gifts. They may even be willing to put in some short-term volunteer time on fundraising activities.

When it comes to the famous folk, your expectations of their actual participation should be minimal. You might be content for them to lend nothing more than their name, so that it appears anyplace that you list people associated with the organization—perhaps on your letterhead, website, and newsletter. Your cause gains credibility, and the person named enhances his or her reputation by appearing to be caring and compassionate. If such people actually show up for your meetings, it's a bonus.

Other Paid Development Staff

Although there's always pressure to run a lean development office (so as to minimize the percentage of the organization's money spent on fundraising), penny-pinching isn't always a good thing. If your potential donor pool is large enough, you may actually become more efficient at raising money by hiring more people.

A first priority is usually to hire a "development assistant," to handle the mail, enter names and other information on supporters into your database, check emails, prepare and mail thank-you letters, and handle other day-to-day tasks. Obviously, these chores could also be handled by a dedicated volunteer or another clerical person in your office, but the person will need sufficient oversight to make sure that the tasks get done on time and that the paperwork doesn't get jumbled with other matters unrelated to fundraising.

A midsize organization may be able to afford a three-person department, adding a "development associate" to the mix. This is typically someone at a junior professional level, who works side by side with the development director, handling similar but less critical tasks. The associate would also have less responsibility for fundraising planning and dealing with key donors, and would be presumed to be "in training" for a director role.

Larger organizations often split fundraising tasks into subject areas, assigning a development officer to each. For example, care and feeding of major donors might be assigned to one person, while another handles grant proposals. A few nonprofits, such as universities, have development officers who spend much of their time just researching funding prospects.

Paid Staff in Nondevelopment Roles

A truly successful fundraising office will always be in close communication with and able to call on program staff as needed. For starters, you want program people to keep your office informed about what they're doing, supplying you with interesting stories (and photos) to illustrate the important work donors are funding.

As a development staffer, much of your job is to explain the importance and success of your organization's work to the outside world. But simply repeating your mission ad nauseam is not going to bring in donations. You need details—colorful, lively stories of difficult situations that your organization confronted and hopefully helped to overcome, for presentation in your appeal letters, newsletter, Facebook page, and more. Here are some examples of compelling stories from my own days as an immigration attorney at a nonprofit:

- a father who literally got off his deathbed to take the citizenship exam and thereby ensure faster immigration for his children
- a Somali youth who was beaten in intertribal violence and who was desperate to get through the immigration process fast in order to go search for his missing mother, and
- a Guatemalan who'd watched his entire village massacred by the army only to have an unsympathetic immigration judge deny his case because conditions had supposedly "improved" in Guatemala.

Because all of these stories so graphically illustrated the important work our group was doing, they were good material to communicate to potential donors—but not all of them saw the light of day. Unfortunately, because few nonprofits foster communication between program and fundraising staff, program staff members don't even recognize their crucial role in the fundraising process. They may resent being asked to weigh down their schedules or dirty their hands with the business of fundraising.

If this is your situation, try gentle persuasion rather than a frustrated lecture. Take a few key staff members to lunch, ask them about what they're doing, and find out what fascinates—or frustrates—them about their work. This information will give you a fuller sense of what your organization does beyond its mission statement, and what challenges it faces day to day. Don't finish dessert without explaining how you communicate with key donors and funders who are likely to give more if they understand why your group's current work is so important.

How Share Our Strength Gathers Its Stories

Between needing content for its fundraising appeals, website, email updates, and several bloggers, Share Our Strength and its No Kid Hungry Campaign are, well, hungry for regular information from program staff. How else will its communicators find out about things like the volunteer who drives around in a non-air-conditioned truck to deliver summer meals to hungry children, or the mother who declared that, thanks to the Cooking Matters class, she could triple the value of her WIC check?

Opening the channels of communication wasn't something that happened by accident, however. As Jason Wilson, Director of Digital Communications explains, "We've deliberately created a culture of storytelling within our organization. This involved bringing in three new people who focus on storytelling—called the Impact Communications Team—as well as identifying key stakeholders throughout the organization who are also responsible for sharing stories. We ask everyone to set aside time to find the stories that represent the impact we're having, and then to connect with the Impact Communications Team, who are putting this information together for the Web or other materials.

"We've seen the effect of this storytelling culture, and the more that people began to see their stories presented—perhaps in an email campaign or as online content—the more they realized the double satisfaction in not only accomplishing something through their day-to-day work, but also through the telling of that story.

"There's no set schedule for sharing—either the staff will pass news along, or the people in charge of content may approach them with questions like, 'We're looking for stories about X, what do you have to share?'

"An effort like this really needs to be organization-wide, and involve accountability. For our team members, storytelling is a formal part of their performance goals."

When you later use information a staffer gave you, be sure to show the staffer the appeal letter, or tell him or her about your successful meeting with a supporter or foundation officer. Some development professionals distribute brief emails or memos to staff describing recent fundraising efforts and successes, or post the classic thermometer to show progress toward a fundraising goal. Though you can do most of this casually and quickly, it's got a name—internal marketing. And it's a valuable tool for getting people within your organization to see how, by working closely with you, they can benefit through increased funding and recognition for their work.

Your next step may be to request something more systematic from staff members. For example, you could ask program staff to write up regular reports on their activities. Asking program staff members to take photographs or videos of their work is also a great way to get them involved.

> **CAUTION**
>
> **Go light on the disaster shots.** Although evocative photos of grieving family members and emaciated victims are undoubtedly moving and can be of some use in fundraising, upbeat pictures showing your successes are usually even more effective. For example, a photo of the new buds of a nearly extinct flower that your group helped preserve will be far more powerful than a photo of the cracked cement that previously covered its habitat.

If your organization holds staff meetings, make sure all development staff attend. If you're a development staffperson, this will give you a chance not only to keep abreast of what's happening, but also to give a regular report on the fundraising office's activities. Such reports should include more than dry numbers, but also convey your hopes, challenges, and disappointments.

Staff meetings can also provide a convenient forum for holding a general fundraising training. Such trainings can cover basic issues like the importance of developing an extensive list of supporters, how staff can help contribute names, how they and their clients can help represent the organization on their Facebook pages or at special events or meetings with funders, and what your organization's strategic plans are for the future, fundraising plans included. Also encourage brainstorming about fundraising. A staffer may have the next great idea for bringing in support.

As program staff hopefully get more attuned to the symbiotic relationship between themselves and your fundraising staff, you'll want to encourage the more charismatic ones to help you with occasional, specific fundraising activities—for example, participating in an important presentation to a potential major supporter or a foundation or writing or editing a portion of a grant proposal. A staff member who works directly with clients or issues is often the most eloquent and credible person to explain your nonprofit's work to the outside world.

Other Volunteers

Many nonprofits begin their lives with an all-volunteer fundraising effort, often led—initially, at least—by a few dedicated board members. Even some established organizations rely heavily on volunteer participation or have more volunteers than paid staff. (Americans volunteer around eight billion hours every year.)

The development office is certainly one place where volunteers can be useful, whether for ongoing office support or for labor-intensive, one-time projects, such as mailings or telethons. No matter what role they play, however, they reduce your need to raise money to pay salaries.

You can advertise volunteer opportunities in your written materials, work with local volunteer placement organizations or online matching services, and check with local colleges and schools, some of which require students to perform community service as part of their curriculum. (See "Online Volunteer Matching Organizations," below.)

What's far more difficult is keeping volunteers around for more than a day or two and managing them effectively. If you're going to inspire volunteers to provide you with meaningful free service over the long term, you must:

- Understand and respect people's motives for volunteering.
- Train volunteers well and ask for a specific commitment.
- Make volunteering as convenient as possible.
- Find ways to allow volunteers to have fun.
- Show your appreciation early and often.

TIP

Big businesses may offer their paid staff as volunteers. While they don't get a tax deduction for these contributions, businesses do get goodwill, an opportunity for employee bonding, and an investment in a more economically stable community. Your best bet is to approach businesses that are geographically near to your organization, especially ones patronized by your staff or clients. Be ready to point out how, through your newsletter or other means, you'll publicly recognize their businesses' contributions.

Cater to Volunteers' Motives

Most people who agree to volunteer for your organization will be drawn to your cause, intellectually or emotionally. But of equal importance to many is the chance to meet new people, develop skills, and feel needed. If a volunteer shows up full of energy and enthusiasm, and you ask that volunteer to photocopy stacks of reply cards for hours, you may never see him or her again.

This can be a hard lesson to learn. After all, the photocopying is crying out to be done, and you don't have the time to create work that will keep every new, inexperienced volunteer happy. But many organizations rely too heavily on their volunteers for thankless tasks, only to find that their volunteers don't stick around for long. And, at a deeper level, being involved in a grassroots, community effort should allow you to make a little room for the community to participate meaningfully.

If you're a development staffer, some, much, or even all the work of recruiting volunteers may fall to you. This makes some sense—your mailings and publicity may ask for donations of time as well as money. You'll soon realize that this is one of those tasks that can turn into a full-time job. If your organization really does plan to rely on volunteers in a big way, you might want to create the position of volunteer coordinator. Because foundations are always interested in leveraging their grant money into maximum results, you may be able to attract the financial support necessary to make this a paid position. Or, if you find a person with lots of energy, time, and savvy, you may find yourself in the happy position of having someone volunteer to be your volunteer coordinator.

Online Volunteer Matching Organizations

Various programs match or recruit and place volunteers with nonprofits, especially online. Such volunteers might be useful in your development office or to substitute for paid positions in other parts of your organization. Some national sites worth looking into include:

- **Idealist, at www.idealist.org.** Nonprofits can enter their own profile and post events and volunteer opportunities.
- **Jesuit Volunteer Corps, at www.jesuitvolunteers.org.** The JVC's long-term volunteers, mostly recent college grads, accept one- or two-year placements where they can provide direct services to economically poor or socially marginalized people. (Your organization doesn't have to be Catholic or religious to use JVC volunteers.) Your organization pays for screening and placement fees and daily transportation.
- **Points of Light, at www.pointsoflight.org,** helps nonprofits find and use volunteers.
- **Taproot Foundation, at www.taprootfoundation.org.** This organization's pro bono project finds skilled professional volunteers to provide nonprofits with consultation or help for a short project.
- **Volunteer Match, at www.volunteermatch.org.** This site is one of the largest online networks of nonprofits recruiting volunteers.

Fortunately, there are a number of relatively simple ways to satisfy volunteers' needs and interests. Asking them at the outset what they'd like to get from their experience is a good way to start! But be prepared to talk with them individually (or to save time, in small groups) about what you can and can't involve them in. Emphasize that volunteers are most likely to construct useful, fulfilling roles with the organization if they commit to sticking around long enough to allow you to help each of them find a good fit.

Another great approach, if you have regular volunteers, is to try to schedule them so that they overlap and can talk with each other. Especially if your organization uses volunteers in nondevelopment roles, arrange for volunteers to split their time between the development office and other work, for variety's sake.

To help with development tasks, you might capitalize on the fact that some volunteers are primarily interested in learning high-level job skills—writing or marketing, for example—and might be interested in interning with your office for an extended time period.

Volunteer Training and Commitment

A formal training process, in which you explain the work of the organization and the volunteer's place in it, will make the experience more satisfactory for all concerned. If the volunteer is willing to help in the development office, briefly go over the annual budget and the fundraising plan. Explain the importance of seemingly mundane tasks such as writing thank-you letters or entering data. Discuss what you normally expect volunteers to do, and what more interesting tasks they might "graduate" to after proven good work. You might also want to create a volunteer manual, something like an employee manual, explaining:

- what you expect of volunteers (in terms of hours, calling when they'll be late or absent, and the like)
- your commitment to making the volunteer experience a positive opportunity for community involvement, and
- basic office policies, such as personal use of the phones and photocopiers.

Unless you are recruiting the volunteer for a one-time effort, ask for a commitment to a certain number of hours per week or month. Be prepared to make this flexible, however. The number of people who work traditional 9-to-5 jobs is declining. Your best source of daytime volunteers may be freelancers who have spare time—but not always at the same time each week.

Be ready to provide feedback on how your volunteers are doing: constructive criticism as well as positive reinforcement. Volunteers who are trying to develop job skills, or will eventually ask you to serve as a reference, need to know how they are really doing. Your feedback will be taken best if you tell the volunteer during the initial training that you'll periodically sit down for a performance review—and if you make clear that the volunteer will then have a chance to give you feedback on the volunteer experience and what would make it better.

Make Volunteering Convenient

If the very mechanics of volunteering for your office are difficult—for example, if the volunteer has to call someone on your staff who's hard to reach—it creates another reason for the volunteer to drop the obligation.

Let's look at how a school literacy program in Oakland developed a volunteer program that's convenient for all concerned. The program is in a public school, in an area with numerous senior care centers. Seniors and others are encouraged to spend one hour a week reading to schoolchildren. No experience is required. To participate, they simply call one of the volunteer coordinators and say they'll be there that week. The coordinators prefer it if the volunteers can make a long-term commitment, but it's not required. For weeks when the program is short on volunteers, it has a list of backup people to call. And, to make sure the program doesn't become too much of a burden for any of the volunteer coordinators, each of them is in charge of managing one day a week.

This literacy program has run smoothly—and succeeded in boosting the children's interest in reading. It creates a system in which no one feels overwhelmed by the amount of work, and people with more or fewer hours to spend can commit accordingly. It also has the virtue that volunteers perform the same task every time, to reduce the amount of oversight needed. This won't always be possible in your office, but it's something to bear in mind.

TIP

Do they really need to come into your office? Online volunteering is perfect for people who have just enough time to sit down at their computer. And you can recruit for such volunteers nationally.

Make Volunteering Fun

Although you don't have to make it a party for volunteers, they won't come back unless they can share in some way in your organization's sense of purpose. One of the most common requests volunteers make is to work directly with the people (or plants, animals, or environment) being served. If they're working in the development office, that won't always be possible.

However, there are other activities that will allow them to work with the public, including:

- canvassing
- asking local businesses for raffle donations
- calling donors to express thanks, and
- participating in telethons.

! CAUTION
Your volunteers are the face of your organization. Be choosy about who you let interact with the public on behalf of your group. If the only human contact a supporter has with your organization is a grouchy high schooler doing mandatory volunteer service and not well-versed in your program, you'll turn the supporter off. (Not that all high school kids are grouchy—some of them are developing interests in community service that will last a lifetime, so giving them interesting and appropriate volunteer tasks is a community service in itself.)

Show Appreciation

Every volunteer wants to know that he or she is making a difference and advancing the cause, so say thank you early and often. For example, I fondly remember volunteering for a school garden tour committee that hardly ever let me walk out empty-handed—I was given a school T-shirt, a pair of gardening gloves, a poster from last year's tour, tomato seeds, and more. I was momentarily embarrassed by their generosity, but I got the message—they appreciated the help. And, most important from the school's point of view, I kept going back to do more.

Try also to plan some organized volunteer appreciation activities: holding an annual volunteer party, for example, or inviting volunteers to your nonprofit's other events, such as a gala or lecture. Don't forget to take advantage of a well-attended occasion by giving a little speech about how much particular volunteers have done for your organization—which you can accompany with awards or certificates.

Outside Consultants and Contractors

To supplement your salaried development staff, it can be useful to hire consultants and contractors. Be warned, however—the hourly rates of well-established writers, designers, accountants, and others may dwarf your own salary. But independent contractors start to look more affordable when you realize that you don't pay for their health insurance or office space, and you don't have to find a way to pay their salaries year-round. You can assign them to a limited task and tightly control the hours they spend.

Consultants and contractors are probably available in your area for just about every task a development office does, from grant writing to direct mailings to individual solicitations to leading board seminars or retreats. Ask other nonprofits for recommendations.

While outside workers can provide valuable expertise and take the pressure off when deadlines loom, you'll want to avoid three common problems. First, make sure you remain the "boss" in this relationship, and don't end up unsuccessfully trying to manage an opinionated and balky consultant. Second, carefully define in advance exactly what the contractor will do on your behalf, when the job will be completed, and how much it will cost. Third, be sure that the services to be completed according to the contract are ethical, honest, and follow fundraising approaches with which you are comfortable.

You've probably heard of scandals where hired fundraisers go out and solicit money (by telephone, for example), then take a healthy chunk for their own salaries and "costs" before turning the remainder over to the nonprofit. Although the nonprofit isn't directly at fault for depriving donors of money that doesn't go where they thought it would, the nonprofit won't emerge unscathed from any resulting negative publicity.

In addition, some states' laws address nonprofits' use of professional fundraisers, for example, by requiring the fundraisers to disclose their status to the people being asked to donate. Whatever you do, don't hire outside contractors on a commission basis—that is widely viewed as unethical and, in some states, is even illegal.

Can You Pitch Your Nonprofit in the Space of an Elevator Ride?

As part of your personal skill building, it's important to be able to quickly engage others about what your organization does, and why it's important. According to Mona Lisa Wallace, an attorney and nonprofit expert, "It's amazing how even some established organizations can't describe what they do—I'll hear vague statements like, 'We're sort of a homeless organization.' But what people really want to hear is who and where your organization is, what you're all about, where you're heading, and how you plan to get there. So, for example, a good elevator pitch might be, 'Our homeless-families support network provides temporary housing and support services to parents and children with no place to go. We help them get back on their feet and find a stable, long-term home. We may never be able to eliminate homelessness altogether, but we're going to keep trying to reduce it, one family at a time.'"

Oakland nonprofit management expert Randolph Belle recommends taking out a stopwatch, and practicing saying what you need to in 30 seconds or less. He suggests practicing succinct answers to follow-up questions, such as:

- "What would you do with $10,000?"
- "Tell me about the needs of your constituency."
- "Who are the other service providers in your field and what makes you special?"
- "Tell me about the composition of your board of directors."
- "What made you get into this field?"

CAUTION

Don't inadvertently turn a contractor into an employee. If you treat contractors or consultants like employees (by requiring them to keep regular office hours and closely supervising them, for example), you're headed for legal trouble. The IRS, as well as state tax and employment authorities, may claim that you should have paid the same taxes and benefits as you would for ordinary employees. For easy-to-access, free information about the legal differences between employees and contractors, see the independent contractor materials on Nolo's website at www.nolo.com. For more detailed information, including a wide selection of sample contracts, see *Working With Independent Contractors*, by Stephen Fishman (Nolo).

Fundraising Skills

This section briefly covers the most important personal characteristics and skills a good fundraiser needs. Of course, there's no one perfect way to raise money—a variety of approaches and styles can work well, depending on your audience, personality, and so forth. Some of these skills may be hard to develop if you weren't born with them, so be patient with yourself, and concentrate on bringing out the things you do best. Of particular importance are:

- interpersonal skills, and
- writing ability.

Interest in Other People

You've probably heard the saying that "people give to people, not to causes." While that may be a bit of an exaggeration, the key takeaway is that a fundraiser's ability to relate positively to his or her fellow human beings is crucial to long-term success. Unless your fundraising office has so many staffers that a few can sit in the back room and write grants all day, everyone should enjoy the idea of interacting with outsiders, be they donors, foundation funders, board members, or others.

If you're interviewing a prospective new development staffer, and the consensus is, "We're not crazy about his personality, but he's smart, writes well, and knows our work," proceed with extreme caution. Your supporters and funders may have the same tepid reaction.

Networking with other fundraisers is also an important part of this job. It's worthwhile for development professionals to join national or local groups such as the Association of Fundraising Professionals (www.afpnet.org).

Writing Ability

The ability to write effectively plays an important role in nearly every aspect of fundraising, whether it's drafting a thank-you letter, an email appeal, or a grant proposal.

Here are my top five tips for effective writing:

- **Write like you talk.** Or better yet, write like you're on the phone with your Aunt Millie, who's a little deaf and wishes you'd get to the point. Too many people think that using long words and convoluted sentences makes them sound professional and authoritative. They're wrong. Turn your writing into a conversation with the reader. Reading your written work aloud is a good way to put it to the test. If the voice you hear doesn't sound friendly, straightforward, and passionate about the cause, try again.

- **Find out what makes your own writing flow.** With all due respect to high school writing teachers, many of them propounded rules that can hinder your subconscious writer—like the one about creating an exhaustive outline before setting pen to paper. I know many excellent writers who simply can't write that way—people who instead begin by writing in bursts, only later weaving them together to discover a structure. In short, if you have your own style of getting your thoughts out, go with it.

- **Be your own editor.** No one I know can produce a finished writing job in fewer than three drafts, and important tasks often take far more. So, when you are finished writing something, read it over with a critical eye. Look for issues like:

  - **overlong sentences.** Any sentence that runs on for more than two lines can probably be chopped.

  - **boring or extraneous words.** Eliminate every word that's not necessary to the sentence. See whether a tired word can be replaced with a more expressive alternative. For example, instead of using "difficult" three times in a paragraph, try "thorny," "obstinate," or "tough." Give your thesaurus a workout.

  - **potentially misleading word order.** We all love to laugh at signs that say "Half Baked Chicken, $7.99!"—but some of your supporters may be less amused if you announce that "Volunteers help burn victim's family."

  - **passive voice.** The passive voice is well named; it sounds as if the writer wearied of the cause long ago. Just say "no" to phrases like "it is of concern that" and "a donation of $xx was received." Instead, use active statements that explain who did what, like "our counselors are worried that" and "the Family Foundation generously donated $xx."

- **Never, ever send anything out without a final read through.** Mistakes and typos can lurk in any document—even one that's been read a dozen times. Ask someone you trust to give your written work a careful going over. Also, if you can, put every document aside for a few hours or days before you finalize it. You'll be amazed at what pops out at you—or what new inspirations arise—with a fresh reading.
- **Lose the lingo.** After you've written a few grant proposals and attended some United Way trainings, your head will be full of terms like "outcomes," "mission statement," and "service-driven." And your organization's own area of expertise is probably jargon laden, too. Learn the jargon and use it when funders or others won't be happy hearing any other terms—but don't let it take over your entire vocabulary. Even funders fall asleep when they read too much jargony stuff.

Fundraising Equipment and Technology

Though good equipment can be pricey, the inefficiencies that result from trying to raise money with tools and technology from the horse-and-buggy era will cost far more. Of particular importance are:

- adequate office space and equipment
- a donor database, and
- credit card capabilities.

Office Space and Equipment

If you're a development director or other high-level development staff-person, it should go without saying that you need a private office, a desk, and a phone to do effective fundraising work. You'll be placing important and sensitive phone calls to supporters and funders, so you'll need quiet and privacy and ideally a landline, for reasons of sound quality and security.

Preparing proposals and mailings are also tasks for which you need adequate space to collect and organize your documents. For example, if you ever have to prepare a grant proposal for the federal government, you may end up with a five-inch-high stack of forms, reports, statistics, and more. If you don't have enough room to sort and organize your paperwork, you might lose track of important documents or leave something out.

TIP

Make sure you're reachable. Put yourself in the shoes of a major donor or foundation officer who is trying to reach you. Can the caller find your number online, and make his or her way through your reception or voicemail system quickly and easily? What if the caller doesn't know or can't remember your last name or your direct line or extension number?

As Lynn Eve Komaromi of Berkeley Repertory Theatre says, "I've had people call me at 10 p.m. on New Year's Eve because they needed to be walked through how to donate on our website. I'm okay with being available in this way—it's important for the theatre, after all, and I've come to consider many of our donors as personal friends—but I don't ask it of less-senior staff members."

Donor and Finance Database

A high-quality database that keeps track of individual donors' names, other information, and gifts can be one of the best investments your organization makes. If you're still working with a homemade database that only you know how to use, lose it now.

New databases are getting progressively faster, cheaper, and easier to use. They offer wonderful opportunities to segment donors into categories for special attention, send mass mailings, and produce reports showing patterns you might never have dreamed of. They can also save you huge amounts of time—a mailing list that might take you two weeks to put together by hand can be generated in 15 minutes or less using a database.

TIP

Get free advice or even funding for your investment in a database. A funder may be willing to offer a grant toward this. Or some organizations may help you locate free or discounted software, such as:

- **Idealware,** at www.idealware.org, with many articles on donor management systems, and
- **TechSoup,** offering free and discounted software to nonprofits, at www.techsoup.org.

Get Your Donor Records in Order First

A database is only as good as the information that goes into it. Whether you are two days or two years away from getting a sleek new database, now is the time to make sure you won't be feeding it garbage. In her work as a database management consultant, Lauren Williams has seen it all in terms of donor record quality—including organizations whose records were in such poor shape that she had to reconstruct donor information from Christmas cards and bank accounts. Lauren offers the following tips for a grassroots organization still working its way toward a database:

- **Keep every last scrap of paper.** "If your office is still very low tech, it's safest not to throw out anything relevant to your donors, because you never know what you'll need later."
- **Write a date on everything.** "For example, if you've got someone's business card, but no one remembers having received it, it doesn't do much good unless a written date shows you how recent it is."
- **Write down your sources for information.** "For example, if your files contain a scrap of paper saying 'Donor may be opening a new business—partnership possibilities?' but the scrap doesn't say who mentioned the possible new business or who took the notes, it won't do your records much good a year or two later."
- **Write down the context in which you gathered information.** "For example, with a business card, don't just date it and sign it; write down the circumstances in which you received the card, and a note about the conversation you had with the person. A collection of thousands of names and addresses, each without context, is useless."

There are literally dozens of online programs available to handle your supporter database (and other technology needs).

If possible, team up with your accounting staff when investigating databases and setting up your website. Many packages include accounting functions (thereby ensuring that donor gifts are tracked smoothly from the mailbox to the bank) and can handle the credit card portion of your website. In any case, make sure any service you choose will interface easily with your other information systems.

Instead of driving yourself crazy with research, talk to your colleagues at other nonprofits. As M. Eliza Dexter, former development director of Oakland, California–based Save The Bay, says, "The smartest thing we did when choosing a database was to call around, ask what others are using, and ask what they've been disappointed in." You might even visit other offices and watch how they use their database—see if you can intuitively understand how they move between screens and whether the visual layout appeals to you. Also ask your colleagues how much they're actually taking advantage of the various bells and whistles—many software packages promise a world of reports, tracking features, and more, but users find the features too hard to use or irrelevant to the organization's needs. (That's why you shouldn't let your tech geek choose the software!)

Once you've got some recommendations, look closer at:

- cost
- what's included
- possibilities for customization
- record capacity
- training
- ongoing technical support
- the company's future
- ease of use, and
- upgrade frequency.

 CAUTION

Pay careful attention to the database's available security measures—and use them. The accuracy of your data is critical—so protecting it from accidental deletions or alterations, perhaps by inexperienced users, should be a first priority.

Service-Tracking Database

In addition to the donor database described above, you'll also want to consider a database that collects information on your outcomes or provision of services. Why is this a fundraising issue? Because your organization will have to send detailed reports to foundations and others on how their money was spent. If you're a development director or another development professional, it will likely be your job to review these reports. And if they're not up to snuff, you're obviously going to have a tough time approaching the same funder for more support next year.

Unfortunately, advancements in data collection software tend to lag behind donor software. This is in large part because the developers who profit by creating standardized software find that service provision is anything but standard. Even among nonprofits providing the same type of service—for instance, shelters for the homeless—one shelter might be accustomed to measuring success based on the number of beds filled, while another might measure the number of hours spent housing or counseling each client. In fact, many software companies throw up their hands, leaving nonprofits to try to develop their own databases.

Again, talk to colleagues at similar organizations, and find or develop a database that makes tracking and reporting simple and accurate.

Online Donation and Credit Card Capabilities

One of the mantras of every fundraiser should be, "Make it easy for supporters to give." To this end, allowing people to donate—or make recurring donations—online or by credit or debit card can be crucial. Fortunately, various providers have made it easier than ever for nonprofits to handle this.

You can approach banks or a third-party provider such as Stripe or PayPal. You'll be seeking to either open a "merchant banking account" or, with a service like PayPal, to have a third-party merchant accept payments on your behalf.

Various services are geared especially for nonprofits, such as DonateNow. And if you decide to invest in a fundraising management product, it will likely come with payment processing capabilities.

You'll likely have to pay a start-up fee, a monthly or an annual fee, and a charge per transaction (flat fee and/or percentage). You may also need to buy hardware letting you swipe credit cards, at least on a mobile device for use when interacting with donors in person.

Shop around for an intermediary that charges low fees and whose overall fee structure isn't so complicated that you find yourself paying high fees without knowing what you did "wrong." It's possible to find ones that waive some of the fees, or return a portion of the percentage normally charged, in recognition of your nonprofit status.

Developing Your Fundraising Plan

Every worthwhile endeavor starts with a plan, and your annual fundraising efforts should be no exception. If I could give you a simple formula, such as "spend ____% of your time proposal writing, ____% on donors, and the rest on special events and planned giving in order to raise $____," I certainly would. But, because every nonprofit has its own strengths and unique position within the community it serves, no such generic fundraising plan exists. It's up to you to create your plan, based on the work you need to accomplish and the financial support you can reasonably hope to attract.

It's okay if you've been operating for a while without a plan—it often makes sense for a new group to focus on the cause first and the funds second. Still, no matter how busy you are now, it's absolutely crucial to reaffirm what works and rethink what doesn't, set goals, and commit to keeping an eye on the big picture.

This will be different than the other types of planning that your nonprofit (hopefully) engages in—strategic planning and program planning, in particular. Every organization needs to make time to plan —and dream—without always viewing things through the lens of, "But how are we going to pay for this tomorrow?"

But as far as figuring out how you'll pay for it, here are the key tasks you'll have to tackle to create your fundraising plan for the next one to five years:

- Determine a reasonable dollar goal to work toward.
- Evaluate your organization's greatest fundraising assets.
- Create a strategy that uses these assets to most effectively reach potential funding sources.
- Write down your strategy in a short, easy-to-understand document to keep everyone on plan in the future.

What Is Strategic Planning?

Done right, a strategic planning process should include researching, collecting community input, and coming to decisions about:

- the current concerns—and needs—of the community you serve
- whether your organization's original mission is still relevant and appropriate or needs to be modified
- whether your programs, products, or policies still represent the best ways to go forward
- whether the community is sufficiently aware of your organization's existence, and, if not, whether further marketing is needed, or if so, whether it supports—or continues to support—your mission and goals
- whether your organization is paying enough attention to its own infrastructure, future viability, and the needs of its management and staff
- the risks and benefits of contracting or expanding your programs
- your overall financial situation, and
- putting this all together, where your organization should focus its energy and fundraising resources in the coming year or years.

Various resources are available to help: See, for example, the National Council of Nonprofits at www.councilofnonprofits.org.

Getting Started: Set Your Fundraising Goal

Every nonprofit should produce an annual budget. When you begin, this may be done informally, with the founding members chipping in a few dollars as needed. But certainly by your second year, the process of creating an annual budget should be institutionalized. Ideally, it should be a collaborative process, overseen by the executive director with input from the board, the accounting staff, and any relevant program managers or other staffers. The resulting budget will reflect all income that the organization takes in and all expenses it foresees paying out.

TIP

Try to create a small reserve fund. Too many nonprofits create a budget in which the total income exactly equals the total expenses. Given the shoestring on which most nonprofits operate, this isn't surprising—but it's still risky. Unexpected expenses may push a nonprofit into the red. Setting aside even a small amount each year—preferably out of donor funds or fees for services—can significantly enhance your organization's stability and limit the risk of a time-wasting midyear financial emergency. Depending on the size of your organization and how quickly it's expanding, it makes sense to create a cash reserve that will keep your organization going for a full 90 to 180 days.

Of course, it would be nice if someone could just tell you how much money you'll need to raise each year. But in the real world, arriving at your total income figure is—and should be—a complex process, in which planners typically look at:

- how much money would be needed in an ideal world to develop programs and infrastructure
- how much money was raised last year (probably a lot less)
- how much more can reasonably be raised this year
- how much the organization's programs and infrastructure can *really* get by on, with appropriate penny-pinching
- whether the reduced figure looks more realistic in terms of fundraising,
- and so on.

Without examining the entire budget process, let's look at the particular and limited role that a development director and other development staff can and should play in developing a budget. This role may include:

- creating the development department's budget
- helping to arrive at accurate and reasonable income projections
- monitoring the percentage of the overall budget that is going to administrative overhead, that is, to nonprogram staff and activities
- identifying places where the group may be able to raise more by better marketing its services, and
- considering whether expensive equipment or services can be obtained via donations, rather than by paying for them.

CAUTION

Don't arrive at your fundraising goal by ratcheting up last year's income. Some nonprofits aim to increase the previous year's number by a set percentage or amount—for example, by deciding that a fundraising effort that raised $100,000 last year can raise $120,00 this year. But fundraising involves too many variables for this kind of approach to be accurate. And if major grants aren't renewed, or other known income sources drop out of the picture, an ambitious goal like this could end up crippling the organization. Look at every revenue source and make a reasonable projection as to how much you're likely to receive this year to arrive at an informed total.

Create a Budget for Development Activities

At some point in the growth of your organization, the development staff may be asked to draft a separate subbudget for their own activities. How, a first-timer might wonder, can you estimate how much money you will spend on photocopying or travel for an entire year? You aren't even sure what events you will have, whether many of your donors will suddenly prefer a full lunch over coffee, or whether the economy will hit a period of inflation.

At the beginning, you'll have to rely largely on your instincts and your careful review of past years' budgets or records of expenditures. Try some simple budgeting exercises. Go through an entire day or week, noticing what supplies you use, how many photocopies you make, how many faxes or letters you send out, and so forth. Then estimate the costs of these items and add up what they'd cost for a month, then a year. Also think about the things you're pretty sure you'll do over the course of the year—send out a certain number of mailings, hold an annual event, and so on—and add up their costs. Though unscientific, these exercises can be revealing, showing that some costs add up faster than you'd think and others are less significant.

Next, look at any budgets or fundraising-expense records from past years. The first thing you'll probably notice is that your biggest expenses are not for incidental items, but for employee salaries and overhead (taxes and benefits, plus the costs of the office space and utilities). You'll see other fixed or regular costs, too; perhaps Web service fees, which give a certain predictability to any budget, year to year. (It also explains why, in tough times, all the cost cutting in the world may not forestall the need for layoffs).

Also look at what fundraising activities your organization undertook in past years, how much they cost, and whether these activities will likely be reduced, repeated, or expanded. Of course, this kind of analysis creates a chicken-and-egg problem—you can't know for sure whether you'll be doing more mailings and fewer grant proposals, or vice versa, until you've developed your fundraising plan. But you can at least get a sense of your operating constraints and, with experience, learn to balance the budget and planning possibilities more naturally.

If you've already been involved with the organization for a year or more, think about what will (or should) change this year. Was there enough money last year to order appropriate stationery and office supplies? Did you have a large one-time expense, such as the cost of renting a hall for a special fundraising event that won't be repeated?

After going through these various exercises and reviewing past budgets, you should be able to fill out the sample cost analysis below (and online, see the appendix for the link). There's a column for "notes," where you might write down the costs you're uncertain about, what might affect them, and the like. For example, if salaries are changing, you'll need to talk to your accounting department about how much the associated employment taxes and benefits will be.

Obviously, no budget will reflect future expenditures with 100% accuracy. Over the course of each fiscal year, keep an eye on what your development department or staff actually spends, to get a sense of what is normal and reasonable and to figure out where your estimates could use a little fine-tuning. Your accounting staff can help here, by putting together regular reports on actual versus budgeted expenditures. If this isn't practical in your organization, it will be up to you to make sure that you either stay within budget or receive permission from the powers that be to deviate from it.

Check Your Income Projections

The income side of your organization's proposed annual budget should include known or projected income from reliable sources such as ongoing grants, annual member renewals, and income that your fundraising efforts will almost surely bring in. For example, if a particular fundraising event has raised between $22,000 and $26,000 for three years running, it's probably safe to assume that it will raise at least $20,000 this year.

Fundraising Worksheet 1: Sample Cost Analysis

Item	Cost per year	Notes
Salaries and benefits	$ _____	_____
		_____
Fees to independent con-tractors and consultants	$ _____	_____
		_____
Travel (trainings, donor visits)	$ _____	_____
		_____
Office supplies	$ _____	_____
		_____
Graphic design/printing	$ _____	_____
		_____
Dues and publications	$ _____	_____
		_____
Staff trainings and networking events	$ _____	_____
		_____
Web, database, and other technical support	$ _____	_____
		_____
Telephone and Internet	$ _____	_____
		_____
Postage	$ _____	_____
		_____
Food (such as coffee or meals with donors)	$ _____	_____
		_____
Special event costs	$ _____	_____
		_____
Other special program costs	$ _____	_____
		_____
Total	$ _____	

Your most important budgeting task is to make sure that the known income figures are accurate. Check to make sure that all of the grants will continue as the budget says they will, and that they don't run out in the middle of next year. Your treasurer or paid accounting staff should be tracking this too, but mistakes can be made.

CAUTION

Be particularly careful when your fiscal year and a grant year are different. If, for example, half of the grant will be received in one fiscal year, and the other half in the next, you'll need to allocate income and expenses accordingly.

Also look at the estimated amount of member donations. Most budget planners estimate this figure based on recent years' results, with adjustments for any known or likely changes. If you have a regular base of members who are encouraged to renew annually, and you can review this history of renewals, you've got a good starting point for your predictions. You can also estimate how many interim mailings or appeals you'll send out to existing members or supporters, and make a realistic assessment of how much these will bring in.

Consider any unusual circumstances that affected recent years' giving patterns. If you know, for example, that individual donations hit a spike last year because of a particular hot issue or disaster, you'll need to make sure that this figure is revised downward. By the same token, if your development office was unusually short-staffed last year and sent out few email appeals, you can assume that individual donations will be at least a little higher this year (allowing for those lost donors whose loyalties shifted in the meantime).

The income projections probably will, and should, have a separate line for the amount of major donations you're likely to solicit. Put any existing estimates through the tests described above—what will be different this year? Was there anything unusual about last year or recent years, like a lapse in stewardship of major donors, a huge one-time gift, or a change in the tax laws?

CAUTION

Actually, there was a major change in U.S. tax laws. By raising the standard deduction beginning in 2018, Congress created a situation where only about 5% of taxpayers (mostly the wealthiest) will itemize—thus the average taxpayer will gain no tax benefit from donating to charity. It remains to be seen how much this will affect charitable giving, but early predictions look troubling. Some have already observed that wealthier donors are occupying a larger share of the giving pie, which may shift the types of causes receiving the most funds. As of this printing, only two states' tax codes (Colorado and Minnesota) provide an incentive for taxpayers to make charitable donations even when they do not itemize deductions.

Another thing to consider is how certain the various anticipated income items are. Identify the areas of greatest vulnerability—where would your organization be hurt the most if money you've included in the budget doesn't come through? You might want to develop a worst-case scenario budget, and think ahead about how you would adjust your organization's fundraising plan accordingly.

EXAMPLE: Save the Banana Slugs (SBS), an Oregon-based nonprofit, has always received half its budget—$25,000 out of its annual $50,000—from a local timber company trying to better its reputation. The company has indicated a willingness to renew that support. However, SBS has heard rumors that the company will be sold to a multinational conglomerate whose motto is "Cut the trees down and get out of town." SBS therefore creates two budgets—one including the projected $25,000 in corporate support, and another that omits the $25,000 (and cuts certain staff and programs to make up the difference).

Watch Out for High Administrative Overhead

Your public relations needs can have a major impact on your budget planning. Every nonprofit must pay careful attention to how much it spends on actual services and programs, versus how much goes to administrative costs—the salaries, equipment, and supplies for people and activities behind the scenes, such as management, accounting, and fundraising. Your grant makers and individual supporters will be keeping an eye on the ratio between these two amounts and will typically cast a wary eye whenever more than 33% to 50% of your total budget is spent on administration.

This doesn't mean that your organization absolutely cannot spend more than 50% on administrative costs. Not only is there no law against it, but for some organizations, it might be appropriate. A new nonprofit, for example, might sensibly spend large portions of its budget on administration while building the very programs, and reaching the very size, at which maximum effectiveness and efficiency become possible. (The percentage of the budget allocated to administrative costs will later drop quickly.)

But you'll have to make sure your group's leaders understand that high administrative costs will make your job as a fundraiser harder. Not only do some foundations and corporate funders limit the amounts of their grants that can be spent on administration, but they may also simply refuse to support any group that spends "too much" on administrative overhead. When you submit a proposed budget with a grant proposal to one of these funders, you'll have to allot an artificially small figure to administrative overhead in order to get the grant.

The pressure will then be on the development staff to make up the difference elsewhere—probably from individual supporters, but you'll also have to explain to them why such a high percentage of their dollars is going right back into fundraising and other nonprogram functions. If you're stuck in this situation, at least make sure that your departmental budget allows for sufficient staff and other resources with which to ramp up an individual donor program.

Don't Undercharge

Nonprofits exist to help others, not to profit from doing so. That means any fees that you charge should be fair. But many nonprofits have taken "fairness" too far: They significantly undercharge for services and end up exploiting their own underpaid staffers. This is a losing strategy—especially when you consider that to succeed in the long run, you'll have to count on those same staffers to stick around and help build your organization.

Client fees have been studied and agonized over in all sorts of contexts, but one conclusion comes through loud and clear: Except when you are dealing with the truly indigent, it's better to charge fees for services than to give them away. For one thing, clients tend to think more highly of services they've paid for. Things gotten for free are seen as throwaways—as evidenced by the phrase I and others heard while providing immigration law advice at a free clinic, "Thanks, but do you think I need a *real* lawyer now?" Later, I learned another valuable lesson: Clients who have paid even a modest fee are more likely to keep their appointments and actively participate in problem solving.

Both your organization's mission and budget will benefit if you charge reasonably for your services. If you've never charged fees before, start by figuring out how much each service really costs you to provide, then survey your client population to consider how much they can reasonably pay. Often, you'll find that people's incomes are spread across a wider range than you at first imagined, which means that a sliding fee schedule may be a good approach. Finally, you'll have to let your clients know why you're imposing fees (especially if you have provided free services in the past) and what you are doing with the money.

Also take a close look at other areas where your organization might be able to charge a reasonable fee for services or benefits it's currently giving away:

- Are you letting a local group use your space at no charge?
- Are you taking members of the public on educational tours or outings that also happen to be fun or much sought after?
- Are you providing speakers for other organizations' events (for-profit or nonprofit) where they're charging the attendees money? Ask them to share!
- Are you providing services to private businesses that could afford to pay for them? For example, if you are picking up surplus food from local restaurants to feed the homeless and prominently listing the restaurants as program sponsors, you may actually be providing them with economic benefits (a lower garbage bill and free promotion). If you explain these benefits to the restaurants, they may agree to chip in for the salary of the person who does the food pickup and delivery.

Factor in Noncash Contributions

Before rushing out to raise every dollar that your organization needs, consider whether you can supplement your fundraising with:

- in-kind donations of goods, or
- donations of professional services.

You've no doubt seen "wish lists" that other organizations place in their websites, event programs, and the like. They're usually for major items of equipment, such as a new or used laser printer, car, or costume for an event. These lists work. Though you can't count on receiving every item on your list, you'll get some of them—and quite possibly from supporters who wouldn't have given money.

An alternative to the wish list is to ask local businesses for equipment or supplies, new or used (but still serviceable). Nonprofits routinely receive donations of everything from computers and desks to flowers for their front entrance by following this approach. The key is usually to contact the owner of the business directly, and be ready to provide the owner with written materials—and, if needed, references—establishing your credibility. Be sure to highlight any place that the business will be publicly thanked, such as in your newsletter, website, or event program. If your organization or its key members are regular customers mention that, too.

Soliciting in-kind donations is an excellent task for board members and other volunteers, particularly in preparation for an auction or a raffle. It's an especially fitting task for those who find asking for objects easier than asking for money.

Your organization should always be looking for ways to get volunteers involved, as covered in more depth in Chapter 2. Just be careful about accepting free services that the provider wants to leverage into a paid relationship. Unless you're clear at the outset about how much you'll pay and for what services, you could find yourself drawn into an expensive or problematic arrangement. Lay out your agreement and mutual expectations in a written letter at the start.

Do Wish Lists Work?

I asked this of Lynn Eve Komaromi, director of development at Berkeley Repertory Theatre, in Berkeley, California. She says, "We've posted a 'wish list' on our website for years, and it has successfully filled important needs, such as furniture and cars for out-of-town actors for whom we've provided housing. "However, a wish list is a passive form of fundraising, and has other down sides, as well. For one, it's rare that we receive exactly what's on our list; though one donor has made sizable cash gifts that were restricted to buying these wished-for items. Last year, we applied this toward an upholstery steam cleaner, which our facilities department had long needed.

"There's also the issue of not wanting to turn away or offend a donor who offers something the organization doesn't need. Nonprofits have been facing this issue a lot lately, as people have been cleaning out clutter the Marie Kondo way. It can get overwhelming—few nonprofits have the storage space to accept random gifts, much less the staff to deal with it all. In fact, Berkeley Rep is itself in the midst of purging items that we aren't using.

"This points to a larger issue—every nonprofit needs a gift acceptance policy, which is a comprehensive, essential guide to both the board and the staff on what types of gifts the organization can accept and who can accept them. It's an important tool when confronted with trickier gift situations, particularly any that might expose the organization to legal liability.

"So, if you create a wish list, do so wisely and list only items that you truly need. Berkeley Rep, for instance, now focuses on requesting in-kind donations that will relieve our budget (and not take up storage space), such as wine and catering for donor events, pro bono legal services, or equipment for the theatre. Those tend to be significant partnerships, and we're able to offer a range of sponsor benefits that make it a win-win."

Evaluate Your Nonprofit's Fundraising Assets

Every nonprofit's mission, property, program, and history are different, which helps explain why there's no one-size-fits-all fundraising plan. Beyond this, however, different organizations also have different fundraising strengths, both tangible and intangible. This section explains how to evaluate your existing assets, with an eye toward strategically deploying them as part of your overall fundraising plan.

Identify Your Assets

An organization's assets come in all shapes and sizes. The reputation you build by running an effective and well-known program is an asset, as is a building or a truck. Skills, people, and experience can also be assets.

Some of your assets would hardly be noticed by outsiders looking at your organization—for example, low employee turnover. With such hidden assets, it becomes even more important for you to identify them and, if and when appropriate, use them to attract supporters or funders.

Although not all assets are suited to every type of fundraising, think creatively about which would best attract your different audiences, among them foundations, corporations, and individual donors. Take, for example, TechSoup, a San Francisco nonprofit that provides technical support for other nonprofits' computing needs. As much as TechSoup might like to recruit a long list of individual contributors, that may not be possible in a world where baby seals, hungry children, and disaster victims are the first to capture donors' hearts. A far more realistic strategy has been for TechSoup to focus energy on foundation grants. This allows it to play to its real strengths, such as providing a hugely needed service to hundreds of other organizations that might otherwise grind to a halt.

Your organization might be in the opposite situation. If you have a program that individual donors can readily understand—such as advocating for urban bike paths or supporting the arts in area schools—but your program doesn't happen to fit neatly into any foundation's niche, you'll want to concentrate on individual and, perhaps, small business donors.

Some organizations have unusual assets or fundraising advantages. A community radio station, for example, has the airwaves—and can request donations from anyone willing to listen during its pledge drives. The International Institute of Buffalo, New York, resides in a classic 19th-century mansion, the gift of a long-ago donor—which it rents out for meetings and parties. The Berkeley Repertory Theatre, after a clean-out of its props and costume warehouse, held a sale of items it didn't think it would need for a future production. Lynn Eve Komaromi explains, "We got lots of folks shopping for Burning Man—they found costumes and bits and pieces for their art displays. It was a win-win."

The people within your organization—your staff, board, and volunteers—may well be its most important assets. Consider their skills and personalities without being either overly judgmental or overly optimistic. Thinking to yourself, "I'm sure Sarita will finally make time for fundraising this year," or "If I can just talk Jay out of his shyness, he'd be great with major donors," is not likely to make the cash register ring. Instead, identify specific and proven strengths, such as:

- personal connections with particular communities (for example, ethnic, political, or interest-based groups) or potential major donors
- personal connections with foundation staff members or potential corporate donors
- good people skills
- reputation—or even fame
- writing or marketing skills
- artistic skills
- event-coordinating skills
- Web or computer skills
- ownership of or access to a nice home, club, or boat, or another facility
- eagerness to participate in a certain type of fundraising (for example, someone who hates to phone potential donors may delight in running an annual silent auction), and
- any other special skills and interests.

Face—And Embrace—Your Organization's Weaknesses

In the course of considering what makes your organization and its people great, you'll have to also consider what it lacks—gaps or weaknesses, personal or organizational, that might undermine the use of a particular fundraising strategy.

If, for example, you've got a great writer on your team, foundation support might be an obvious fundraising choice—but if you know that you've already tapped every possible foundation, you'll probably have to find some other uses for your writer's talents. Or, let's say there's a famous person on your board who could be the keynote speaker at a fundraising event—but that person is controversial or, even worse, disliked by a significant number of your supporters. It will be of little long-term benefit to run a successful event that alienates a significant part of your constituency.

Consider how to turn supposed negatives into positives. Such creative thinking has been a central theme in the fundraising work of Lupe Gallegos-Diaz, who teaches fundraising courses at UC Berkeley and once worked with a national Chicano studies organization. That group had a large membership, but most—about 80%—were financially challenged undergraduates, with the remaining 20% mostly underpaid faculty members. Because this population was not ripe for major gifts, the group instituted a campaign asking members for donations of at least $1. They educated every donor about the importance of giving even a little. Although they didn't bring in big dollars the first year, they got people into the habit of giving, thus laying the groundwork for continued—and larger—gifts in the future.

Another example Lupe cites is of a group whose members were mostly stay-at-home mothers. Because they were neither socially prominent nor affluent, they didn't feel ready to reach out to rich and powerful donors. But they did know plenty of people in their own community who would enjoy a good meal. To start their fundraising, they held a series of in-house dinners, hosted by their own members, with everyone helping prepare food and sell tickets. Later, they used the goodwill developed through these small events to put on a bigger, more elaborate dinner event—by which time the prospective guests knew each other and were eager to attend. The group raised significant funds and educated many community members about their excellent work.

List Your Assets

As soon as you're ready, take a piece of paper and write, in a column, all the relevant assets—whether people, property, or abstract qualities—that you can identify within your organization. When it comes to people, you might want to mention individuals by name, and give each a separate line. Next to each asset or strength, list the types of fundraising it could support.

The worksheet below (and online; see the appendix for the link) will help you create a list of your nonprofit's assets and their possible fundraising applications. Don't just fill this out on your own and put it in a drawer. Take a blank version and meet with staff, board members, and other stakeholders. Ask them to brainstorm and record their ideas on it.

Remind them about the various tasks and activities involved in fundraising, and ask them to think specifically about what and whose skills and advantages might be helpful. Explain the reasons behind listed items—for example, under "physical facilities," a boat could be used for a special event, or a weekend at someone's lakeside vacation home could be offered up during a silent auction. Your brainstormers may come up with something you didn't think of—or didn't even know about. For example, a board member might say, "You know, my brother's wife is part of a famous band that sings about social justice issues—I bet they'd do a benefit concert for us!"

After you've collected input, create a master chart of your organization's assets and their fundraising applications (using the same format as before). You'll use this to develop your fundraising strategy, as described next. You'll also probably want to refer to this chart again during next year's planning process.

Fundraising Worksheet 2: Fundraising Assets

Asset Type	Asset Description	Possible Fundraising Use
Organization's mission	_____	_____
	_____	_____
Organization's programs	_____	_____
	_____	_____
Organization's reputation or history with certain foundations or individuals	_____	_____
	_____	_____
Organization's access to certain members of community	_____	_____
	_____	_____
Organization's physical facilities or resources	_____	_____
	_____	_____
Physical facilities or resources owned or accessible by board, staff, or volunteers	_____	_____
	_____	_____
Executive director	_____	_____
	_____	_____
Development director	_____	_____
	_____	_____
Development assistant	_____	_____
	_____	_____
Other development staff	_____	_____
	_____	_____
Board members	_____	_____
	_____	_____
Board fundraising committee	_____	_____
	_____	_____
Particularly active individual volunteers	_____	_____
	_____	_____
Volunteer program generally	_____	_____
	_____	_____
Other friends of your organization	_____	_____
	_____	_____

CAUTION

Special events aren't always so special. When you get volunteers together to think "fundraising," you'll often see most of the excitement and ideas generated around proposals for special events. "Hey, we could do a carnival, with a dunking booth, and I'll bake 1,000 cookies … it'll be great!" In part, this tendency is natural: Most people have more experience with events, from bake sales and raffles to silent auctions and wine tastings, than with any other kind of fundraising. And who wouldn't rather plan a party than write a grant proposal or call ten major donors? Too bad that when you figure all the time and energy that goes into them, special events are, on average, the least profitable form of fundraising (though they have their other benefits; see Chapter 8 for more information). Try to keep your brainstormers focused on the overall goal, the full breadth of fundraising methods needed to meet it, and the assets that might support those methods.

Develop Your Fundraising Strategy

Now that you know how much income you'll need for the coming year's activities and you know your organization's fundraising strengths and weaknesses, it's time to figure out how you'll get the money.

From the total needed for the coming year, subtract the amount that you can count on receiving, such as committed grants and fees for services you're fairly sure to provide. The number that's left is the amount you'll actually need to raise.

You're now ready to decide on a fundraising strategy—that is, to identify which of the fundraising techniques or sources described in this book can be tapped for maximum advantage. You'll have to consider some general tactical issues, such as what your core assets are and how much you'll need to diversify your funding sources. Then consider how your assets match up with the possible range of fundraising methods. Finally, make sure the board and key staffers are enthusiastically behind the final plan.

> **TIP**
> **Fundraising must be an expression of a group's philosophy and identity.** For example, the Mayflower Historical Society would probably not do too well with a rock concert, and the West Flatbush Neighborhood Improvement Association might concentrate on getting new individual members who live in and care about the neighborhood, not on soliciting large donations from celebrities.

Tactical Considerations

Your fundraising strategy should depend, in part, on your organization's purpose and goals. Stick with fundraising activities that are time-tested or core to your organization's identity; stay within the boundaries of your organization's strategic plan and mission; and otherwise try to diversify your funding sources and activities.

Although you should engage in an open-ended planning process, that doesn't mean that your whole fundraising strategy has to change. For instance, there's no point in junking a well-run individual member program (ever) or a much-loved annual event (unless it's truly draining other resources or you feel you've gotten into a rut).

In fact, donors appreciate a certain degree of consistency. Just as with fast food restaurants, there's a certain value in letting people know what to expect in terms of offerings and quality. Some supporters may even mentally plan around your traditional fundraisers, thinking "I'll buy my greeting cards from X organization again this year, and take my friend Cynthia to its annual auction." If you bounce between an auction one year, a holiday tree sale the next, and a walkathon the year after, you may confuse and frustrate your most loyal supporters.

> **TIP**
> **Focus on individual donors.** No matter how else you plan to raise money, virtually every nonprofit should be trying to increase the number of people who support it each year and the amount of money each of these individual donors gives. Not only does increasing member support send an important signal about your organization's vitality to larger donors, it's also an important hedge against economic hard times.

You should also try for a certain level of diversity among funding streams—we all know the risks of putting all your eggs in one basket. It's sad to watch all the work and energy that went into building or developing a program that serves your mission go down the drain because the funding faucet gets turned off. (Sometimes the staff who get laid off are the lucky ones—the remainder have to pick up the workloads they left behind, because of promises made to the remaining funders.)

Diversify thoughtfully, though. Having numerous baskets each holding one egg can be problematic, too. If many separate sources of funds have their own time, staffing, and reporting requirements, you'll be pulled in too many directions to be effective.

Maybe that's why a study of the nation's largest nonprofits—with revenues over $50 million—came to the surprising conclusion that concentrating on just a few funding sources helped their success. The National Wild Turkey Federation, for example, found hunters to be its biggest and best funding source. (See "How Nonprofits Get Really Big," by William Foster and Gail Fine, *Stanford Social Innovation Review,* Spring 2007.)

The ideal is to have a manageably sized mix of stable sources providing the bulk of your budget, with some additional sources to provide balance, create future potential, and fill in the fundraising gaps. Author and expert Kim Klein recommends that no more than 20% of your total funding come from any one person or source. (See *Fundraising in Times of Crisis,* from Jossey-Bass.) She also recommends that no more than 20% to 30% of your total budget come from foundation or government sources, because foundation money tends to dry up after a year or two, and government funding is notoriously affected by recessions and elections.

RELATED TOPIC

Information on developing donor diversity. Diversity among the race, ethnicity, and lifestyles of your donors is also worth striving for. Refer to Chapter 4 for information on developing such diversity.

Spread Out Fundraising Responsibilities Among Your Staff

The goal of diversifying applies not only to your fundraising sources—where the money is coming from—but also to the people who go after it. If you've ever worked in an organization where the ED or development director quit, and all development efforts went stagnant for a few months because no one else had any idea what was planned or underway, you know all too well what this principle means.

If you are unable to hire a large development staff, it's even more important that various members of your board, as well as other volunteers, are committed to your fundraising program. There may even be times when you want to build activities into your fundraising program specifically to keep certain board members enthusiastic and involved—sort of like writing the script to fit the actors.

Your First Draft Plan

Now it's time to make important decisions about your future fundraising activities. This is not a task to handle alone; instead, bring in some combination of the ED, development staff, and key board members (depending on your organization's size and number of paid staff).

Pick up your final version of Worksheet 2, showing organizational assets and possible fundraising applications. You'll use it to create another chart, shown below, in which you choose the best fundraising activities for your organization and make sure that these activities will help you reach your goal without draining your budget.

Using this chart (also available online; see the appendix for the link), play around with various scenarios. Start by choosing a promising fundraising activity, such as "proposals to foundations," in Column 1. Estimate how much you'll be able to raise through that activity in Column 2. Then estimate any new or unusual costs the fundraising activity will require in Column 3 (which is there to make sure you don't render your departmental budget irrelevant). Particularly if you're shifting course toward a strategy

Fundraising Worksheet 3: Fundraising Strategy Chart

Activity or Funding Source	Amount It Should Raise	New or Unusual Expenses	Total Amount (Column 2 minus Column 3)
_____	$ _____	$ _____	$ _____
_____	$ _____	$ _____	$ _____
_____	$ _____	$ _____	$ _____
_____	$ _____	$ _____	$ _____
_____	$ _____	$ _____	$ _____
_____	$ _____	$ _____	$ _____
_____	$ _____	$ _____	$ _____
		Grand Total:	$ _____

that requires a high up-front investment, such as a new direct mail program or special event, you'll need to estimate the added costs carefully and make sure that they aren't going to break the bank. Subtract the amount entered in Column 3 from the amount in Column 2, and enter the result in the fourth and final column.

As you go, keep a running total of the amounts entered in Column 4, until the Grand Total equals (or preferably exceeds!) the amount you need to fundraise for that year. (To get even more scientific about this, go back to your department budget to see if there are any costs you won't be incurring because you've shifted strategy away from the activities with which those costs were associated.)

Let's say, for example, that your organization is a clinic. Its greatest asset may be satisfied ex-patients and their family members, who already support a successful major donor program. The major donor program is no doubt worth continuing—or better yet, increasing at a realistic rate. Enter the likely fundraising proceeds in Column 2 (and, if you're expanding, any new costs in Column 3).

However, even an expanded major donor program probably doesn't cover all of your monetary needs. Moving on down your assets chart, you may see that you have a volunteer who is willing and able to take patients' artwork and turn it into greeting cards and another volunteer willing and able to market the cards. This may, however, require some up-front investment (unless the cardstock and printing are donated). Enter the amount this strategy could realistically raise in Column 2, being sure to estimate the new expenses in Column 3.

Check your running total from Column 4 to see how much that leaves to be raised from other funding sources. Grant proposals to foundations, corporations, or government are a likely prospect for most nonprofits. In the clinic's case, submitting proposals would be particularly appropriate if the organization's assets include a good reputation, any history of foundation support, current board or staff members with inside contacts, and someone who can write up a compelling proposal.

Keep matching up your organization's greatest strengths and their corresponding fundraising uses, being sure not to assign more tasks to any one person than he or she can handle.

Also remember that your department will have to take on responsibilities that don't raise money directly. You'll need to decide what tasks the development office will carry out that won't have an immediate payback, such as preparing an annual report, setting up a new database, or planning donor forums or volunteer appreciation events. Make sure you've left time for someone to take care of these activities, too. Play around until you've found a way to raise all the needed money.

Finding a balance that seems to work is incredibly satisfying—but it's no cause for complacency. In fundraising, as in everything else in life, things can and will go wrong. Pick up that chart one last time, and ask, "What if?" For example, what if several major donors don't contribute this year? What if your board member with the party yacht takes it on a yearlong trip to New Zealand? What if donations to your silent auction aren't as generous as in past years? Focus only on the greatest, foreseeable risks—there's no point in obsessing over plagues, floods, or pestilence. But now that you're scared a little, modify your plan so that you have an adequate financial cushion if things go wrong.

Strategize With—And Seek Buy-In From—A Larger Group

Creating a fundraising plan involves estimating how much help, and what type of help, you'll get from the people involved in your organization. Before chiseling your plan in stone, make sure that all these folks will happily support it. You should have already enlisted their voices at the brainstorming stage—now it's time to go back to them at the commitment stage. Draft your preliminary fundraising plan and present it to staff and board members, at the same or separate meetings. If there are key volunteers outside the board, meet with them separately.

You have three principal objectives in holding these meetings. First, you want to give people a clear idea of what it will take to raise a particular amount of money. Second, you want to give them an opportunity to be heard, so that you can, if necessary, adjust the plan based on their ideas. Third, you want to be sure that they buy into the plan and will commit to doing the necessary work.

To facilitate this process, create a final version of your fundraising strategy chart. Distribute copies, labeled "Draft," to everyone in attendance. Go through each intended fundraising activity one by one, explaining whose help will be needed, how much work will be asked of them, how much up-front investment the organization will be adding, and the risks of failure. If there are alternate plans you considered and rejected, or are still considering, describe these as well.

Then sit back and listen, as open-mindedly as possible. One effective strategy is to start by writing down everyone's ideas on a whiteboard or an easel-mounted pad. Use just a few words for each, saving discussion for later. Once this is done, come back to those ideas, one by one, to consider them as a group. Be clear, however, about who will make the final decision on the fundraising plan.

If you are hearing major resistance to a particular element of the plan—especially if it's from the very people on whom you're relying to carry it out—it may be time to rethink. Try to gauge the level of resistance. If you're hearing embarrassed laughter about the prospect of soliciting in-person donations, then a pep talk or training may be all that's needed to tip the balance. If, however, you've got a room full of stone-faced board members who think that starting a car donation program is the worst idea they've ever heard of, it's time to reconsider—unless you want a parking lot full of used cars and no one to deal with them but yourself.

If, at the end of this planning process, you realize you don't have enough staff or volunteers to raise the needed funds, talk with the leaders of your organization. You may need to invest time and resources in finding this help before setting your budgetary or fundraising goals. In the worst-case scenario, your organization may have to scale down its programs or ambitions or look into merging with another organization. These can be painful decisions, but ones that will be better in the long run than hobbling along without sufficient staff or funding.

Create the Final Plan

Write your fundraising plan down, so that you and others can remember what you decided and refer to it later. But this isn't like school, where more pages get you a higher grade. Keep it simple and usable, choosing a format that will work for you and your staff. Some helpful components to include in your plan are:

- **An indication of the time duration of the plan.** One year is the standard, but it can also be helpful to include less detailed projections for the next few years.

- **A narrative description of its major goals.** For example, if the plan is to continue on your current course, say so—or if it's to reduce donor mailings by a certain number in favor of spending time on special events, describe that. And again, include goals that support fundraising indirectly, such as staff training, projects involving your Web presence, and the like.

- **A calendar showing what you'll work on month by month.** This should including mailings, grant proposals, events, and whatever else you've decided on. Start with the deadlines you can't change, such as for a year-end appeal or a particular foundation's grant-proposal due date, then fit the rest around them.

- **A breakdown of responsibilities.** Describe who will lead each task, who else will be involved, and if appropriate, approximately how much time the person will devote to this task. For staff persons, this can be expressed as a percentage of overall time.

- **How you'll measure interim success over the year or years.** Plan on revisiting your plan at least quarterly, to see how reality is measuring up to your projections.

- **Descriptions of backup plans if particularly risky strategies don't pan out as hoped.** The picture is sure to change over the course of the year, and having a Plan B is a great way to minimize any shock or need for new planning meetings.

Once you've written the plan down, make copies for the appropriate people and slip these into colorful folders. Also post the plan on your shared drive, and do whatever else it takes to make sure that everyone can find it. Emphasize your commitment to making this a living document by bringing it to board or management meetings, reporting back on progress toward its various goals, and asking for feedback on what's working and what isn't. (And realistically, plan on issuing some individual reminders of tasks to be done.)

Preparing a detailed fundraising plan once a year is a good idea. This doesn't mean reinventing the wheel or overturning your strategy every year—it will get easier each time.

Fundraising Pros Start With a Plan

With 30-plus years of development experience, consultant Christine Grumm has come to appreciate the importance of planning ahead. "People go wrong by not having a plan—they start out assuming that they should simply write a grant or ask for money. But they've forgotten to do the up-front work of understanding the various possibilities. It's a very systematic process. You can't just look at a grid of fundraising techniques and say, 'I'll do some of this and some of that.' Unless there's a connect between the financial need and the assets that you have to support that need—such as a board contact, or interest on the part of foundations—it's not going to happen."

Attracting Individual Supporters

The day-to-day work of a nonprofit can feel isolated. Your staff may be toiling away on research projects, meeting one-on-one with low-income clients whom society seems to have forgotten, or worrying about an indigenous population a continent away. However, you have a nearby constituency and a support network you may never see: your donors and dues-paying members. I'll call them "supporters" or "donors." Some people also use the term "investors."

Think about organizations that you have given money to—didn't you feel that you personally were helping to clean up a waterway, save a dog or cat from being euthanized, or release a political prisoner? Until every member of your staff realizes that these unseen supporters are a vital part of your work and learns to communicate with and actively solicit more of them, your organization will be heading toward stagnation.

Why Not Call Them "Members"?

In some states, the word "member" has a specific legal meaning in the nonprofit setting: It indicates a person with legal rights to participate in and sometimes vote on important organizational decisions, such as appointments to the board of directors, amendments to the articles and bylaws, the sale of certain assets, or mergers with other nonprofits. Most organizations don't want this many people involved in such decisions. Therefore, they go without a formal membership structure (stating this in their articles and bylaws), and avoid using the term. For more information, see Anthony Mancuso's *How to Form a Nonprofit Corporation* (Nolo).

From a practical standpoint, recruiting individual supporters is particularly worthwhile, because their donations come with few strings attached. While a grant from a foundation or the government may yield a lump sum of tens or even hundreds of thousands of dollars, such grants can come with enough restrictions to significantly hamper your work—and paperwork requirements that gobble up precious staff time. Many foundations insist, for example, that an unreasonably low figure be allotted to the costs of managing your organization or pressure you to prove immediate success in settings where it can't be realistically measured. New or smaller nonprofits may have difficulty attracting grant money in the first place. Also, a grant may be here one year and gone the next.

The question for most nonprofits is not whether to solicit funds from individuals, but how to go about doing it. This chapter will address both subtle and more direct approaches to attracting new supporters, including:

- demonstrating that your organization can meet individual supporters' high expectations
- understanding why people give—and what will encourage them to give to your organization, and
- using direct mail, email, and other techniques to solicit new supporters.

 CAUTION

Just how much of your nonprofit's income might come from individual donors? The unfortunate answer is, probably far less than the 75% that was typical in past years. That's due primarily to the Tax Code changes described in this chapter. Also, explains Krista Tuomi, professor of economics at American University, "Tepid wage growth will likely further reduce individual giving. Nonprofits will need to both diversify their funding sources and explore alternative ways for individuals to support them, for example through legacy gifts or IRA donations (which are not deductible, but count toward the retiree's required minimum distribution)."

Make Your Organization Look Support-Worthy

Individual supporters don't normally attach conditions to their donations, but that doesn't mean they don't have expectations. Just the opposite—a number of forces are driving them to expect more and more from nonprofits in terms of efficiency, results, and reporting—and to be suspicious if they don't get this information. Of course, your supporters don't have the time or energy to poke around behind the scenes to see whether your nonprofit is really what it claims to be. They'll have to rely on more external indicators, such as your publications and media coverage. This doesn't let you off the hook—the true quality of an organization's work and people becomes known in the community one way or another, and its reputation eventually affects its ability to attract financial support.

Although there are a number of metrics by which nonprofit performance can be evaluated, many use one ratio: the proportion of funds being recycled into administration and fundraising instead of fueling the core work of your organization. A ratio of more than 50% of your funds going to administrative costs is widely considered too high. The Better Business Bureau (BBB)'s Wise Giving Alliance recommends that no more than 35% of total funds raised be churned back into fundraising—and that 65% of a nonprofit's budget be spent on program activities (unless the group has a good reason, such as being new).

One study of wealthy individuals found that 56% said they would give "a great deal more" to charity if they knew that the organizations were effectively managed. That makes financial accountability and organizational efficiency cornerstones upon which your fundraising hopes and plans must be built.

Of course, taking the time to build a support-worthy organization is easier said than done. I know firsthand the frustration of having outsiders fussing about your so-called "efficiency" when you're putting in long hours with bare-bones staffing, antiquated equipment, and the world's least ergonomic chairs. People who can carry out fundraising and other managerial activities are absolutely necessary to keep an organization running; at a minimum, someone has to be there to comply with the various demands for reports and other accountability measures!

Nevertheless, your organization should try to meet or exceed generally accepted guidelines measuring nonprofit efficiency, even as a start-up with few resources. As your organization grows, careful attention to financial procedures and reporting should help you guard against sloppiness, self-dealing, or worse, embezzlement by a bad apple on your own staff. Developing good financial tracking systems will quickly alert you to instances where you're spending more money than is appropriate. And knowing that you can back up your assertions about well-spent donations will make you and your volunteers more confident when it's time to raise funds.

Once you have taken steps to ensure that you are spending donated money responsibly and well, how can you make that apparent to your supporters? This section discusses four ways to do so:

- Deliver accurate, up-to-date reports to foundations, the IRS, and other watchdogs.
- Open your books and be willing to share financial information with individual supporters.
- Be courteous and efficient in your dealings with supporters.
- Set realistic but visible benchmarks for success.

Responsible Reporting to Foundations and Government

Running a nonprofit means dealing with a mountain of paperwork. At a minimum, you'll be required to submit reports to your grantors, to the federal government (the IRS), and possibly to your state and local government throughout the year.

Whenever you get a grant, whether from a foundation or the government, you'll likely be asked to write a report, in a very specific format, detailing how you spent the money. These reports may be due once a month, once a year, or somewhere in between. Some funders even require you to provide a financial report before they write a check. While some of the material you provide in the report will be general and narrative, you'll also have to supply an up-to-date accounting of actual costs and expenditures.

For the IRS, your organization will probably need to fill out a Form 990 annually (an informational form, used to assess compliance with the tax laws). Organizations with receipts normally less than $25,000 can e-file on IRS.gov a short form or "e-postcard" called a 990-N, while those with gross receipts between $25,000 and $999,000 can use a simplified "990-EZ."

Select types of organizations can avoid the 990-filing requirement altogether, including faith-based organizations, subsidiaries of larger nonprofits, foreign nonprofits, nonprofits not registered with the IRS, federal corporations and state institutions, and private foundations. (For details, see *Every Nonprofit's Tax Guide: How to Keep Your Tax-Exempt Status & Avoid IRS Problems*, by Stephen Fishman, J.D. (Nolo).)

On your Form 990, you'll need to supply information about where your revenues came from and where they were spent. The Form 990 then becomes a public record. You're obligated to give a copy to anyone who asks for it or to post it on the Web.

Some state governments also monitor nonprofit finances. Most states now require registration by nonprofits that solicit money from individuals there (including online). A few states also require financial reports in connection with nonprofits' regular reregistration. All of these reports may become public information. For more information, see Anthony Mancuso's *How to Form a Nonprofit Corporation* (Nolo).

Apart from these registration requirements, many states also require registered nonprofits to submit reports (annually or in connection with each fundraising campaign) detailing how much they spent on fundraising activities in order to bring in a certain amount of donations. These states also tend to require that, along with any request for support, the organization disclose to prospective supporters the percentage of donations that will be used for fundraising purposes.

Will your individual donors ever see these various reports? Probably not, unless they're savvy enough to look up your Form 990. But that doesn't mean the information won't come to them by other means. For example, investigative reporters doggedly check out Form 990s, looking for the latest, hottest nonprofit ripoff. And a number of watchdog groups evaluate and compile data on nonprofits, using the Form 990s and other reports, publishing the results on websites such as:

- **www.charitywatch.org,** founded as the American Institute of Philanthropy, which provides grades on selected nonprofits based on their financial practices and efficiency
- **www.charitynavigator.org,** which rates nonprofits on a four-star system based on their financial health, accountability, and transparency

- **www.give.org,** by the BBB Wise Giving Alliance, which provides reports and information on nonprofits, reviews them against a list of 20 standards, and acts on complaints about U.S. nonprofits, and
- **www.guidestar.org,** (by Candid), which gathers 990s and other information on virtually every nonprofit in the United States, creates reports, and allows nonprofits to register and post information about themselves.

Have a look at these websites. Search for a few organizations that you know, and see how well—or poorly—they appear onscreen. Notice how half-hearted it looks when a nonprofit has an opportunity to register on a site but doesn't—and vow never to make the same mistake.

Share Financial Information With Supporters

Your organization already has to compile financial reports and statistics for funders and the government. There's no reason not to make this information available to individual supporters. Doing so will enhance your credibility and convey that your organization is committed to good planning, wise spending, and rigorous oversight practices. (This may require your fundraising staff to keep in regular contact with your accounting staff—always a good idea.)

The data supporters are most likely to want are the spending ratios described above, as well as your budgets for particular projects. It's also helpful to your donors—and very effective for fundraising—to break down expenses on a per-unit basis, such as "every $4 allows us to feed one hungry person for a day." Your website is an excellent place to post this sort of information.

Also include financial information in solicitation mailings or any newsletter you regularly send to supporters, perhaps in an article entitled "Where Your Money Goes" or "How Your Gifts Support Our Services." If discussing a particular program, you might discuss the challenges of raising funds when "bus rentals to transport the children cost $250 alone." Specific dollar figures catch people's eyes and make them better understand why you're tackling an ambitious financial goal.

Also include financial and budgetary information in any written material you present in individual meetings with potential major supporters, as discussed in Chapter 6.

Be Professional in All Contacts With Supporters

Supporters will see every interaction with your organization as a reflection of how well you actually deliver services or fulfill your mission. A donor who gets a thank-you letter from your marine mammal protection organization three months after contributing probably won't think, "Oh, they must have been too busy saving the whales to get to my letter"; instead, he or she will probably wonder, "Hmm, if this place can't get its act together to send one little letter, how are they going to save a whole whale?"

Other ways to demonstrate good management and interest in donors include good writing and careful editing of letters, emails, and website content; returning phone calls courteously and promptly; handling supporters' checks and credit card pledges responsibly; and demonstrating an obvious desire to treat supporters as both friends and, at some level, customers.

Knowing that you're under this kind of scrutiny can raise your stress levels—but it can also give you a sense of purpose as you engage in the tedious tasks of printing out supporter acknowledgments, checking your supporter database for mistakes and duplications, entering new data quickly, and so on. Make sure your staff and volunteers understand the importance of such tasks—and thank them profusely when they do them well.

Focus on Your Organization's Successes

Focusing the public's perception on the great work that your organization is doing can defuse concern over ratios. Who's going to quibble about how much you're spending on services if it's clear that you're getting a giant bang for your buck? Sit down with program staff and look hard at what you're really achieving. Try to break things down—look not only at your long-term goals, but at the step-by-step or indirect successes that you achieve along the way.

EXAMPLE: A youth project runs an after-school program that gives kids who might otherwise join gangs an opportunity to build friendships and leadership skills and to learn about their ethnic heritage. One of their funders has asked them to prove that they've measurably changed society and reduced teen violence. Because it's hard to prove this kind of major impact, the group is understandably nervous. However, when they sit down to consider successes they can share with the funder, they come up with the following:

- the number of students who voluntarily join their program each year
- the percentage of students who regularly attend the program
- the number of students who have voluntarily met with counselors on a long-term basis
- the improvement in their students' grades relative to the rest of the students in their school, and
- the community service projects that the students have successfully completed.

All of these are legitimate successes. If their program wasn't really providing a valuable service, the kids wouldn't be coming, improving their grades, and giving something back to their community.

Part of your job as a fundraiser is to identify these successes and communicate them effectively to your supporters and the public.

Understand What Motivates Your Supporters

The question of what motivates donors has been examined in excruciating detail, but at some level, this discipline will probably always be in its infancy. After all, understanding givers' motivations doesn't directly lead to knowledge of which fundraising techniques will tap into those motivations. Almost as soon as a particular technique achieves outsize returns, it becomes overused.

Still, it helps to have some understanding about what leads people to give, and especially to give to one type of cause over another. This section looks first at the more abstract, altruistic reasons for giving, then at the more tangible benefits you might offer donors in return for their support.

Why People Give

Evidence is mounting that humankind possesses a sense of altruism, and gives to charity accordingly. Some claim that an instinct to help others is hardwired into the human race, as a way of ensuring group survival. The statistics certainly look good. Though the U.S. economy has its ups and downs, Americans tend to be generous in their giving: Over half of U.S. households typically give some money to some causes. And total giving was over $281 billion in 2017.

It's not just the rich who give. In fact, studies consistently find that the typical donor is middle or lower income. So you should feel comfortable approaching people with the sense that their hearts and minds may be generally open to giving. It's just a matter of finding the supporters who will give to your organization.

> **TIP**
> **Entrepreneurs are a valuable donor segment.** According to a 2018 report by Fidelity Charitable, people who founded or own a business typically giving 50% more to charity each year than others, and are far more likely to volunteer. It's seems to be due to a mix of philanthropic instincts (and perhaps the knowledge of how hard it is to run any business, much less one not designed to earn a profit) and a realization that they can enhance their own reputation and that of their company with acts of generosity.

Why Altruistic People Choose One Cause Over Another

People's motivations for giving become clearer when you look at how they decide how much to give and how they choose between the various good causes seeking their support. People seem to give when they feel they will get something in return—in most cases, something that satisfies them at a deeply personal level. Although the giveaway baseball cap or coffee mug might tip the balance for a few, most are looking for something loftier, but no less tangible. These rewards might include:

- feeling good about themselves
- returning a favor, if they or their family has been helped by a particular organization

- getting a tax deduction (though very few will, after the 2018 Tax Code revision)
- helping solve a social, environmental, political, or medical problem that they find personally important or that has affected their friends or family
- sending a message about their beliefs
- receiving quality information about a topic that interests them
- aligning themselves with friends, peers, or a community, or
- bringing about justice, or even vengeance, in an area where they or their loved ones have been hurt.

If the length of this list surprises you, remember that people are complex and often have more than one reason for giving. For example, you might give to your college alumni association because giving makes you feel good, because you feel that supporting quality education will help society, and because your alumni friends asked you to give!

By the same token, if you get a letter from an organization within which you have no prior friends or contacts, which supports a cause that has never touched you or your family personally (say, the restoration of a landmark in a city you've never visited), and whose message you might not feel strongly about, you're unlikely to support it.

> **TIP**
>
> **Guess who's telling the men to give?** A survey by the Fidelity Charitable Gift Fund found that over 90% of men cited their spouses as their primary influence in deciding which charities to support and how much to give. The women surveyed named a broader range of influences, including extended family, friends, and coworkers.

Understanding your supporters' motivations can help you devise ways to interact with them and hook into their personal interests.

Although some people's links to an organization will be obvious—for example, they are former patients of your clinic—others can only be accounted for by the vagaries of personal taste. Just as some people like chocolate ice cream better than vanilla, some people will be drawn toward environmental causes, not human rights issues. There's not much you can do to convert people on such fundamental matters. But you can learn more about the general characteristics of the type of supporter your own organization will attract.

> **TIP**
>
> **People may choose one group over another based on its marketing.**
> Particularly in major cities, you'll often find a number of groups addressing the same cause or issue. In such cases, people may choose the group with the best reputation, or the one in which they know people, or simply the one that got to them first. Virtually all of the advice in this book is intended to help you distinguish yourself from the competition.

Don't Expect Everyone to Give

Finding supporters isn't like winning an argument—you'll rarely convince people to part with cash against their early inclinations. And no one has an obligation to support you, no matter how great your work.

If you're nodding your head, or saying "I knew that already," reflect on how easy it is for an organization to give the wrong impression. You've probably seen nonprofit marketing or social media posts whose stridency implied that everyone should support them now, or feel bad if they didn't.

I've even heard nonprofit staff shrilly proclaim that all wealthy people should feel guilty about their relative comfort, and therefore give money to their causes. The unfortunate truth is that most affluent people either don't realize how good they've got it, aren't listening, or are already major nonprofit donors. In none of these instances will a guilt-based pitch help—and it might end up breeding resentment.

> **TIP**
>
> **How much money in the bank does someone need to feel financially secure?** A study by sociologist Paul Schervish asked this of people with a net worth of at least $25 million. The answer: $20 million! Good thing philanthropic giving appears not to be just something people do with their spare cash.

Find Out Why Your Supporters Chose Your Organization

Focusing on why people have chosen to give to your organization in the recent past will help you predict where you might find additional supporters. Prepare for some surprises.

As an obvious example, your research might show that most of the people who support your battered women's shelter are women—no surprise there. But you might additionally find that a number of your supporters are the fathers of women who have been abused by their spouses or partners.

Or, if your organization works on an age-related illness such as Alzheimer's or macular degeneration, you might not be surprised to find that most of your supporters are in the over-55 age range—but your research might also unexpectedly reveal that a significant number of your supporters are in the medical profession.

Your first step in this exploration is to develop a "donor profile." This is much like the market research that any business does to learn how and where to sell its product. For example, you might gather the following information about your existing donors:

- household income
- educational level
- job or profession
- neighborhood of residence
- family status (for example, whether they have children or are caretakers for elderly parents)
- experience with social or medical issues that your organization addresses, and
- recreational activities and hobbies.

Once you decide what you want to know, there are a number of ways to gather the information. The simplest is to survey your existing donors. You can collect information from them along with their pledges of support; call them to say thanks after you receive a contribution and chat a bit; or request that they take an online survey.

Negative information can also be useful—you may occasionally wish to survey lapsed donors, asking for honest input on how they felt about your organization's performance and why they elected to end their support.

At a more personal level, some organizations set up focus groups, in which a selected group gathers to talk for an hour or two about why they care enough about your organization to support it financially.

If your organization can afford it, you can hire outside experts to do your donor profiling. Plenty of consultants will analyze organizations' existing donor pools, as well as their goals and subject areas, and match these with descriptions of potential new supporters. This matching will become particularly important if you embark on a program of finding donors through the mail, as discussed later in this chapter.

When Donors Gain Tax Deductions

As a nonprofit corporation organized under Section 501(c)(3) of the Internal Revenue Code, you are eligible to offer tax deductions to those who give you cash or certain other gifts. Many nonprofits throw the word "tax deductible" around when asking for gifts, but not all of them have a clear idea of what this means for the supporter.

This is especially problematic given that not every donor can make use of the tax deduction for charitable contributions—only those who itemize their deductions using Schedule A. This means that their itemized deductions must be higher than the standard deduction available to all taxpayers. And that's going to be only a small minority of taxpayers going forward, owing to changes made by the Tax Cuts and Jobs Act ("TCJA").

The new law, which took effect January 1, 2018, roughly doubled the standard deduction. It's now at $12,000 for single filers and $24,000 for married couples filing jointly. For around 95% of taxpayers (according to the Urban-Brookings Tax Policy Center), taking that standard deduction is a better deal than itemizing. (Say goodbye to the rush of gifts on December 31, when taxpayers were trying to maximize their deductions for the year.)

This isn't a change that will affect all donors, however. Historically, plenty of the people who contributed to nonprofits weren't the wealthiest in our society; they never had any use for a tax deduction, and got no tax benefit from donating to charity. The new law changes nothing about their motivation to give.

Meanwhile, for the few who can use the tax deduction, the benefits remain significant. Taxpayers are allowed to deduct the full amount of their charitable contributions, up to 60% of their adjusted gross income.

Exactly how much a particular donation will be worth in tax deductions depends first on what type of tax return the donor will file (single, married, and so on) and then on which tax bracket the donor falls into. (The tax bracket is the percentage of income a taxpayer must pay in tax; those who earn more fall into a higher brackct and, therefore, must pay a higher percentage of each dollar they earn in income tax.) For every dollar contributed to a charitable group, the donor will save what he or she would have had to pay in tax on that dollar—and because wealthier taxpayers pay more tax on the dollar, they also save more tax by taking tax deductions.

Tax deductions for donations of property. Donors may deduct gifts of both cash and property (land or personal property). However, special rules apply to setting a value on property, as described in IRS Publication 561, *Determining the Value of Donated Property (*which explains how to value anything from used clothing to Old Master paintings). If you're planning a vehicle donation program, be sure to see Publication 4302, *A Charity's Guide to Vehicle Donations*; you'll need to tell the donor the eventual sales price for tax purposes.

Supporters have a particular incentive to donate property that has gone up in value since they bought it, such as stock. If they sold the property for cash, they might have to pay capital gains tax. By donating the property directly to charity, however, they can deduct the full, current fair market value of the donated item, without worrying about the capital gains tax.

> EXAMPLE: Arif bought stock 12 years ago for $100. The stock is now worth $2,000. By donating the stock directly to the charity of his choice, Arif can (if he itemizes) take a $2,000 tax deduction. If he sold it instead, he would owe capital gains tax on his $1,900 profit.

 RESOURCE

Need more information on tax rules? The IRS provides an information line for tax-exempt organizations, at 877-829-5500. Also see *Every Nonprofit's Tax Guide*, by Stephen Fishman, J.D. (Nolo).

What About State Tax Deductions?

In response to the federal tax changes, various states have been looking into or proposing legislation to create a state-tax based incentive for making gifts to charity. It also happens that some states have separate charitable deduction laws on their books, or basically track the federal code and don't have any disincentives to claim the deduction. California, Minnesota, and Colorado are three examples.

California law basically adopts the federal standards for tax deductions on gifts to charity. (See California Revenue and Tax Code § 17201.) One important difference is that California has a 50% limitation on charitable contributions based on federal AGI, as compared to a 60% limit under federal law.

Because California's standard deduction is lower than the federal one, however, many taxpayers can and will want to itemize their charitable contributions on their California tax returns.

Taxpayers in the state of Minnesota who don't itemize deductions on their federal return can, on their state tax return, reduce the amount of their income that's subject to tax by 50% of total charitable contributions over and above $500. (See § 290.0132 Subd. 7 of the Minnesota Statutes.) The standards for which types of charitable donations "count" toward the subtraction follow the federal guidelines.

Colorado law (§ 39-22-104(4)(m)) says that taxpayers who have claimed the basic standard deduction on their federal return, and who thus can't benefit from a federal itemized deduction for charitable contributions, can take a subtraction on their Colorado return for the full amount of their charitable contributions over and above $500, limited only by a percentage of their adjusted gross income (AGI). The limitation is 50% of AGI in most cases. The subtraction means that Colorado taxpayers can literally lower their taxable income from the amount shown on their federal return. As in Minnesota, the standards for which donations "count" in this situation track the federal ones.

Consult a local tax expert about the law in the state where your nonprofit is located.

Tax deductions for volunteer work. Separate tax rules apply to people who volunteer their services and itemize deductions. The market value of the services themselves is not tax deductible. So, for example, if a licensed massage therapist donates services at your health clinic, or a lawyer gives your organization a free consultation, neither can claim a tax deduction. They can, however, deduct the costs of their unreimbursed expenses, including the use of their cars on behalf of your organization (gas, oil, parking, and tolls or a per-mile rate of 14¢), incidentals (such as treats with which to help train a shelter animal or art supplies brought to teach a Sunday school class), and travel expenses if they're away from home (transportation, meals, and lodging).

When receipts are required for tax purposes. You're required by the IRS to send donors a receipt for any gift valued at $250 or more, for them to keep in their tax files in case they're audited. But as a matter of good donor stewardship, you should send thank-you letters that also serve as receipts for all gifts. The receipt can simply be a letter, or even an email, but should always specify the value of the gift. (See Chapter 5 for more about thanking and providing receipts to donors.) For more information, see IRS Publication 526, *Charitable Contributions*.

Return Gifts to Donors

People don't give to good causes solely because of the promotional items they commonly get in return—but they might act faster or more decisively because of them. For example, if you were planning to give to your favorite public radio station anyway, but by pledging within the next hour you'll get a Bulgarian music CD that you can't get anywhere else, you might just get out of your chair and pick up the phone. And, because so many of us procrastinate, this might make the difference between the station's receiving your gift right now—or never.

Many organizations offer promotional items in return for donations, particularly when they're asking for an annual renewal of support. The lowest level of donation usually receives a token item (such as a poster) or nothing at all, but each higher level of donation comes with a gift of higher value. It's customary to list the gift premiums on the reply card right next to the suggested dollar amounts.

Make sure to include a box to check if the person doesn't want the gift (perhaps because they want to maximize the amount of their donation going toward services or they want the full tax deduction).

From your standpoint, the best promotions are the ones that don't cost anything to produce. For example, those radio station gifts are usually solicited in advance from publishers, stores, and restaurants, which realize that they'll get free advertising in return for giving the station some free or reduced-price products. Some organizations create their own low-cost gifts—for example, artworks or greeting cards with images drawn or photographed by their clients.

The value of a donation of cash or property must be reduced, for tax purposes, by the market value of anything substantial the donor receives in return. And, if the gift was worth $75 or more, you must send the donor a written statement with your good-faith estimate of how much he or she can deduct, after subtracting the fair market value of the item. For example, if a supporter sends you an $80 check that entitles her to a calendar with a fair market value (the amount it normally sells for) of $15, her contribution is valued at $65. It doesn't matter whether your organization paid anything at all for the item—the donor must subtract the value of what he or she receives.

> **EXAMPLE:** A soup kitchen holds a silent auction to raise money. One of its board members donates a weekend at her cabin. Roger and Allison put in the winning bid, at $60. They're excited, because this is a bargain—weekends at cabins in this area usually go for at least $150. However, if they were also hoping for a tax deduction, they're going to be disappointed. Because they didn't pay anything over and above the fair market value of what they received in return, they cannot claim a charitable donation.

Token or low-cost items, like stickers or bookmarks, need not be subtracted from the donation. (For 2019, a "token" item's cost to your organization could be no more than $11.10 and the contribution received must have been at least $55.50.) Token items must also bear your organization's name or logo. To qualify as "low-cost," the items must either have a fair market value of $111 or less, or be worth 2% or less of the donor's payment, whichever is lower. But the cost of raffle, bingo, or lottery tickets is never tax deductible (perhaps because every buyer is hoping for the grand prize). For more information, see IRS Publication 557, *Tax-Exempt Status for Your Organization,* and IRS Publication 1771, *Charitable Contributions: Substantiation and Disclosure Requirements.*

> CAUTION
> **Be prepared to market any homegrown items separately.** The costs of producing items like bumper stickers, mugs, or T-shirts usually mean that you're best off creating a large number at once. However, these could end up in a stack on your floor if not enough supporters respond to your appeal. See Chapter 9 for more on marketing and selling goods for your organization.

Bring in New Supporters

In the early days of an organization's life, finding supporters is usually a grassroots effort. Friends, fellow activists, fellow community members outraged by the prospect of a new, local supermall or the like, relatives, and people met on the street while getting petition signatures are among those who might be inspired to help. These early supporters might, in fact, be some of the most loyal ones, because they will feel a stake in an organization they helped found and a deep personal connection to the issue or cause.

As an organization grows, however, you'll need to look toward building a broader base of support. (Much of your communication may then be by mail. This is an ongoing task—there will never come a day when you can safely say, "That's enough, we have all the supporters we need to keep us going."

Most of your rank and file supporters probably won't stick around for more than two to three years. That may have nothing to do with the quality of your nonprofit; it's just an average based on other nonprofits' experience of people's giving patterns. In part, it's because many people who give to charity actually prefer to spread their giving around and will deliberately withdraw their support when they think it's someone else's turn. It's also partly because many nonprofits do a mediocre job at donor retention!

Your goal should always be to turn every casual supporter into someone who will stick with you over the long haul (see Chapters 5 and 6 for more on them). Treat every supporter as a potential major donor in the making.

But it's also important to be realistic. As your organization grows and your relationship with supporters becomes more distant, so does their level of loyalty. Even in a healthy organization, the majority of supporters will be of the "here today, gone tomorrow" variety; and you don't want to spend too much time chasing after a $25 gift.

Where do you find the new supporters who will replace those who move, die, or just have a short attention span? Here are some possibilities:

- individuals contacted personally by your board members, volunteers, and staff
- overlooked ethnic, racial, and other diverse communities
- the people your organization serves, their caregivers, or others in close contact with them
- people you meet in face-to-face solicitations
- people who hear about your organization through traditional and social media
- people you bring in through special events, and
- people you locate through direct mail solicitations.

TIP

Don't limit yourself to these techniques. Attracting new donors is an area where tapping your own creativity is key. Your entire staff, not only your fundraisers, should be encouraged to speak out positively about the work of your organization (including in their online social networks) and to collect the names, addresses, and other contact information of people who might want to help.

Your Circle of Friends

The most likely people to take an interest in your organization are those you know or are connected to. They may be living in the same community, commenting on the same social media pages, dealing with or personally interested in the same social, political, health, environmental, or other concerns, or perhaps just moved by hearing you talk about your cause. They may be the vendors who sell you paper or coffee!

Don't forget people who were once part of your community, but have moved on. Alumni of a school, class, or performance arts group are the most obvious example. Less obvious examples are people who have moved away in search of better opportunities, perhaps from a low-income or rural community. Such people may still feel the tug of their roots, and be willing to help—and their local friends and family are the ones likely to know how to reach them.

It should be a regular policy of your office to ask staff and board members for names and contact information of potential prospects. If this sounds like a lot of work, remember that the most effective way to raise money is through personal contacts. For an example of how one organization put this theory into practice, see "Zen Hospice Project Mobilizes Volunteers," below.

Zen Hospice Project Mobilizes Volunteers

The Zen Hospice Project, a San Francisco organization whose collaborative services include residential hospice care, volunteer programs, and educational efforts to foster wisdom and compassion in service, was facing a common challenge: The economy was down, individual donors were feeling exhausted by desperate appeals, and every nonprofit in town was trying to drum up new support. Lisa Ruth Elliott, then the development manager, described how Zen Hospice conducted one of its most successful campaigns ever:

"Mailing is generally a good strategy for us, since our organization touches people in a very personal way. However, we decided to take this approach one step further. We really engaged our volunteer caregiver corps—about 150 of them. These are people who ordinarily spend their time in the residential care part of our hospice, interacting on a weekly basis with terminally ill patients. Now, we asked them for their help in taking their stories to their communities, meditation groups, families, and friends and obtain their support. We put together fundraising packets for them that included talking points, newsletters, brochures, a sample fundraising letter, and a reply envelope. Some of the volunteer caregivers crafted letters based on their own experience— these were particularly effective.

"There was a bit of resistance at first. Some volunteer caregivers said things like, 'This is not something we should have to do,' or 'I'm scared; I can't fundraise.' However, we gave them a lot of support and the opportunity to ask questions as the campaign went along. Once they started to see the generosity of their communities, they got excited about the process. The results were impressive—the volunteer caregivers raised over $35,000 and contributed about $18,000 among themselves."

The name givers shouldn't have to worry that you'll hassle their buddies. You can approach potential new prospects with anything from a simple invitation to an event to an in-person meeting, depending on what seems appropriate. For further information on personal meetings with potential major donors, see Chapter 6.

Your circle of contacts also includes anyone who volunteers for your organization—even if it's just a one-shot deal. If, for example, a local company sends a crew of its employees to paint your building, staff a telethon, or provide other services, don't just say "thanks" and "goodbye"—get names and contact information from each and every person who arrives, then put them on your mailing list. (Studies show that people who spend time volunteering are almost 40% more likely to donate to a cause than those who don't.) Your first mailing should start with individual thank-you letters; then follow up with information on how they can become further involved.

New Friends in Diverse Communities

There's been much study lately on how to increase donor diversity—not only ethnic and racial diversity, but also diversity of lifestyle, age, gender, and physical ability. What the emerging findings show is that you may have to throw some of your old fundraising practices out the window in order to succeed with diverse donor groups.

When it comes to certain ethnic minorities, for example, research shows that their altruism is traditionally directed at groups other than mainstream nonprofits, often staying closer to home with family, church, and community groups. And contributions are often made in forms that fly under the traditional fundraising radar, such as collecting clothing or food for distribution to recent immigrants, or making small cash contributions directly to friends or community groups. Some of the supposedly tried-and-true methods of attracting new members, such as the direct mail approach we'll describe below, may seem distant and cold—and, therefore, may not be effective.

Where and how you focus your diversification efforts obviously depends on the community in which you're located as well as the clients or constituencies you're serving. If this is a new outreach effort for your organization, you have a lot of learning to do and shouldn't expect overnight success. You'll need to think carefully about who your most likely allies are and incorporate a long-term strategy to attract them into your fundraising plan. As part of this effort, you'll need to identify ways to increase the relevant community's trust in your organization, such as visibly participating in ethnic and community festivals and celebrations, advertising your job openings or special events in ethnic or group-based media, and recruiting diverse staff and board members. In other words, you need to get out and make friends before you can start turning people into donors.

A nonprofit whose own staff and board aren't representative of those from whom they seek support may have a tough time establishing credibility within a new group. Without a history of working together, you may encounter understandable suspicion that you're not "one of them" and are hoping only for a quick new cash source. The most natural way to break through this perception is by strengthening preexisting, natural relationships among your staff, board, and community members. This, too, will have to involve long-term planning—you can't just fire and replace your trusted staff and board members.

People Your Organization Serves

You may already be overlooking some of your most obvious supporters.

> **EXAMPLE:** An agency that helps immigrants and refugees opens its phone lines once a week for questions from the public. A woman calls, identifies herself as Kathy, and expresses concern that her children's nanny, who is from El Salvador, has been waiting years to hear whether she'll be granted political asylum. The nanny has a work permit, but nothing more. The staff lawyer explains that this is a normal delay and describes how to send the immigration authorities an inquiry just in case. Kathy is relieved, says, "Thank you, I couldn't seem to find this information anywhere else," and they politely end the call.

You can probably guess what went wrong in this example. The lawyer completely missed an opportunity to make Kathy, an already concerned (and possibly affluent) citizen, an active supporter of the organization. It's an understandable mistake—the lawyer is focused on providing direct services to the public, the next caller is already waiting, and the lawyer probably thinks fundraising is "not her department." But it would have been quite simple for the lawyer to get Kathy's full name and address, explain that thousands of people are in her nanny's position, and ask whether she could send Kathy more information about the organization. That's one more name on the database and at least one more potential check in the mail.

Look at your own organization's procedures and contacts with the public—are there people with whom you're missing a chance to connect? Not just your own clients, but people who call or visit your organization for information, buy a craft article at a fair, or even bring their kids trick-or-treating at your front office can all be given information and an opportunity to become supporters.

Also, think broadly about your indirect beneficiaries—for example, if you provide child care training services, the parents who hire your graduates are also benefiting from your organization, and should be given an opportunity to support your work. You're not twisting their arms; they can always say no.

What if your organization provides direct services to low-income clients who you believe can't possibly support you now, either by paying fees or making donations? Don't underestimate their value as supporters. For example, if you provide great services for homeless people, who knows better than they the value of your organization? They may even enjoy seeing the endeavor as a team effort in which they have a role to play. Some organizations have found that, until they got better at telling their clients about their fundraising needs, the clients just assumed the money flowed from the government or other source on high—and may have wondered why their service providers often seem frazzled and overbooked.

Even if they are truly penniless, your existing clients may provide help as volunteers, particularly on one-time projects, such as painting your facilities or participating in a special event. Longer term, it's possible that their economic and life circumstances may improve. (That may well be part of your goal in helping them.) Though keeping in touch after the immediate crisis is over can be difficult, try your best.

In an immigrants' services organization with which I worked, one of the staunchest supporters was a man from the Sudan whom the organization had helped gain political asylum. He happened to be a highly educated professional; once he got on his feet, he become a board member and tireless advocate.

What if your organization doesn't provide direct services at all and, so, doesn't have a client base to mobilize? There may still be ways in which you benefit a sector of the public that doesn't even realize it. Your job is to find those people while they're getting the benefit at issue. An organization in Utah, for example, was working to save an unprotected canyonland from mining and other development. While it relied on some of the traditional techniques for garnering interest and members—such as publicity and mailings—it realized that loads of potential supporters would probably never hear about its existence. To help reach them, the organization took the simple but brilliant step of posting volunteers outside the entrance to one of the area's existing parks. The volunteers briefly explained to people coming to enjoy the park what the future might hold and asked for financial and other support. In this way, they reached visitors from far and wide who might never have seen or responded to their local efforts—but who were concerned enough to support the cause.

Looking Beyond Your Client Base

Fundraising guru Tony Poderis tells the following story, which aptly illustrates how a little creative thinking can turn up potential supporters based on their existing links to your organization. (Check out his website at www.raise-funds.com.)

"One of the first organizations I ever worked with was Big Brothers of Greater Cleveland. At the time, it served more than 500 boys who did not have fathers at home. The boys' mothers weren't able to give much, but we did a little research and discovered that more than 10% of the women were employees of a local utility. Our funding request to the utility pointed this out and came complete with endorsements from many of those employees. The gift we got was far larger than the utility's usual contribution."

Grassroots Methods of Reaching Out to Supporters

Potential donors become tired of the barrage of indistinguishable emails, direct mail letters, and intrusions by professional telemarketers. In this climate, meeting an enthusiastic volunteer outside a grocery store or coffee shop can seem like a breath of fresh air. (But if the person is pushy or not well-trained, it can seem like an annoyance.)

Another grassroots technique that shouldn't be forgotten is leafleting. A simple one-page explanation of the issue at hand, what your organization is doing about it, and how people can get involved may be all you need— particularly for urgent or local issues, such as a pending development, a movement to restore a local landmark, or a need to support a local team or school. Don't forget to distribute your leaflets to local business owners, particularly if it's an issue in which they have a vested interest, such as neighborhood aesthetics.

If sending volunteers to wander outdoors seems a bit random, try more targeted presentations. Ask your board and staff whether their church, service organization, or other club would be open to a presentation from your organization. Make your presentation colorful and fun, then tell people how they can join in your exciting efforts through volunteering or donating. People's workplaces are also potential venues for such presentations, particularly if there's a thematic tie-in. For example, I was first introduced to immigration law while sitting around a conference table in a corporate law firm, listening to how nonprofit lawyers whose time was spent helping people who'd fled persecution presented their political asylum cases to judges. Like many corporate law firms, mine then allowed me to spend numerous hours helping these clients for no fee.

Supporters From Traditional and Social Media Outreach

Getting your name into the public's eye can have both direct and indirect fundraising benefits. Hopefully, at least a few of the people who watch an online video or read a news story about your work will be moved to contact you afterwards and offer financial support or volunteer help.

Young people in particular are most likely to first connect with your organization via social media—and to throw the snail mail letter described later in this chapter into the trash.

At an indirect level, the more exposure people have to your organization's good name, the more credibility they'll attach to it if and when you solicit them individually.

Because social media and other outreach are such important tools for reaching many types of funding sources (not just individual supporters), they're addressed separately, in Chapter 11.

Crowdfunding Campaigns

Tell people you're trying to raise money for your nonprofit, and they're likely to ask, "Have you tried Kickstarter?" (Or Fundraise.com, CauseVox, Fundly, Mightycause, StartSomeGood, Indiegogo, Chuffed, or some other crowdfunding platform.) Such sites are getting lots of buzz—and they've raised plenty of money for the nonprofits (as well as artists, filmmakers, and businesses) that know how to use them. (Your organization could also, by the way, set up a crowdfunding campaign on its own website, but you'd need someone with technical expertise to set it up, and to devote some resources to monitoring it.)

Crowdfunding can be particularly effective for reaching millennials who, it's often said, are more motivated to give to issues or causes than to organizations. And by 2025, according to a study commissioned by the World Bank, the global crowdfunding market could reach $90 billion or more.

Is Your Nonprofit Ready for Crowdfunding?

Crowdfunding is a tool, not a magic wand. For one thing, crowdfunding is not meant for ongoing fundraising. The usual idea is that after you've paid some combination of fees for setup, monthly use, and transaction processing, you get to post a page on one of these websites saying, in essence, "Hey, we're trying to raise $X by X date to do X-and-such, can you all pitch in and tell your friends? Also (*according to the rules of some sites*), you'll get X as a thank-you gift or 'perk,' and if we don't raise the needed amount, you'll get your money back!"

Users donate online, and if all goes well, the hosting platform transfers the proceeds to you at the end of this minicampaign, minus a percentage.

CAUTION

Return gifts have tax implications. Your organization (or the host platform, if its services include it) will not only need to send out thank-you letters and receipts, but, under the IRS's quid pro quo contribution rules, tell donors the fair market value of any non-token goods or services they received. Some nonprofits have gotten around this concern by having the gift come directly from a third party who is participating in the campaign.

As for giving money back if you don't reach your goal, that's not the norm on all sites; and you need only *offer* the money back. (Many people would probably allow you to keep it.) On Indiegogo, you choose in advance whether or not to keep all the proceeds; though if you choose that arrangement, you'll have to pay a higher commission to the site.

Another issue is that, unless your campaign is hugely lucky and instantly goes viral, you've largely got to find your own "crowd." Depending on which platform you use, you may not only be competing with other nonprofits, but with savvy artists and entrepreneurs, all trying to attract the same bunch of people. In her experience giving workshops on crowdfunding to nonprofit leaders and other entrepreneurs, Professor Krista Tuomi has found that, "Almost everyone thinks theirs is the project that's going to go viral. But the sad reality is that, depending on the platform, only 11% to 31% of crowdfunding projects reach their financial target. There might be a silver lining; the group might bring in new supporters or learn what works for next time; but still, I'd recommend doing the background work required to hit that goal."

It's not easy to make your voice heard or to come up with an idea that will take off. Unless your nonprofit already has significant online contacts through its email list, website, and social media, and a good sense of how to create compelling online content that they will want to share with their own circles, it may not be ready for crowdfunding.

Of course, there are consultants who can help with your crowdfunding campaign. (Some nonprofits report that the first people they hear from after launching a crowdfunding page are consultants wanting to help them improve it!) They typically charge a percentage of the amount raised.

There are, however, situations where a crowdfunding effort might work, namely where your nonprofit:

- has a particular, tangible, urgent goal in mind—such as a new vehicle or piece of equipment, a trip to a project site, medical care for one individual, or production of a film; or a time-delimited concept around which to fundraise, such as a matching grant or the birthday of a celebrity supporter who makes a personal request for donations
- can confidently predict that the goal is sufficiently exciting, moving, or fun that a specific audience within your existing supporters and social media contacts will tell their friends about it; and they, despite knowing little to nothing about your organization, will be moved to pitch in (campaigns that incorporate a personal story and an emotional component tend to do best)
- has the skills to present the idea in an attractive way, preferably complete with photos, graphics, and video, and
- has loyal supporters who will create tangential pages connected to your nonprofit's master page (as is allowed on some sites), on which they ask friends and connections to give.

TIP

What if your crowdfunding earnings exceed the goal? Any extra that's legally considered "restricted funds" can be used only for the specific purposes the donor gave. As attorney Jean Tom (with Davis Wright Tremaine in San Francisco) explains, "It would be a shame if you, for instance, raised twice the money needed to buy a van and then had to return the extra." To avoid such scenarios, she suggests, "If the platform allows it, it may be helpful to include language in the crowdfunding pitch along the lines of, 'Projects listed are just some examples of how funds may be used to fulfill _____ goal.' Or, you might briefly describe what will happen to any extra funds (e.g., 'Any funds that exceed our goal will be used to support our other critical education programs'); or indeed to any and all funds if it later turns out your organization can't pursue the project. The safest bet is to work with legal advisers to incorporate appropriate language into your crowdfunding pitch, your contract with the platform, as well as into contracts between the platform and your donors."

By the way, it doesn't necessarily have to be your nonprofit that sets up an original crowdfunding page. Any of your supporters may do so, if they are motivated and have a wide personal network to tap into. Of course, you'll do best to provide advice and support for such efforts. In fact, you might want to noodle around the Internet to see whether people are trying to crowdfund for your organization without your knowledge. If so, check on whether you're happy with how your work is being represented. You may need to contact the person who posted it with corrections or requests for changes. If it's truly unacceptable, you can ask the platform to take the listing down.

Choosing a Crowdfunding Platform

To learn more about and choose from among the various crowdfunding sites, visit them yourself. Pretend you're a potential donor, and check out the various projects and campaigns vying for funding. The "most popular" projects will give you a sense of whether yours might measure up. Look at the less popular ones, too. You'll probably notice things to avoid, such as the tendency of nonprofits to simply say, "Please support our work; our mission is this." Such messages lack any sense of urgency, and appear dull by comparison to the others.

Also take a careful look at each crowdfunding site's reputation (check their BBB ratings), features, fees, ease of use, terms, and level of success being achieved by other nonprofits. You're looking in particular for:

- Ability to customize your organization's page with its own branding, so that it will look familiar and trustworthy to visitors. Better yet is if the host will list your organization's name, not its own name, on donor credit card statements—however, this may depend on whether the crowdfunding site is serving as your agent in raising the funds or is itself accepting the funds and then regranting them to your organization.

- A feature allowing your supporters and volunteers to set up their own subpages, to which they can send their friends.

- Access to donor contact information, allowing you to import it into your organization's database for follow-up cultivation. (Some platforms claim donor privacy, which could mean you'll receive only one-time gifts from "Anonymous" or a batch of unattributed gifts from the platform.)

- Lots of help with administrative tasks, such as sending donation receipts, advising viewers of the latest donation total, and so on.
- Attunement to the needs of nonprofits. Some platforms are themselves 501(c)(3)s, which can be helpful. If you choose one that's not, make sure the cause-related nature of your pitch doesn't get buried. For instance, attorney Jean Tom cautions, "On some sites, viewers have to be pretty savvy (checking the FAQs and so forth) to figure out whether their contribution will be to a nonprofit. Your campaign may be mixed in with pitches from individuals seeking medical care, businesses seeking start-up cash, and so on."
- A fair and simple system for charging you fees and commissions, as well as quick transfer of donor funds. Watch out for per-check charges if this is how you choose to receive your money.

Both before and after you choose a host platform for your campaign, do a test run, click by click, pretending you're a donor. Read any and all fine print.

Supporters Through Special Events

Any event that you hold or participate in—whether it be an arts or entertainment event, lecture, crafts fair, walkathon, petition drive, or annual dinner—is an opportunity to inspire and bring in new donors. Because special events are an important fundraising tool of their own, and not merely useful for bringing in new supporters, they're covered in detail in Chapter 8. But now is a good time to remind yourself that every special event provides a great opportunity to collect the names and contact information of potential new supporters. (Perhaps you will have already captured this information from the main ticket buyers, but not from their guests.)

There are various ways to collect this information without seeming intrusive. For example, I once attended a concert given by a nonprofit musical society, at which attendees were invited to enter their names and addresses into a raffle for free tickets to a future concert. Not too surprisingly, I've been receiving newsletters and fundraising appeals from them ever since. (An alternative raffle prize might be items donated by local businesses.) I fell for a similar technique at a theater event, in which audience members were invited to "vote" on the outcome of the plot. The ballots asked for our name and address and also offered a raffle prize. And yes, I'm on yet another mailing list.

Also remember that personal checks you receive from ticket buyers and others usually have addresses on them. Don't cash them without first making a photocopy, so that you can enter the information into your database. (But keep such copies in a secured file.)

Be sure to make people aware of your organization's name at any event. I've attended a number of benefit concerts where the charitable organizations never made it clear who they were and what they planned to do with the money raised. Perhaps they just weren't very efficient, they assumed that most attendees were long-time supporters, or they were shy about intruding on people's "pure" enjoyment of the event. But, in fact, many audience members' enjoyment is enhanced by hearing that they are helping a good cause.

If there's an intermission, the opening of the second half is a good time to have a representative of your organization speak briefly but directly about its work and how donations help. Also make clear where people can pick up brochures or learn more, and put out a clipboard so people can, if they so desire, sign up to be on your mailing list. A collection basket by the ticket desk doesn't hurt, either. And, of course, the event program should mention your organization's name, website, and other contact information and give a brief blurb on the activities the benefit is helping fund. Many people bring these programs home!

Donors Through Direct Mail

There's one more possibility for attracting supporters—a direct mail campaign.

Soliciting new supporters by mail is a small subset of all the types of mail your organization might send out, which include brochures, newsletters, or appeal letters you send your existing supporters. A direct mail, new-supporter solicitation is one in which you beg, borrow, trade, or buy a mailing list that comes from another organization or a marketing specialist. You then send letters to all the names on the list—or to a test sample (usually 1,000 to 10,000 names) from that list—explaining the work of your organization and asking for support.

In theory, you could do the same thing via email, rather than U.S. mail—and of course, do it much cheaper. However, because of the backlash against spam, email is better reserved for follow-up with people who have already indicated some interest in your organization.

> CAUTION
>
> **Don't misuse membership rosters.** Many professional, social, and alumni groups publish lists of their members, with contact information—and it can be awfully tempting to borrow one. However, read the fine print: Many such rosters specifically warn the members that letting the list be used without permission will be frowned upon, or worse. Also, you are implicitly invading people's privacy— something that is sooner or later (probably sooner) going to anger key supporters.

Most everyone has mixed feelings about direct mail fundraising. We all receive too much of it, it kills trees, and we're increasingly hip to all the tricks—the "urgent" stamps on the outside, the seemingly handwritten envelopes, the promises of free gifts inside, the little see-through windows trying to fool us into thinking it's a check.

Even if the letters your organization sends out are understated and honest, the majority will be thrown in the trash. You'll be lucky to break even on your first mailing, and you'll probably have to invest a few years in trying out various lists and refining your methods before you see a return in immediate and long-term support.

Despite all this, however, direct mail can be a cost-effective way to reach donors who might not hear of your organization by any other means. If you've designed your letters well and sent them to the appropriate recipients, a certain percentage of them will be opened and read. One percent is considered a respectable number, and 0.8% is more normal.

While these immediate returns may seem negligible, look at the longer term. Small-time supporters whom you initially find via direct mail may turn into your long-time contributors and major donors—and all for the initial cost of some staff time, some paper, and a stamp.

CAUTION

Don't start a direct mail campaign until you're ready for major donors. This discussion assumes that you're in a position to handle donor steward-ship and major donor solicitation. If you're not, be wary about investing heavily in direct mail now. If you back out halfway, those initial letter and stamp costs will have been wasted—and they add up fast.

Direct mail solicitation involves much more than simply sending out a bunch of letters. You'll have to choose the right mailing lists, design and write an attractive appeal—or two, if you want to test out different approaches—have them printed and packaged, and deal with arcane postal regulations if you send the letters bulk mail. Then comes opening the return letters, cashing the checks or running the credit card donations, entering the results into a database, sending out thank-you letters—and just when you think you're ready for a rest, starting all over with another list.

Create or Choose a Mailing List

One of your first steps is to find a mailing list and decide how many people to solicit. In some situations, you can create your own list. For example, if you've just held a special event and you have the names of the ticket buyers, they should go on your list. Similarly, names collected from board members and other volunteers can be added to a mailing list. You can also cull your organization's old records for the names of donors who haven't given for a few years and have thus been dropped from recent mailings.

Your next best bet is to trade lists with another nonprofit organization. Though that may sound entirely counterintuitive—like everyone trying to take bites out of the same cookie—studies have shown that many supporters give to more than one organization anyway. There's usually no direct harm in revealing the names of your supporters to others, or vice versa. That said, you may sensibly conclude that you want to avoid direct competition with a very similar group. Your best bet is to look for an organization whose work is complementary to yours in a way that reflects underlying affinities to your donors. For example, an ethnic arts organization and an immigrants' rights organization might be logical trades, or a women's musical group and a women's political group.

After a little testing, you can expand your list trading to groups whose members have less obvious affinities to your members. The concept of affinity is both psychologically simple and ultimately unpredictable. Your goal is to locate lists of people who are most like your typical donors—whose hearts are not only in the right place (because they give to charity) but are in similar places when it comes to choosing a charity. With enough testing, you're likely to find affinities you wouldn't have expected. For example, Project Open Hand, a Bay Area organization that provides home-delivered, hot, nutritious meals to homebound people with critical illnesses, has found that donor lists from arts and environmental organizations yield particularly good results for them.

> **CAUTION**
>
> **Watch out for duplicate names.** If you're combining lists to get to the number you want, some names may appear more than once. You may want to run what's called a merge/purge to identify and delete the duplicates.

If you've already run through these options, your primary remaining avenue is to rent a mailing list. Sometimes this is loosely referred to as "buying" a mailing list. However, mailing lists are valuable property—you probably couldn't afford to buy the whole thing for keeps. But many are made available for a one-time rental, from sources including other nonprofits, magazines, businesses, museums, schools, and many more. Again, you should be looking for lists of people with likely affinities to your group, but who are preferably not already donors of organizations nearly identical to yours.

Mailing lists vary widely in price because they vary in quality. The closer the list is to what you need, the more you're likely to pay for it! Before agreeing to rent any list, ask questions to assure yourself of its quality, such as when it was last updated, and whether qualified professionals do the data entry.

To prevent you from copying the list, you will probably never actually get your hands on it—the list will be handled by a go-between. Even if you are given direct access to it, however, most organizations plant a couple of "seed" names into their lists, addressed to their own staff or board members, so that they catch anyone who tries to use their entire list a second time. When your organization gets around to trading or renting your list, you should implement the same security measures.

CAUTION

Your own list is a commodity, too. As your own list of supporters develops, you'll naturally feel very protective of it. You should be—never just give your list away for free. But also consider this: You've got a commodity that can bring in rental fees, and such a source of revenue shouldn't be ignored. You definitely don't want to rent the list out too frequently—both because you'll anger your supporters, and because a less-frequently rented list has a higher value. But with some careful thought, and screening of the list renters to ensure that they are appropriate and not too competitive with your own organization, industry expert Mike Maxwell explains, "You should feel comfortable doing list exchanges—it's how the fundraising business is done." For the sake of your supporters, be sure to honor any of their requests that you not include their names on any shared mailing lists.

The result of the one-time use practice is that you've got only one chance to turn the names on any one list into supporters. But once a mail recipient responds to your mailing, you're free to continue the relationship. You can see why direct mail solicitation is an ongoing process: You'll need to keep trying out various lists, homing in on the categories of recipients that seem to produce good results, and so on.

Finding a mailing list to rent is a less mysterious process than you might think (although, because of the costs and level of effort, it's probably not appropriate for newer, low-budget organizations). In fact, a whole profession has grown up around matching nonprofits and other businesses with mailing lists, known as "list brokers." Ask your colleagues at other nonprofits for recommendations of good brokers who specialize in working with nonprofits, or look for ads in the *Nonprofit Times* and *Chronicle of Philanthropy.* The great thing is, you not only save time and gain the list broker's expertise about what works, but you don't usually pay the broker directly for his or her services (though you'll pay for the rental of the lists themselves). The broker is ordinarily paid by arrangement with the organization that rents you the list.

How large a list should you start out with? That depends mostly on the size of your organization and how much you're willing to invest in initial test mailings. However, the prevailing wisdom is that an initial mailing should include no fewer than 2,000 names and as many as 500,000.

Prepare the Letter and Remainder of the Mailing

Now you have to come up with something to send to this select group. The standard direct mail package comprises four or possibly five parts, including:

- outer envelope
- letter
- reply device
- envelope in which to send the reply back, and
- insert (optional).

 TIP

There's no magic formula—testing is the key. Below, you'll find various suggestions for how to draft and design compelling parts of a direct mail package. But, particularly because every added element can also add expense, you've got to set aside any assumptions and test to see what works on your own donors. As your direct mail program develops, this will literally mean dividing every mailing list in two and sending your basic, tried-and-true "control" package to half the list, and a "test" package containing anything new to the other half. Or, divide your list into thirds if you're mailing one control and two test packages. As an example, says Mike Maxwell, "I've seen compelling teasers and photos on outer envelopes work extremely well, but I've also seen instances where they depressed the response rate. Test to see which works best—you may be surprised by the results."

The outer envelope. Most people—and some say *all* young people—will take one look at your mail package, decide, "Oh, it's just a request for money," and toss it into the trash unopened. So consider how your outer envelope can induce recipients to actually open it. Printing a photo or a few words about your cause may be helpful. Or you can make the package look more official, with see-through windows and warnings such as "TIME-SENSITIVE MATERIALS ENCLOSED." Some organizations have even tried putting a nickel inside! Keep it simple, however—splashing too much text and imagery across the envelope reminds people of cheap commercial marketing.

The letter. The central item should be a letter, on your organization's stationery, between one and four pages long. Exactly how long is best continues to be debated by fundraisers. Some say one-pagers are better for today's attention-deficient readers, while others say that only the heft of a four-page letter conveys authority and substance. If you're going to go for a four-pager, it had better be a real page-turner (or start out so strong that only a few people will feel the need to keep reading before donating).

Mike Maxwell, drawing on his 20-plus years of direct mail experience, reiterates: "I've seen donor solicitation packages get simpler and shorter. Years ago, you could send long letters with multiple inserts and people responded. Today, there's greater competition in the mailbox for donor dollars. Many donors seem to appreciate you getting to the point in an honest and succinct fashion. Every page or component that you add may unnecessarily raise your production costs. While you should always invest enough in your mailing to build a compelling case for support, you may find that a two-page letter raises—or at least nets—just as much money as a six-page letter, perhaps more. What's most important is that you test these assumptions over time."

Even if you're getting help from a direct mail professional, it's best to keep control of the process, by writing the initial draft of the letter yourself or suggesting detailed material for it.

Before you even get to the text, you've got to figure out who your letter will be addressed to. In fact, you might get hung up on the "Dear So and So." If you've got the technology, it's best to use the person's name rather than "Dear Friend." Here's the first reason why it's important to use a quality mailing list, however. People whose names are misspelled may toss the letter right then and there. ("Dear Friend" sounds far better than "Dear Mr. Carolyn Reeeed.")

A number of nonprofits don't even wait for the "Dear" line to launch into their story, but capture people's attention with a "teaser" paragraph, known as a "Johnson box." It's usually in a different font, in the upper-right area of the letter.

TIP

Make the letter from "me" to "you." This is a personal letter, not a college essay or an academic paper—so make liberal use of personal pronouns and ditch any overly long words or flowery language! The letter should address the reader as "you," and be written in the honest voice of the "I" who will sign it. Any other personal links you can mention—even simple statements like, "I know you share our concern for urban creek protection," will also help to draw the reader in.

With or without a Johnson box, the opening paragraph of your letter can be the hardest to write. Nonprofits have tried every catchy opening in the book. However, the type that seems to draw people in the most effectively is a personal story. This isn't just a quirk among people who donate to charity—human nature makes us all particularly interested in other humans (or animals). If your organization doesn't work directly with living creatures, don't worry—there's always a way to connect it to something alive. For example, one of your volunteers could describe why she has devoted every Saturday afternoon for the last several years to your cause. Personal quotes, either from clients or others participating in your work, are also a powerful way to remind people that you're not just making this stuff up.

In the rest of the letter, you'll want to build on the opening story, so that the reader comes to appreciate:

- the scope of the problem
- why your organization is well placed to help solve that problem
- why this should capture the reader's heart or mind, and
- how the reader can make an immediate, measurable difference, primarily financially, but possibly with volunteer and other opportunities as well.

In a way, your letter is like a mininovel. There's a conflict, or perhaps a person in distress. (That someone should be your clients or the cause you serve, not your own organization—potential failure doesn't sell well.) Then there's a duo of heroes—your organization and the person you're reaching out to. The plot you are constructing should also point to the prospect of a happy resolution. This is particularly important, because people's usual reasons for giving often include a healthy dose of self-interest—they want their voices to be heard, and to help create a world that's more in tune with their values and dreams.

Unlike a novel, however, your letter's reader is not going to be curled up in a chair with a cup of hot cocoa. More likely, he or she will be ripping open the envelope while shedding coat, bag, and groceries after a long day's work. Your main points need to stand out strong and stand out fast.

Some helpful tools for this are old-fashioned underlining and bullet points. You can underline a few key important words or phrases, such as "<u>While our theatre productions are ever more popular, ticket sales cover only 60% of our annual expenses.</u>" (But don't overdo it!)

Also avoid one of the most common mistakes made by fundraising letter writers: loading the text down with big, thick paragraphs (particularly in a small font). Eliminate extra words, and break these into shorter, even single-sentence paragraphs so that the eye has somewhere to move. Or, if an important list of items is buried in a long string or separated by many commas, think about using bullets to highlight them. For example:

"Instead of having nothing to do after school, youth in our program can:
- participate in our basketball team
- volunteer in community activities, or
- receive one-on-one support from trained counselors."

> **TIP**
>
> **If your letter is good enough, use it more than once.** There's no need to rewrite your letter every time. Once you hit on a content and presentation that inspires donations, keep using the letter—or its basic structure, with some freshening up—for as long as it's effective. Some respected organizations have been using the same letter for years! But also keep testing out alternatives, so that you can retire the letter after you've outdone it with an even more effective one.

At the end of the letter, there's no need to be subtle. The reader probably already guessed you were going to ask for money. Come straight out and say something like, "We hope you'll help us with your contribution," or "Now we are asking you to make a tax-deductible donation," or "Every $_____ you give will put a meal onto the table of a housebound senior."

In the past, there was much brow knitting on the subject of who should sign these solicitation letters, with nonprofits frantically looking for a famous person to lend his or her name. However, the consensus that has developed is that your executive director or a board member is the most natural signer and will get as good a response as anyone else. The exception is if a famous person is intimately involved with your organization and eager to speak out about it.

Most organizations end their letters with postscripts. They do it for a reason: It adds a sense of up-to-the-minute urgency that the rest of the letter doesn't have. And because of that, it often gets read first. For example, your PS might say "Every gift that we receive before [_date_] will be matched by a gift from the _____ Foundation," or "Eighty percent of every dollar you give goes straight to helping people in need."

Even better is to organize your volunteers to come in and handwrite personal notes as PSs—though this will preclude you from using bulk mail, because all the letters will no longer be identical. The personal touch may be worth a first class stamp, however.

> **CAUTION**
> **You may have to run your letter past a local government body.** Check with your lawyer, board members, or other organizations for more information.

The reply device. For those who wish to give by mail, include a reply card, on which the person indicates how much he or she is giving and by what means (check, credit card, monthly installments, or whatever you're prepared to offer). You've seen a thousand of these reply cards before—the format is fairly standard. The card should be attractive and self-contained—some people toss the letter, but keep the reply card around in case they decide to donate.

If you have a website, list its URL on the reply card and mention that supporters can donate online. This will be the preference of many donors, particularly young ones. Make sure your website is a welcoming place for first-time visitors; highlights the same topics as mentioned in the letter; and provides a quick path to a donation page. (For more on making your website attractive to donors, see Chapter 11.)

The biggest decision you'll make is simply what gift amounts to suggest (for example, "☐ $25 ☐ $50 ☐ $100 ☐ Other"). Starting out with too low an amount may encourage people to take advantage of that option. On the other hand, I know of an organization that suggested $1, simply as a way of building their membership, in accordance with a strategy of approaching foundations with a strong showing of community support. You'll need to choose suggested donation levels based on your sense of your potential supporters' giving capacities and your ability to credibly ask for high amounts.

Some organizations like to attach names to the various giving levels, such as "bronze," "silver," and "gold." This helps inspire people toward higher gifts and allows you to group donors' names in publications such as your annual report. Naming the giving levels can, however, be tricky. Each giving level needs to sound appropriately recognized, with no one falling into a category like "tin" or "aluminum alloy."

Some groups get around the ranking problem by assigning value-neutral names. Bryn Mawr College, for example, names its "donor societies" after historic college buildings, such as Cloisters, Pembroke Arch, and Goodhart. Yet another alternative is to give a quick summation of what each gift level will fund, as in "☐ $500 (funds one student fellowship for four weeks)."

If people will receive something in return for different gift levels (a fleece vest or baseball cap, for example), your suggested amounts should of course bear some proportional relation to the value of this return gift.

The reply envelope. The reply card should fit neatly into an addressed reply envelope (which has to be small enough to fit into your cover envelope). But should you provide return postage? Fortunately, most people willing to donate to your organization are also willing to put their own stamp on the letter. You'll add a lot to your costs if you put first-class stamps on the envelopes. Organizations with higher budgets and more experience at direct mail may wish to send preprinted, business reply envelopes (with those postal seals that say "No Postage Necessary If Mailed in the United States"). But believe it or not, the postage on these is actually higher than a first-class stamp, though your overall costs should be lower because you only pay for those envelopes that donors actually mail back to you.

Optional inserts. You can also include things like a Post-it® note with an urgent or "late-breaking" message, a relevant news clipping, or a "freebie" such as return address stamps or a bumper sticker. All of these will, of course, add to the costs of your package. If you're new to direct mail, you might as well go without them—particularly the freebies, which are getting so common that people feel less and less obligated to give anything in return. You can always try adding such extras later.

Eventually, however, you may find that certain types of extras are very effective. For example, Project Open Hand, a Bay Area nonprofit that provides nourishing meals to seniors and people living with AIDS and other serious illnesses, saw response rates go up by 7% when they included a donor involvement device in the form of "meal certificates" with acquisition mailings. They're actually a combination of reply device and insert. Donors choose an amount to give to a person in need of food, such as $35 for a "Certificate Good for 1 Week's Worth of Meals." The certificates are expensive to produce, adding 2% to overall costs. But with the high return, they're clearly worth it. And they feel tangible to people, who can see that they're giving something specific. (See a sample of Project Open Hand's meal certificates below.)

Meal Certificates From Project Open Hand

Reprinted with permission

CAUTION

Don't add extras to some letters and not others. If you're planning to mail via bulk mail, the U.S. Postal Service (USPS) demands that each of your letters be of the same weight.

Make the final product look professional. With new technology and in-house publishing programs, assembling professional-looking packages on your own is getting easier. A staff or board member who has photographic or artistic abilities (not just amateur) may come in handy to add visuals to the package. A compelling picture can be worth pages of explanations.

If you'll be using a professional printer or mail house, get recommendations from other nonprofits. Some printers specialize in working with nonprofits and will help you figure out ways to keep down costs and produce something in line with your own values. For example, an environmental organization might want to use obviously recycled paper—but still have the mailing package look classy and be affordable.

CAUTION
Whether you'll be using a professional or printing in-house, proofread everything several times. Professional printing is not like photocopying; a word that you typed perfectly in your version can transmute into something else through the "miracles" of scanning or program conversions. And be alert for sins of omission— for example, the one board member whose name was left off, or a photo without explanatory text.

The Mechanics of Mailing

Getting a mailing out creates a busy time at a nonprofit, whether you're handling it in-house or through a printer and/or mail house. No matter which, you'll want to give everything one last looking over—or two. Then have everyone—including volunteers and possibly staff members who don't normally participate in development activities—ready to kick into high gear.

If someone at your organization or from your board is going to personally sign the letter, make sure he or she won't be on vacation that week, and can spare an hour or two. Someday, of course, your group will use printed signatures, though it makes the letter one step less personal.

If you're doing the mailing in-house, several boxes of paper will arrive from the printer, and you'll need to have staff and volunteers lined up to deal with them. Depending on what services you ordered, you may need to have volunteers fold the letters and combine them with the reply cards and envelopes before placing them in the mailing envelope. Give your workers a clean space, miles away from any coffee or snacks. Carefully train everyone in the assembly process. Letters should be neatly folded and placed in the envelope so that the greeting is the first thing the reader sees upon opening it, with the other inserts behind.

As a nonprofit, you can take advantage of the USPS reduced mailing rates if you're sending 200 or more identical pieces of standard domestic mail (same size and weight, up to 15.999 ounces sorted by zip code). You'll need to plan for this in advance, first by getting a permit, using USPS Form 3624, *Application to Mail at Nonprofit Standard Mail Rates,* available at pe.usps. com. (Click "Nonprofit USPS Marketing Mail Eligibility.") Your permit will lapse, and you'll need to reapply if you don't use it at least every two years. The exact postal rates will vary, depending on the size of your letter and the rate for which you qualify.

Be warned, however, that the nonprofit regulations are tricky. In fact, people usually attend trainings just to find out how to organize and prepare mail in a way that meets the postal service's requirements.

And you can't just go to any post office once you're done—you'll have to work through the one where you filed your application.

Various software programs (either within your fundraising database program or separate) can make preparing your bulk mailing—in particular, the envelopes and labels—easier. Nevertheless, mail houses are the choice of many nonprofits, despite the added costs. As Lisa Ruth Elliott (formerly of Zen Hospice) points out, "With a mail house, there's less chance of the process dragging on. You can ask them to have it done within a certain length of time. If you do the mailing in-house, the paper can build up and consume your office. At least make sure to have a number of experienced volunteers on hand if you go this route."

After assessing and comparing the time and costs of a mail house and of learning to use and handling bulk mail yourself, you may discover that first-class stamps are actually your most cost-effective option. This isn't a cop-out—many organizations decide the same thing (take a look in your mailbox and see). First-class mail can also be forwarded if the addressee has moved; bulk mail doesn't offer this advantage.

 RESOURCE
Want more detailed information on bulk mailing? Take a look at these resources:
- The U.S. Postal Service's website at pe.usps.com. Look for Publication 417, *Nonprofit Standard Mail Eligibility*.
- The Alliance of Nonprofit Mailers. See www.nonprofitmailers.org.

Follow Up

After your mailing goes out, you can collapse—for no more than ten days, however. With any luck, replies will be rolling in steadily by then. I don't need to tell you to rip open those first envelopes quickly. But you'll also have to keep up a steady pace, carrying out these critical follow-up tasks:
1. Photocopy the checks and forward these and all credit card information to your accounting department.
2. Enter the supporter information and gift amounts in your database.
3. Send thank-you letters (discussed in detail in Chapter 5).

Each of these should be done within 24 hours to two days of receiving the replies (the sooner the better). For one thing, some people don't balance their checkbooks and will keep drawing out money until it's gone, unless you get there first. For another, developing an up-to-date system of data entry is crucial at every stage of your organization's activities; once you start getting behind on this, you may never catch up. And third, supporters who aren't thanked immediately can take it personally.

CAUTION

Quick thank-you letters are that important. I once heard a radio show debate over whether a charity-based bicycle event had become too corporate. One person called in for the sole purpose of announcing that she'd stopped her support because it took the event organizers two months to send her a thank-you letter. It's easy to understand how this might have happened: Events take up staff time, the data entry person perhaps quits and is replaced by a part-time temp, and the reply cards pile up in a corner with the most recent tossed on the top as the bottom ones molder. But the supporter in this example doesn't know about all this, nor should she. She simply views a thank-you letter as an indication of how well an organization is run and how much it appreciates her support.

If you don't think you can handle rapid follow-up, either hire a professional, or delay soliciting supporters by direct mail until your organization is better prepared for the aftermath. You can inspire even greater donor loyalty by combining a thank-you phone call with the letter.

Most supporters will send their replies within about the first month after you sent the mailing (though some people will literally add them to a pile that they'll hold for their end-of-year decision making). Wait until your replies have fallen to a mere trickle, then evaluate the success of your mailing by filling out the Mailing Evaluation form below (also online; see the appendix for the link).

For **Item B,** include not only the costs of printing, postage, and materials, but also any special staff or professionals hired to help. You don't, however, need to include the hours put in by development staff who would be working anyway. For **Item F,** don't be surprised at a low percentage—a 1% response rate is considered successful. Hopefully, **Item G** will be a positive number, indicating that the mailing at least broke even. But if it isn't, focus your (and your board's) attention on the number of new supporters. With proper cultivation and renewal efforts, one of them could turn into your next $10,000 donor.

Fundraising Worksheet 4: Mailing Evaluation

For mailing sent [*date*], consisting of:

_____

_____

_____

_____

Describe appeal and any special enclosures:

_____

_____

_____

A. Number of letters sent out   _____

B. Total expenses of mailing $ _____

C. Number of new supporters   _____

D. Total amount of donations $ _____

E. Usual donation amount $ _____

F. Percentage of response (C divided by A)   _____ %

G. Net profit (D minus B) $ _____

H. Cost of acquiring each new supporter (B divided by C) $ _____

Comments:

_____

_____

_____

_____

_____

How to Keep the Givers Giving

A first-time donation is an opportunity, not a fait accompli. Typically, it means that the person was momentarily persuaded to contribute, by one or another of your organization's fundraising efforts. It probably wasn't a huge amount, either. According to Blackbaud, the median donation amount for gifts under $1,000 is $20. Unfortunately, without your creative intervention, the donor's impulse may well turn out to be not only low-budget but fleeting.

Studies of lapsed supporters have found that a significant number couldn't remember having supported the particular organization in the first place! Given the high cost of finding a first-time supporter, this is not what you want from your own supporters.

Retaining a supporter costs only one fifth of what you'll spend to attract him or her in the first place, which makes donor retention a relatively low-cost source of untapped potential for many organizations.

This chapter will help you figure out how to keep a healthy percentage of your donors giving and how to increase their support over the years. Some people refer to this progressive process as moving supporters up a giving ladder, or bringing them closer and closer within concentric circles of engagement. Eventually, your most committed supporters should see that your organization is the most effective instrument by which they can carry out their hopes to improve at least a little corner of the world. Currying this relationship with donors is known as "stewardship."

Your organization will also, inevitably, lose some donors along the way. As Lynn Eve Komaromi of Berkeley Repertory Theatre, observes, "With widening income inequality, we've seen the donor participation rates of our general theatre audience decline, while major gifts have been on a tremendous rise. This echoes across the field. It has led us to redirecting resources to invest more heavily in cultivating and soliciting our major donor prospects—though seeking broad support remains crucial, in part to discover who possesses a philanthropic impulse and may one day become a major donor."

The most effective strategies for keeping supporters—and drawing them into an increased sense of engagement with your organization—include:

- communicating with donors frequently, through regular mailings, newsletters, and annual reports (covered in Chapter 11), and social media and other outreach (covered in Chapter 13)

- offering them other ways to contribute to your work
- thanking them for gifts, immediately and appropriately
- periodically analyzing your donor base to look for trends, groupings, and weaknesses, and
- contacting supporters personally by telephone.

Regular Communications

In an age when we're being barraged by information, you'll have to send powerful, directed communications to remind donors of the great work your organization is doing—hopefully without joining the ranks of the bombardiers. A number of different methods are available to convey these important messages. (Some are discussed at greater length in other chapters of this book, including newsletters, annual reports, social networking, and media outreach, covered in Chapter 11.)

This section covers the mail, both traditional "snail mail" and email. It will help you develop a strategy for mailing communications to existing donors over the course of your funding year, covering:

- how often to send appeal letters or emails
- crafting your annual appeal
- designing special appeals
- what to say—and what not to say—in an appeal, and
- when to stop mailing to unresponsive donors.

How Often to Send Appeal Letters or Emails

It's impossible to come up with a cut-and-dried formula for how often to appeal to donors. What's appropriate for your nonprofit depends in part on the frequency with which you are reaching out with informational and marketing communications.

Among grassroots nonprofits, Eric Talbert of MedShare observes, "Current practices tend to include sending existing donors one or two snail-mail appeals per year, plus two to four emailed appeals (in addition to any Giving Tuesday emails). This assumes, however, that prior to any appeal, the group has reached out with two to three emails containing information of interest to the readers, updates or videos about the group's work, or a call to action (such as a request for volunteers). These aren't fundraising emails—at most, they should include a passive ask, such as a donate button at the bottom." So, if you're still struggling with the marketing end of your communications, a weekly barrage of emails that mainly appeal for more funds will likely turn donors off.

> **TIP**
>
> **Give the donor control.** The simplest approach is to ask donors their preferences about how often they'll receive communication of various forms. For example, you might tell donors at the outset that you'll typically contact them once a year to renew their annual membership, and four times more for targeted solicitations—then give them a chance to elect to hear from you less often. If asking seems like too big a risk, at least respect and follow the wishes of donors who speak up and request fewer communications.

You may need to experiment a bit in order to develop the most effective possible mailing calendar. And we mean the word calendar literally. Eric Talbert explains, "Whether your fundraising staff handles all communications (not only mailings, but social media posts or interactions) or your nonprofit has separate teams handling communications and fundraising, it's crucial to plan ahead. Create an annual editorial calendar, stating what messages will go out and when. This avoids sending conflicting messages, and it creates a balanced, engaging experience for donors and followers."

Programs such as Lightbox or Hootsuite can help with the nuts and bolts of creating this calendar. Of course, you may need to rejigger the calendar in response to unexpected events or breaking news, either by adding a mailing or a social media post, or delaying one while the public's attention is occupied.

> **TIP**
>
> **What is Giving Tuesday?** It's a designation given to the Tuesday after Thanksgiving; a date when many people are beginning to focus on gift-giving, both charitable and non. Nonprofits are encouraged to reach out via email and social media on this day, spreading the word about their projects and asking for help in reaching a specified, realizable goal. See www.givingtuesday.org. Should your nonprofit participate? Definitely!

TIP

Create a gift donation program. More and more families are substituting gifts to nonprofits for yet another round of holiday gifts. And it's becoming popular to ask guests at weddings and other celebratory events to make a gift to a designated charity instead of to the people being honored. (This is especially true for second marriages, when the allure of all those new toasters may have worn off.) Savvy nonprofits let their supporters know that they are happy to establish special-occasion gift programs. Don't forget to send acknowledgment letters to both the donors and the people who inspired these gifts.

Annual Renewal Letters or Emails

Of course, you'll want to send at least one communication per year asking for a "renewal" of support. This is a good time to remind donors of their long-term commitment to your organization and about the vital work that you continue to do. Start by sending one or more emails, then mail people who don't respond within a week or so.

Whether or not you have a formal membership program, try styling your appeal as a renewal of their alliance with your group—and remind them that their newsletter subscription and any other benefits will expire on a certain date. Also let them know what benefits would come with an increased gift.

TIP

How should you handle "renewals" for supporters on your automatic giving plan? Whether you've got supporters whose credit cards you're authorized to draw donations from on a monthly, quarterly, or yearly basis, be sure to remind them of their upcoming annual renewal. It's not only basic courtesy, but an opportunity to reach out with a personal message thanking them and generating excitement about what's ahead—that is, what activities, programs, or change their ongoing contributions will help bring about.

Project Open Hand's then-Director of Development, John McArdle, explains, "With renewals, I like to remember that different donors will respond to different types of messages. And, of course, it often takes more than one letter to get a response."

In fact, it can take four or five communications before a past supporter is moved or remembers to renew. It rarely pays to send more than eight or ten renewal requests; better to put these donors in the "lapsed" section of your database and wait a decent interval before trying them again. But if your lapsed supporter received a newsletter or another benefit of membership, make sure to cut it off when you said you would.

TIP

Make renewal appeals obvious. Some nonprofits send out so many fundraising appeals every year that donors have no idea when they're due for an actual renewal. Try to protect the integrity of the renewal cycle by clearly indicating that other solicitations are special-purpose appeals. Also, it's a great idea to tell donors the date their last gift was made and how much it was, or better yet, set forth their giving history over the last few years; studies show that most donors mistakenly believe that they gave more recently than they actually did.

What to Say in an Appeal to Donors

In drafting an appeal, some of the tools you used for your initial solicitation letter (described in Chapter 4) will be helpful. However, you shouldn't speak to the reader as if he or she has never heard of your organization. Opening with a reference to your organization's recent history and the important role of your supporters is one way to set an appropriate tone: for example, "As we enter our second theater season, we know that you're as excited as we are by these rave reviews …" or "We're truly celebrating, as support from you and others has allowed us to move into our new space."

TIP

"Our job is to meet donors where they are." Those are the words of John McArdle, former Director of Development at Project Open Hand in San Francisco. "Some enjoy factual data, some are more visual, and some may need a refresher on who we are in the first place. We try to be conscious of who our various letters will appeal to, and to vary the letters up if the same person will be receiving several appeals from us."

The most important elements to include in your appeal letter or email are:

- **A defined project or event with an attainable goal.** This is your reason for writing. For example, a holiday gift drive, in which you collect and wrap gifts for low-income children, would both make for a good story and provide an understandable reason for sending this separate letter. Even if you're asking for help to fund ongoing activities, find some new, seasonal, or otherwise special concern to highlight.

- **A personal story or hook.** Personal stories that illustrate how your group makes a difference are always good for drawing people in. For example, a group collecting and organizing lightly used sports uniforms and equipment in the United States, and then transporting and distributing them to children in South American villages, might feature accounts, quotes, and even before-and-after pictures of a particular low-income team.

- **The financial challenge ahead.** Be clear about the costs associated with the project and how people's donations can make a difference.

- **A reminder of your organization's overall mission and how your current appeal fits into it.** Make sure to tie your appeal to your group's purpose and goals. When you ask for a contribution at the end, it will be in the spirit of asking the donor to reaffirm support for your underlying mission.

- **A request for a donation (as well as for volunteer help, if appropriate).** Always be direct in telling people what they can do to make this project or event happen. Depending on your organization's technological capacities, you may want to refer specifically to the amount of the supporter's last gift and ask him or her to increase it by a certain amount. Don't make the mistake that one San Francisco organization did, however, and simply ask all supporters to give the difference between their previous donation and a predetermined amount (in this case, $1,000). Someone who'd donated a mere $25 to the organization got a letter saying, "Won't you increase your donation by $975?" She thought it was a good joke, but the letter clearly didn't add to her sense of personal connection with the organization.

For a sample of how all these strands can be woven into a complete—and not overly long—letter, see below.

Sample Appeal Letter

TVNewsMonitor
1234 Fifth St. NW
Washington, DC 20000
www.tvnewsmonitor.org
(212) 555-1212

Dear Friend:

Were you as outraged as we were about the television news' recent coverage of our state election? Once again, issues were ignored in favor of gossip, and voters were left with little to go on except the candidates' misleading attack ads.

With your support, however, we at TVNewsMonitor were able to turn our collective outrage into positive action. In keeping with our mission of increasing viewer awareness and applying pressure to the television media, we:

- sponsored well-attended voter forums for presentation and discussion of the issues in nine cities

- mobilized nearly 2,000 viewers to send critical letters to television news outlets

- disseminated critiques of dozens of news shows with suggestions on how to do better, and

- prepared a list of ten important, overlooked news stories and overlooked resource suggestions and sent them to producers at 31 alternative media outlets.

Now, we are at a critical juncture. Our research has shown that in order to get our media reform message to a broad cross-section of people, we will need to buy advertising space on a cable television channel—at a cost of several thousand dollars per airing.

Will you join in taking this exciting next step? Already, one of our longtime members has pledged $25,000 in seed money. We know we can raise the remaining $100,000 with the help of supporters like you, who realize that the longer we wait, the less accountable our media will become—at an incalculable cost to our free society. Every $50 tax-deductible gift will buy two seconds of airtime. It may not sound like much, but working together we can make those seconds add up to a powerful pro-democracy message.

Thank you, and be sure to check our website and Facebook page for the latest news critiques and reports on TVNewsMonitor's activities.

With best regards,

Warfield Watcher

Warfield Watcher
Executive Director

P.S. As a special thank you, all donors who increase their past gifts by $35 or more will receive free passes to our next showing of "Collected Worst News Clips"; and all who donate $125 or more will receive a video of this hilarious and horrifying collection.

TIP

Any holiday can create a basis for appeals. At the end of the year, people really do seem to experience a spirit of giving. However, this needn't be the only seasonal event to which you tie your appeals. Check the calendar for other holidays whose theme is linked to your nonprofit's work; for example, an African-American studies group might send an appeal around Martin Luther King Day, or a comedy troupe might have fun with April Fool's Day.

After every appeal, tally up your returns and compare them with past ones of the same type. Also keep track of any comments you get from recipients, to help you assess how well you did with the content and presentation. Of course, events beyond your control may play a role in your returns—a month of bad weather or a disaster such as an earthquake, a war, or a terrorist attack can focus people's giving sympathies elsewhere.

Tips for Email Appeals and Outreach to Donors

Email is a cheap, fast way to communicate meaningfully with supporters. But you've got to give them a reason to be interested in your emails—rather than to simply delete them on sight or request removal from your list. So, mix fundraising-related emails with:

- **quick updates,** such as news or a link to a video about how all of the eagle chicks whose rescue was the subject of your previous appeal letter survived and were released
- **follow-ups to an appeal letter,** for example containing a similar message about a campaign or an issue, as a subtle reminder and a way of making payment easy, with links to your website
- **surveys,** for example, requesting input on where to focus your work
- **newsletters** (digital or via a Web link) discussing recent projects and achievements
- **alerts on issues requiring member action,** such as attending an upcoming vigil or demonstration or to sign a petition, and
- **requests and reminders for volunteer help, upcoming special events, and more.**

CAUTION

But will people read your emails? The statistics don't look great. According to the 2018 M+R Benchmarks Study, average "open" rates of nonprofit fundraising emails are at about 15%, and click-through rates have dropped to 0.42%. Ouch. Perhaps the rates look worse because nonprofits are failing to weed out non-responsive recipients from their lists (remember, people change email addresses a lot more frequently than they change street addresses) but nevertheless, you'll want to work extra hard at making your emails stand out.

Here are a few guidelines to remember when sending messages via email:

- **Confine mailings to existing supporters who have either expressed an interest in receiving email communications ("opted in") or who are given a chance, in every message, to opt out.** (And make sure to process opt-out requests immediately.) As you collect email addresses from supporters, let them know your policy on sharing that address with others. The policy most likely to please supporters is to never rent out your email lists unless you've gotten people's advance permission.

- **Personalize the "sender."** Readers are much more likely to open an email that comes from "Ilona Bray, Fix Everything Foundation" than the name of the organization alone. That sense of personal communication should be carried throughout the message. Use different staff names for different types of messages or different segments of donors, as appropriate. Even better is if you can incorporate the sender's photo and a graphic of his or her signature into the message.

- **Make the subject line brief and catchy, yet specific and clear.** Even existing supporters have to be convinced to open a message. A bland heading like "News From Our Nonprofit" is easy to ignore. An overly general title like "What's New" may sound like spam. Create interest or excitement with something like "Otter Born in Captivity," or "Invitation to KidsOrg's 10th Anniversary."

- **Time your emails so as not to cannibalize snail mailings.** Allow enough time not only for mail delivery, but for people to read and consider the appeal.

- **Consider creative ways for emails to support mailed appeals.** For example, at Project Open Hand, John McArdle said, "We did an appeal around our senior lunch program. Attached to the mailed reply device was a perforated note on which we asked supporters to write an encouraging personal note to one of the seniors receiving services. We followed up our mailing with a series of four emails saying, in essence, 'Touching base about our senior lunch program, we'd love it if you'd reply and send a note to a senior client.' Sending a written message is as easy via email as via hard copy—though not all such involvement devices translate so easily to email."

- **Don't get caught in a spam filter.** First, be careful about subject line words or phrases that might trigger content filters. These are set to prescreen the spammers' latest favorite words or tricks. Though these are ever changing, surefire trouble words are any that sound remotely sexual (watch out for double entendres), strings of capital letters or punctuation marks, mentions of debt, baldness, or popular health remedies, and even the words "free," "limited time," or "opportunity." Second, try to avoid volume filters—that is, filters that interpret all messages sent to large numbers of people as spam. Talk to your email provider to make sure it has negotiated an exemption for your organization with the major Internet service providers or use a service like Mail Chimp.
- **If a particular message might resonate with a wide audience** (for example, a proposed development could impact a popular national park), encourage recipients to forward the email to friends. But be sure to date the message, and to tell people about any deadlines for action. You don't want your email to bounce around the Web for years.
- **Include enough information to clue in anyone who's never heard of your organization.** If your email is forwarded beyond your immediate supporters. They'll need the bigger picture: who you are, what you do. And it never hurts to remind donors exactly what their contributions are funding.
- **Informality doesn't mean sloppiness.** Typos look just as bad in an email as in a letter. And, keep the emojis to a minimum.
- **Keep messages short and readable.** A few paragraphs, with lots of bullet points, is plenty. If you have the capacity to put the message in HTML format, great. If not, use a large font, put spaces between paragraphs, and review the text from the viewpoint of someone who will open it and give it a few seconds' quick scanning.

- **Be ready for two-way communication.** Your readers are only a click away from the "reply" button. They may have questions or concerns, or wish to respond to your requests for information or help. They likely expect someone at the other end to answer right away. Make sure you've got someone lined up—if not with a full answer, then at least with a note saying "Thank you for your [comments, concerns, *or* offer]. I'll look into this and get back to you within the week."
- **Encourage readers to click through to your website or Facebook page.** While your email message should be interesting on its own, it can also legitimately act as a "teaser," compelling people to learn more.
- **Don't send emails encouraging donations until your website is equipped to handle credit card transactions.** If you ask readers to write a check and put it in the mail, you'll irritate the very ones who are most accustomed to doing things at the speed of email.

Another smart way to use email is to send messages to segmented groups from your mailing list. For example, you might share a quick success story with donors or volunteers who recently helped with a project. This won't prevent you from fleshing out the full story in a letter, a newsletter, or another communication later.

When to Give Up on a Donor

As you continue corresponding with supporters, you'll notice that few of them respond to every appeal with a gift. Some will inevitably drop off. After a year without any response, you may start to wonder whether it's worth keeping the person on your list at all.

At what point do you give up? If you encourage supporters to think of themselves as members, then their lack of interest will become clear after your intense efforts at renewal fail. For those not on a renewal schedule, the dividing lines aren't so bright. Unless the supporter has died or joined an ascetic monastic order, you could choose to keep him or her on your list until you receive a request to remove the name. (Don't do this without analyzing your annual cost of mailing to lapsed donors, however.) The general rule is to continue correspondence until a year and a half has gone by, then take a rest.

CAUTION

Be vigilant in removing deceased donors from your database.
Remember, someone still gets the letters, even if the former donor isn't around to read them. A friend of mine who was responsible for tying up her deceased aunt's affairs wrote letters—for 20 years!—asking a charitable organization to take her aunt off its mailing list. The organization's appeal letters kept on coming. The bad news for the organization is that my friend had formerly been a donor too—but, as she said, "Even if they're a good organization otherwise, how can I support them when they're wasting so much money sending letters to dead people?"

Some supporters shouldn't be relegated to the "lapsed" file even after a year or two has gone by. In particular, try to stay engaged with supporters who have:

- **made large gifts.** Donors who've made gifts of hundreds of dollars or more have felt strongly about your organization's work at some point. Perhaps more mailings aren't the best strategy—try a phone call or an invitation to a lunch, meeting, or small event.
- **given for a long time.** If the donor has given to your organization for five years or more—regardless of the amount given—don't give up hastily. The donor may be a little worn out, but not necessarily uninterested. You could reduce the number of appeals, but continue sending event-related notifications, and other pieces to reignite interest.
- **a personal tie to your organization.** Some people should be kept on your mailing list whether they give frequently or not. These might include former staff members, clients, or alumni. Again, you can tailor the type of communications to the person or group.

CAUTION

Never call someone a "lapsed" donor. Sounds like some sort of failure, doesn't it? Few people who haven't made a donation for a year or two would describe themselves as "lapsed"—especially those who don't subscribe to your belief that they should give early and often. Your correspondence can forever simply refer to its recipients as "members," "supporters," or whatever term you customarily use.

RELATED TOPIC

Some supporters clearly have the interest or ability to give frequent or larger gifts. These will require more than the occasional letter, as described in Chapter 6.

Invite Supporters to Get More Involved

Money may not be all that your supporters have to give, nor all that you want from them. In your various communications—thank-you letters, phone calls, emails, newsletters, and so on—be sure to describe other ways to support your organization's work. These could include volunteering, either on a regular basis or at a special event; participating in a campaign of writing letters or emailing congressional representatives; attending lectures and events that you sponsor; and more.

Author Kay Sprinkel Grace recommends contacting supporters twice with an invitation to get involved—perhaps to attend a lecture, tour, or reception—for every one time that you contact them for money. (See her book *Beyond Fundraising*, published by Wiley, for further suggestions on donor stewardship.)

Whether or not your supporters' participation in these activities helps your organization directly is not the point. It develops a relationship and makes them part of your inner circle. The more a supporter gets involved in your issue, with heart, mind, and body, the more the supporter will feel he or she "owns" it—and continue or increase support as a result. (See Chapter 2 for more on volunteer involvement and Chapter 8 for more on special events.)

Analyze Donors' Giving Patterns and Interests

As your base of support grows, you'll want to analyze your supporters' giving patterns and segment them into groups. The purpose is to tailor your appeals and stewardship accordingly. Most nonprofit organizations sort their supporters by financial levels. Some also create groupings based on particular interests or connections with the organization.

Segmenting Donors by Giving Level

Traditionally, grassroots nonprofits divide their donors into three financial categories:

- **regular donors,** who give less than $100, or who give less frequently than once every two years
- **midscale donors,** who give between $100 and $500, or who give once or twice a year, and
- **major donors,** who give more than the high end of your midscale donor category ($500) perhaps, or who give several times a year. This category would also include people who have made your organization a beneficiary of their estates.

You don't have to create three tiers of donors or divide them along the dollar amounts suggested above—your groupings should depend on the giving levels among your organization's own supporters. You could also create a fourth category, perhaps of "top donors" whose gifts run to the thousands of dollars.

CAUTION

Never call someone a "minor" or "small" donor! The terms by which you segment donors are, for obvious reasons, for internal purposes only.

In creating these segmentation lines, consider how your donors view their gifts. Research has shown that people see themselves as having made a major gift if they donate $500 to $1,000.

If you're lucky enough to have so many high-dollar donors that you've stopped thinking about the $500 givers as "major," you may need to think again. This year's $500 to $1,000 supporters are your most likely source of next year's larger gifts—but only if you've treated them with due respect along the way. Very few supporters leap directly from gifts of a few hundred to several thousand dollars. They usually inch their way toward the large gifts. To truly cultivate your donor base for next year's growth, and to keep your pool of givers full (as protection against slumps in the economy), keep a sharp eye on supporters who seem to be positioning themselves to become major donors.

Where you draw the dividing lines between supporters may depend on how much time you and your staff and volunteers can devote to communicating with them. Include as many people as you can handle within the midscale and major donor categories—even if their gifts were fairly modest—and then lavish attention on them to encourage their continued or increased support. You'll find information on how to do this in Chapter 6.

> ⓘ **CAUTION**
> **Are too many of your donors stuck at a certain giving level?** If your donors seem to be in a giving rut—particularly if it's at a low level of giving—you may need to look again at the message you're sending through your publications, marketing, and suggested gift levels. Make sure your communications encourage giving at higher levels—and explain exactly what these larger gifts will fund.

Segmenting Donors on Nonfinancial Bases

Giving levels are not the only possible distinctions you might draw among your donors. Equally important to your fundraising concerns are their subject matter interests. At an immigrant rights organization, for example, donors may be clustered into different ethnic groupings. At a musical or an arts organization, you might distinguish between audience members and present or past students or participants. At a health-related organization, patients and their families might form a separate and important grouping.

This segmentation can be taken to a micro level, especially as artificial intelligence gets adapted for use in analyzing donor databases. For example, fundraising expert Eric Talbert explains, "Instead of just thanking all donors for past gifts to help save cats and telling them 'Many cats were saved,' you could thank donors living in particular cities and include an image of a cat in that city that was saved thanks to their help. That's a powerful way to get people to personally connect with your mission." For an example of how one fundraiser identified and cultivated a nonobvious subgroup, see "Reunion of the Founders," below.

Also, keep an eye on trends within your donor base. Where are your new donors coming from? Is there a group that seems to be unmoved by your appeals? Such observations can help you tailor your publications and solicitations.

Tailored Appeals to Select Supporters

Tailoring your communications to different segments of donors, and to different donor interests, is another good way to make sure your mail is read with interest. For example, you could customize appeals or send entirely different ones based on characteristics like gender, age, socioeconomic class, original connection to your organization (for example, people who attended an event as opposed to those who follow you on a social media site), or behavioral criteria, such as typical amount donated or frequency of giving.

Reunion of the Founders

M. Eliza Dexter, then-development director at Save The Bay, relates the following: "We'd always known that an unusual number of our members had been around for 30 or 40 years, but we hadn't fully focused on what this meant. The more I got to know Save The Bay's donors, the more I realized that this group of early members was something special. They had been true environmental leaders in the '60s, when the movement was still in its fledgling stage. They were out there monitoring things, calling each other to say, 'Did you hear what they're going to do to this watershed?' or 'Let's organize something around that.'

"So, we decided to hold an event just for these 'founding members.' It was a tea party at the Berkeley Yacht Club, and included a speech by a former UC Berkeley Chancellor who had himself been a founding member of Save The Bay.

"I'll never forget watching people arrive—you would have thought it was a high school reunion. People were hugging each other. They were so excited to catch up and reflect on how far they and the organization had come together."

This segmentation may affect not only the substance of the appeal, but also how much you ask for. At Berkeley Repertory Theatre, for example, Director of Development Lynn Eve Komaromi says, "Why send out emails asking everyone for a $100 donation when, for example, we can ask members of our audience who always buy the best seats in the house for a higher amount, and ask the bargain-seat buyers for an amount closer to their range of comfort? Even within a segment, we'll sometimes test three different giving amounts to get a sense of where the sweet spot is, and factor that in next time we do a similar appeal. With every successive appeal, our data gets more and more refined, so that we've been able to successfully grow our average donor gift over time." Or, you can tailor letters to different donors by asking board members to write personal notes on the letters.

RELATED TOPIC

Information on major donors. For more on working with midscale and major donors, see Chapter 6.

Thank Your Supporters (and Satisfy IRS Rules)

The IRS requires nonprofits to send receipts for any donations of $250 or more. But really, anyone who makes more than a token pledge or gift to your organization should receive a prompt thank-you communication. If sending a written letter, it should go out no later than within 24 hours or a few days. An emailed thank-you should go out instantly, if possible (and it *should* be possible for any online donations). In any case, remember that the quicker you act, the more engaged and excited your supporters will be, potentially leading to more gifts later.

For smaller gifts—say, $15 or under—an email or postcard is sufficient or even preferable to a formal letter; you don't want the donor to feel like you spent the entire gift on return postage. For example, see the postcard sent by the San Francisco Mime Troupe (a theater group that performs political satire in the parks of the Bay Area and beyond) reproduced here. According to Peggy Rose, former general manager of the San Francisco Mime Troupe, "It's important to thank people, but we don't want to waste the resources they've just provided us with. People want to see that you're using their resources in the best way you can. Plus, the postcards are colorful and fun."

For larger gifts made online, however, it makes sense to double up on thank-yous, sending not only an instantaneous email, but a follow-up letter or card. Or, pick up the phone!

Your thank-you communication serves three important functions:

- It lets the supporter know the gift was important to you.
- It gives your supporter proof of the gift in case they're itemizing deductions and an IRS auditor ever pays your supporter a visit (especially important if he or she gave cash)
- It offers your nonprofit a chance to connect in a meaningful, personal way.

The thank-you need not look like a receipt or follow any special format. (Avoid starting with "Dear Member" or something equally impersonal.) In fact, you're encouraged to make your thank-you communications interesting, for example by using handmade cards crafted by your clients.

As an example of fostering personal connection, Eric Talbert (Western Regional Director of MedShare) suggests, "You could start your thank-you letters to new donors with something like, 'We know this is your first time giving to us.' That helps recipients feel heard; they're not just part of a faceless mass." Try to tell the donors something they haven't heard before—like how many other donors joined in on this recent effort, a one- or two-sentence success story, what

Reprinted with permission

progress is already underway on the project to which they gave, or what upcoming projects and events you have planned. Better yet, once you have the capacity to "segment" your donor lists, so as to identify which donors are from which constituencies (former students, volunteers, and so forth), send letters tailored to their particular interests and type of involvement in your organization.

TIP

Test your nonprofit's donor-response experience. It's hard to know, from where you sit, what it's actually like to make an online donation to your organization. You might ask a friend or relative to do so (a few bucks is enough), then to tell you (honestly) how well your organization followed up. Did the "thank-yous" come as promptly as expected? Was the person made to feel like he or she had played an important role in your work, and affirmed in feeling that, "Yes, that's why I give to this organization"? Did the person find out something new about your organization and become curious to learn even more?

No matter what else you say in your thank-you communications, include the following information in order to meet the IRS's requirements:

- your organization's name
- the amount of the donation
- whether the donor received anything in return in cases where the gift was $75 or more; if nothing, "No goods or services were exchanged for your donation"
- no mention of token items of insubstantial value (such as a membership sticker, pen, or refrigerator magnet that cost your organization $11.10 or less if the contribution received was $55.50 or more; or if the item's market value is either up to $111 or 2% of the amount of the contribution, whichever is less) or a membership privilege worth less than $75 a year (such as event tickets or free parking at events), and
- in cases where the giver received something substantial in return ("substantial" meaning it has a fair market value of $111 or more, or exceeded 2% of the amount of the donation, whichever is less), a good-faith estimate of its value, and notification that the donor will need to reduce his or her tax deduction by the value of what was received.

If the gift was very large, you'll want to take extra steps to thank and otherwise recognize the donor, as discussed in Chapter 6.

Below is a sample thank-you letter from a fictional organization. Notice that it's one page long. There's rarely a reason to go longer than this.

Sample Thank-You Letter

Sand Dune Restoration Project
5432 Beachside Way
Oceanside, LA 12345
123-555-1212
www.ladunes.org

Mary Doane-Orr
2345 First St.
Oceanside, LA 12345

Dear Mary Doane-Orr:

We were delighted to open today's mail and find your generous gift of $80. Your support will help our staff and volunteers bring native plant life back to Oceanside's sand dunes for the enjoyment of present and future generations. Community support for this phase of the restoration project has been very encouraging—already we've received gifts from 120 people.

And, there's exciting news to report: Just yesterday one of our volunteers spotted some new shoots of one of the native flowers that once dominated these dunes—but have recently been threatened with extinction due to development and other problems. Our staff and volunteers will continue their efforts to weed out nonnative species and put protective cages around the new, native growth.

Please save this letter, which will serve as your receipt for tax purposes. [*Alternatively, depending on circumstances*:]

To comply with Internal Revenue Service regulations, this letter also confirms that you are receiving no goods or services in return for your contribution.

[*or*]

We'll be sending you the sand sculpture that you requested as a recognition gift, by separate mail. For tax purposes, your contribution must be reduced by $10, the value of this sculpture.

Again, thank you. We hope you'll come see the difference your gift has made, at our celebratory evening ceremony this June 25th—on the beach, of course! Look for more details in an upcoming mailing or on our website at www.ladunes.org.

Very truly yours,
Rocky Beech
Rocky Beech
Executive Director
Sand Dune Restoration Project

How About Holding a Donor Celebration Event?

Yes, you've got plenty to do already. But a small party celebrating your organization's supporters offers an instant way to increase engagement and long-term involvement. Here's how Ligia Peña, CFRE implemented this strategy when she was Director of Development at the MOSD Foundation (Montreal Oral School for the Deaf):

"I was working with a small budget, so I needed a cost-effective way to generate excitement among our donors and help them connect with our mission. I got $100 out of the budget and a board member found me a food sponsor. We held a simple celebration, from 5 to 7 pm, in the conference room of the school. It must be noted there had not been any donor recognition done since the end of the capital campaign seven years prior to this event, so many donors had not visited the new building.

"The main idea was to get people in the door, to share hugs and stories. We also invited a few students from the Montreal Oral School for the Deaf, and their families, so that donors could talk with them face to face and see how the MOSD was changing their lives. We planned two testimonials from parents as well as guided tours of the school.

"As an additional touch, we created individualized donor name tags, saying 'Proud Donor Since [year].' These were a great conversation piece, and people liked seeing their giving history. It provided everyone with a conversation starting point.

"I enjoyed the celebration, but more importantly, my skeptical board chair was no longer skeptical about the importance of celebrating donors! The event provided me with a lot of interesting nuggets of donor information that I diligently entered into our database and included in the 'thank you for coming' cards I sent following the event."

TIP

Don't forget to regularly change your thank you letters. At a minimum, it's worth reviewing and changing your letters (both online and written) every campaign or season. Swap out any success stories contained within. Consider how you'd feel, as a supporter, if you gave to two campaigns in a row, and realized that the second letter was not only identical to the first, but referred back to events that you heard about long ago.

TIP

"Our board and staff members call and personally thank everyone who's made a contribution of $100 or more," says Peter Pearson, president of The Friends of the Saint Paul Public Library in Minnesota. "It's a great way to nurture donor relationships. They're so happy to hear from us, and often say things like, 'Yours is the only organization that's ever called me!'" (This task also a great way to engage board members who are new to or uncertain about fundraising-related activities.)

When to Call Your Supporters

Many nonprofits try to incorporate the telephone into their donor communication efforts—but we all know how irritating unwanted calls can be.

No wonder telemarketing models of fundraising simply don't work for many nonprofits. Lynn Eve Komaromi of Berkeley Rep says, "For years, we used to telefund and telemarket to our general theatre audience. Two years ago, however, we abandoned that practice. The ROI no longer made sense. Instead, we've invested in new technologies that allow us to solicit donors in ways that make it easy for them to give. For instance, we contracted with a company that allows donors to quickly make a donation by texting a keyword related to one of our shows or a special initiative."

However, there are some ways to use the phone as an effective and inoffensive way to raise funds, including:

- to thank a donor for a gift
- in combination with a letter, and
- to follow up on an appeal.

Thanking Donors by Phone

As discussed earlier, everyone who gives more than a token contribution should receive a written thank-you letter. In addition, for larger gifts, a phone call can be a nice added touch. Chances are, the donor will remember your call long after the form letter is buried in his or her files.

If you can muster up the volunteer resources, calling everyone who sent in a reasonable-sized gift will yield results in terms of donor loyalty and potentially larger gifts later. However, a "big-name" person—such as the ED, development director, or a board officer—should always be the one to call the major donors.

> **TIP**
>
> **Voicemail can be your friend.** Chances are, the person you're calling won't pick up—in fact, he or she may be screening calls. This isn't necessarily a bad thing. If you're calling with a thank you or another simple message, leaving it as a recording is all that's necessary. Give the supporter a way to contact you, but make clear that calling back is entirely at his or her option. If your message requires a return call, at least you'll know that the donor will be calling at a time that's convenient for him or her.

FTC Efforts to Stop Telemarketing

In 2003, the Federal Trade Commission took steps to protect Americans from constant calls by telemarketers. It created a national "Do Not Call" list, for which people could register online or by phone (at www.donotcall.gov or 800-382-1222). The website and phone lines were swamped as soon as they opened—about 370,000 people registered within the first 12 hours.

Charities are not prohibited from calling people on the Do Not Call list. However, the public is clearly fed up with solicitors who intrude on their private life and space. Even if your group name shows up on their caller ID, many realize that this technology can be spoofed, too. The lesson is to use the phone judiciously.

Fundraising Calls Introduced by Letters or Email

A highly effective strategy to use with midscale donors (or donors not quite major enough to warrant a personal visit) is to send a brief letter or email explaining that you'll call to talk about how the donor can take part in supporting an upcoming plan or project. This is known as a "lead letter." Studies have shown that this combo yields greater returns than either mail or telephone used alone.

Your letter should tell the donor approximately when to expect your call (in a few days or a week, most likely). The key, of course, is not to get too busy, because you must follow through on that promise to call!

This combination can also be done in reverse, by making phone calls alerting donors to expect a letter. This is slightly more sensitive, of course, because they aren't expecting the call. It's best to have a script that also includes a thank-you for past gifts, and a quick word on what's new and interesting at your organization. You might also try calling when you know the person is unlikely to answer, with the intention of leaving a message!

Calls to Follow Up on Other Appeals

If you've mailed or emailed an appeal or sent a renewal request without results, it makes sense to follow up with a phone call. This is another good time to mobilize your volunteers, so you can reach as many people on your list as possible. Train them on the contents of your appeal. They should be ready to summarize the issue for the callers, and be willing and able to answer questions about it—or know who's available to handle any difficult questions or concerns.

It's best if your callers identify themselves (truthfully) as unpaid volunteers. This distinguishes them from the masses of telemarketers and makes the person on the other end more likely to stay on the line.

To give supporters an additional reason to donate when called, volunteers should remind them of what an early gift will mean—an immediate and needed boost for the project, and for the caller, freedom from future mailings on this issue! If you have a premium you can offer to the first several donors, all the better.

Midscale and Major Donors

Chapters 4 and 5 discussed how best to appeal to a broad base of individual supporters, most of whom you hope will donate between $15 and $250. These donations add up. But for most nonprofits, larger gifts—around $500 and up—are crucial pieces of the fundraising pie. So, where do you find people who will give your organization thousands of dollars? Though you might dream of sending out a newsletter and getting a $10,000 check in next week's mail, that dream seems to come true only for the nonprofit across town.

To get donors to write big checks, you'll have to approach them individually. Most often, you'll be approaching existing supporters, asking them to upgrade their giving levels. In rarer cases, you may persuade people who haven't supported your organization in the past to give a large donation.

Either way, to inspire gifts at this level, you will need to enter into a close personal relationship with the supporter. Fortunately, this won't require you to assume the role of a beggar. As any successful development professional will tell you, the donor-donee relationship that works most effectively can best be described as one of collaboration. You and the supporter work together, with shared excitement, toward the same goal: that of making a major, potentially visible or measurable difference in the world. Your organization serves as simply a pass-through entity, through which the donor's generosity is transformed into social, educational, environmental, or other worthy change.

Still, you'll need to convince a good-sized group of major supporters that your organization is the best pass-through entity to achieve their goals. As discussed later in this chapter, an important part of doing this is showing the donor just how important his or her funding is to your results.

Does this sound frightening, or like hard work? Actually, it can also be a lot of fun. You probably didn't get involved in fundraising because you like counting money, but because you care about furthering a cause. Sharing your conviction and interest with like-minded people who can afford to help that cause—who may even have been waiting and looking for a way to use their financial means to make a difference—can be a joy, not a chore. In fact, you generally shouldn't ask anyone for a major donation unless and until:

- The person is not a stranger, but a friend or someone with a demonstrated interest in your organization or the type of work it does.

- You know that the amount you request will be in line with the person's financial capacity or past giving history.
- You've laid enough groundwork so that the person won't be surprised, shocked, or offended by your request.
- You can convincingly explain exactly why the money is needed, how it will be spent, and what you hope to achieve with it.

The items on this list don't have to be accomplished in a day, week, or even a month. It's not unusual to spend two or three years cultivating a potential major donor until all of these conditions are in place.

This chapter starts with the most comfortable and low-pressure parts of relationship building and works up to the more challenging. This gradual approach isn't for your comfort alone—studies of major donors have shown that when they feel rushed to give, they're more likely to say no. The chapter covers:

- doing background research on supporters
- getting to know your midscale and major supporters
- asking supporters for annual renewals
- designing special events for major supporters
- meeting with supporters one on one, and
- organizing a campaign in which you and your volunteers schedule numerous meetings with supporters.

Background Research

You've just walked into a nonprofit as a new development staffer. If you're lucky, you'll have a database of supporters, which you can use to generate a few reports. (If you don't have a database, look into getting one—see Chapter 2 for suggestions.)

The most useful reports will tell you who the most generous and most frequent donors are. But the names may still be meaningless to you. Perhaps one of them sounds like an acquaintance from high school, and another has the same last name as a half-forgotten 18th-century author, but that's about it. You're going to need more information to figure out how best to approach each supporter in the future.

Learning more about your organization's biggest supporters will help you find common interests, personal connections, and shared history between them and your staff and board members, which, in turn, should help you decide who in your organization each major supporter should meet and which projects to highlight. In addition, doing background research will help you screen for wealth levels, and thus decide what size and type of gift to request, when the time comes.

Start your research in your own building, by talking to staff members. Ask them to name any supporters with whom they've had personal contact and to tell you their knowledge and impressions. Also check your development office and ED's records for notes on previous meetings with supporters, personal correspondence, and lists of people who participated significantly in special events or projects. Compile these notes for your database and files. Put together a list of the hottest prospects, for further research and cultivation.

Now do the same thing with key board members (past as well as present, if possible), especially those who have been long connected to your organization or the community it serves. Board members probably haven't kept systematic records, but their friendships with major donors may be deeper. In fact, board members may have been responsible for bringing certain supporters into contact with your organization in the first place.

Even after tapping into your organization's knowledge base, your database reports may contain mystery names or supporters about whom you know little more than names, addresses, and giving histories. Also, you may receive names of new prospects, from board members, for example. This is the time to do some digging, starting with the obvious Google search and likely continuing on to sites like LinkedIn (for professional affiliations), TruePeopleSearch (for biographical information including places lived and family relations), and imdb.com (for film industry profiles). If you're still coming up dry, check www.indorgs.virginia.edu/portico, which offers links to websites containing information of interest to donor-prospect researchers. Lauren Brown Adams (a fundraising consultant with over 30 years' experience in working with major donors), explains, "The information you're collecting should be in service of building a picture of what your organization's prospects value; who they associate with, where they spend their time and money, how they wish to be seen by others, how they view themselves, and what they care most deeply about. That helps determine whether there's a point of connection with your organization—which is vastly more important, in most cases, than whether or not the person owns a plane, for instance."

CAUTION

Don't be a snoop. While research on a donor's background is legitimate, invading privacy clearly is not. For thoughts on where this sometimes wavering line should be drawn, see the Association of Professional Researchers for Advancement's Statement of Ethics, available at www.aprahome.org (click "APRA Community" then "Professional Standards"). One of their key guidelines suggests recording only information that is relevant to your fundraising effort. ("Getting caught up in reading about scandals is a waste of time anyway," reminds Lauren Brown Adams.) APRA also suggests never pretending to be someone else when seeking information and checking carefully to make sure that your sources and the information you glean from them are reliable.

RESOURCE

Subscriptions are available. If you'd rather pay someone to do the research or wealth screening for you, several Web-based services offer subscription packages—sometimes with free trial demonstrations using actual names from your database! For example, you might check out:

- **iWave,** at www.iwave.com
- **"Intelligence for Good" Analytics,** at www.blackbaud.com
- **Wealthengine**, at www.wealthengine.com
- **NOZAsearch**, at www.nozasearch.com, (calls itself "the world's largest searchable database of charitable donations"), and
- **Foundation Center,** (by Candid) at www.foundationcenter.org, whose subscription-based directory (free if you visit one of its libraries) will tell you if your prospect sits on the board of a grant-making foundation, in which case, you may quickly ascertain what causes that person believes most deserving (especially if it's a small, family board, and your prospect is the only member making grants in a particular geographic area).

Get to Know Your Existing Supporters

In a perfect world, you'd have time to meet and get to know all of your supporters, even those who send you only $10 carefully saved from their pension checks. Of course, that's probably not possible, particularly in growing organizations. The most practical alternative is to focus your personal attention on supporters who have given donations in the major and possibly midscale range.

To put your relationship with these supporters on a solid footing, and to identify personality matches between them and your board or staff members, look for meaningful ways to establish personal contact. Your early interactions should not involve a request for cash; it doesn't hurt to be patient at the start. Three good ways to foster your relationship are:

- conveying your appreciation for a supporter's recent gift
- inviting supporters to get an inside peek at your organization, and
- creating forums where supporters can come together to share thoughts and ideas about your work.

> **TIP**
>
> **Know the names of your top supporters.** You (and others who interact with the public) need to be ready for spontaneous calls or visits. Imagine your embarrassment if someone who's steadily given substantial gifts to your organization calls or stops by, and hears, "Sorry, what exactly can we help you with? Could you repeat your name? How do you spell that?" Far better to say "Wonderful to hear from you, Mrs. So-and-So. Your support is helping the kids already." Make up a list of these top supporters and put copies where you and other people in regular contact with the public can access them when they pick up the phone (but keep them out of public view). Of course, you should also be friendly to anyone who calls, but time probably won't allow you to memorize all of their names.

Express Appreciation for Recent Gifts

What better time to get to know a midscale or major supporter than when he or she has just made a gift? You know that your organization is already on the supporter's mind, and you don't need to do anything more elaborate than show your thanks. Make sure your database and office procedures are set up to let you know when an unsolicited midscale or major gift arrives.

Midscale gifts in particular may arrive without personal contact, perhaps through a mailed appeal or an event, or as a result of positive publicity. But you can make the contact personal by simply picking up the phone—preferably on the very day when you receive the gift. Thank the donor graciously, then follow up with a few friendly questions, such as, "What got you interested in our organization?"; "Is there a particular branch of our work that interests you more than others?"; and "What can I tell you more about?"

 TIP

Read your file before reaching for the phone. In the words of development professional M. Eliza Dexter, "I read through everything I've got on a donor before I pick up the phone, even for a simple thank-you call. It's common for them to ask questions, or to refer to something, like 'I remember that great coastal walk with David [the ED].' The last thing I want is to sound surprised!" And don't forget to review the reply card that came with the donation. It could tip you off to an important fact—for example, that the donor recently moved and changed her last name (as would be common for a woman after a divorce).

Even if you don't learn anything earthshaking, the conversation will give you valuable insights into the supporter's personality and motivation for supporting your organization. You might slip in some relevant personal questions, such as "Are you an artist yourself?" or "Do you spend time hiking in our state parks?"

At the end of the call, you'll probably want to suggest further involvement with your organization, again without asking for money. For example: "I'm sure you'll enjoy the information in our next newsletter, coming out in two weeks—if you'd like to help with any of the volunteer activities, give me a call and I'll connect you to the coordinator."

If you receive a solicited gift after a personal meeting or other direct contact, then your phone call obviously need not dwell on these preliminaries. Simply pick up where your last conversation left off. However, the person who solicited the gift should absolutely follow up with a personal thank-you (in writing or by phone) when the gift arrives. For example, if your ED inspired the gift after making a talk at a local service club, the ED should be the first to convey thanks.

Especially if your organization receives many donations, you may, if you're a development staff person, want to handle the follow-up on only the most promising donors yourself, delegating the task of thanking others to a board member or savvy volunteer. Be sure to use volunteers who have a pleasant manner and good interpersonal skills. This may be the first human contact some supporters have with your organization.

> **TIP**
>
> **Train your volunteers.** They might need a word or two on proper phone manners. For example, remind them to ask, "Do you have a moment to talk?" before launching into the conversation. Also explain what issues or recent achievements the supporter might want to hear about. If the gift was made in response to a mailed appeal, for example, volunteers should expect questions about how you're progressing on the issues described in the appeal letter. And listen to new volunteers' first few calls to make sure they don't sound like they're merely reading a canned speech.

When a thank-you conversation is concluded, you or the volunteer should enter detailed notes on the donor's interests and background into your database or the donor's file. Don't forget to record the name of the person who made the call.

Other Special Ways to Thank Supporters

Reaching out and showing appreciation increases a supporter's sense of connection to your organization. For example, if the supporter has mentioned his or her birthday to you, a card can be a nice gesture.

If you're on a business trip or vacation in another city, check your database to see whether any major supporters live there. Yes, it's your personal time, but you might enjoy squeezing in one lunch with a major donor. (Use it as an excuse to take a long lunch with a friend when you're back at work.)

The year-end holiday season is also a good time for general supporter appreciation. For example, the Allerton Estate in Illinois (a historical home and park) celebrated the end of one year by sending select donors jars of honey made by local bees, together with handwritten notes from the group's development director.

Invite Donors to Watch Your Organization at Work

Once you've made your thank-you call, the next step is to broaden and deepen this personal contact. (This is also appropriate even if you've had no opportunity to place a call.)

Fundraisers often rack their brains for the perfect way to excite donors about their organizations, when the answer is right under their noses: Invite a donor to watch what your organization does. Makes sense, doesn't it? If you were a donor, would you rather see glossy marketing materials and a staged event, or the real people or places that the organization is working to help? One of the best examples I've heard of is Save The Bay, which invites major donors (and foundation staff members) to get into canoes and see the watersheds they're working to preserve. (For more on that, see "Giving Donors a Canoe's-Eye View," below.) Activities involving children, arts, nature, or animals also tend to be popular. If your group teaches foster parents how to raise good kids, the graduation ceremony from one of your courses might be a similarly inspiring moment.

Of course, if you work with a think tank where people sit at computers all day, or at a hospice or shelter where visitors aren't allowed, this strategy may be harder to implement. But keep it in mind. If, for example, your researchers receive an award and you'll be filling a table at the ceremony, see if you can make room for a supporter or two.

Inviting potential major donors to an event requires forethought. For example, if you're planning a trip or an outing, don't invite more than a few new supporters along. The focus should be on keeping things real and reasonably intimate. Be sure that staff members and others in attendance know who your guests are and behave or reach out appropriately.

Because most real events—whether it be a morning at a clinic, listening in on a course, or helping at a shelter—won't offer you and the potential major donor much opportunity for one-on-one conversation, it's not the best time to ask for specific support. If the donor is asking financial questions, however, by all means give the answers, and tell the donor what a difference financial help could make. Being too nonchalant may give the impression that financing is the last thing on your mind.

Giving Donors a Canoe's-Eye View

Save The Bay works to restore and protect the San Francisco Bay and Sacramento-San Joaquin Delta Estuary. Founded in 1961, the organization has spent more than 50 years fighting to stop unnecessary fill, unwise construction, toxic chemical dumping, and invasive plant and animal life. To further that mission, Save The Bay has acquired a fleet of canoes, which it uses to create "outdoor classrooms." Adults take tours, children learn to take water samples, and teachers attend institutes where they get ideas for bringing water ecology concepts into the formal classroom.

All of this offers a prime opportunity to get supporters interested. Save The Bay arranges to bring donors, as well as foundation staff members, along on its educational tours. Or, sometimes it will create special outings just for donors—including short coastal walks for those who don't feel up to canoeing. M. Eliza Dexter, former development director at Save The Bay, remembers one donor who took a canoe tour and shortly afterward gave a higher donation than ever before—but said, "I'm not giving this just because you took me on a canoe trip!" The way Eliza figures it, the canoe trip probably helped the donor "get" why Save The Bay's work was important and increased her sense of connectedness to the organization—even if she didn't realize it!

Create Donor Forums

In addition to inviting potential donors to see the good work your group does, you may want to involve them more systematically, by creating small meeting or discussion groups, either on a one-time or an ongoing basis. For example, The Women's Foundation in San Francisco created donor circles—small groups focused on grant making in issue-based areas, such as race, gender, and human rights. Each member of the circle makes a commitment of both time and money. Circle members educate themselves about the chosen topic and decide what they'd like to support with their pooled contributions.

Although your organization probably doesn't make grants, there's no reason not to adapt this model to your own purposes. You might, for example, create a donor group around a particular project, such as a community outreach effort or an arts event. The important thing is to give the group members the freedom to make some real choices—in other words, don't just tell them to round up money for a health awareness campaign, but ask them to research and discuss what type of campaign they would be willing to support.

Annual Renewals of Support

Your organization may or may not have formal "memberships," in which supporters receive annual benefits—such as a newsletter or gift—for certain levels of support. Regardless, the one-year anniversary of a gift is usually an excellent time to ask for a renewal of support. When it comes to midlevel and major donors, you'll be talking to people who have already demonstrated a willingness to make substantial contributions—and an entire year may have passed since their last contributions.

Your database should tell you when supporters will reach their one-year anniversary, or you can check your records each month.

Once you've figured out who to ask for support renewal, you'll have to decide how to ask. A letter is okay for rank-and-file supporters, but for your midscale and major supporters, a more personalized request is appropriate.

The midscale supporters should receive, at a minimum, a personalized letter, signed by the executive director and mentioning relevant personal details such as, "We'd love to hear more about your trip to Kenya," or "The summer program that you helped sponsor is attracting record numbers of participants." At the end of the letter, ask for continued support and suggest that, if possible, the person raise his or her donation amount. One good technique is to suggest an appropriate percentage increase above the last gift. But do the math, and tell the supporter what the new amount would be (rounding the number to the nearest sensible amount).

Include a reply envelope just as you would with an ordinary mailing. If you don't hear from the supporter, a personal phone call is typically in order.

For major supporters, send a similar letter, but also suggest a personal meeting—perhaps over lunch—to discuss the supporter's renewal. Say that you'll call in a week, and then be sure to do so. The supporter may well renew before the lunch date or meeting. But if he or she instead schedules a meeting with you, it's still a good sign; it shows the supporter's potential interest and gives you an opportunity to reignite that interest and increase the supporter's involvement with your organization. For tips on conducting such a meeting, see "One-on-One Meetings," below.

> CAUTION
>
> **Beware the holiday rush.** You may find that a number of your supporters' giving anniversaries fall toward the end of the year. Try to plan ahead and schedule meetings as early in the season as possible. With this flurry of activity, it is also especially important that gift information is entered into your database immediately. The last thing you want is to telephone a supporter asking for a renewal when the check has already arrived.

Lectures, Small Events, and Parties for Major Supporters

If you don't have ready-made opportunities for donors to see what you do, then why not arrange one? Some organizations sponsor supporter appreciation events, such as a complimentary "major supporters only" dinner preceding a publicly open fundraising lecture or performance. You could also take a donor or small group of donors to lunch, invite them to a reception with your actors, artists, researchers, or others, or do something else that resonates with your organization's mission or shows off its work. Note that we're now transitioning into occasions at which it can be appropriate to issue a general request for financial gifts.

For example, an immigrants' rights organization with which I worked invited about 20 major donors and board members to an informal luncheon at the organization's own office. The group selected well-spoken clients to join the group, including a Guatemalan who had survived a massacre and was receiving help to apply for political asylum, and a Laotian student participating in an after-school program that offered a positive alternative to gang membership. Both spoke briefly about their personal circumstances and how they'd been helped by the organization. There was also time during the meal for chatting and getting to know one another personally. When the executive director stood up at the end, thanked everyone for participating, and asked for financial support, one impressed donor wrote a $10,000 check on the spot.

> **TIP**
> **Lunches don't have to drain the budget.** There's no need to pay big bucks for catering or even restaurant take-out. The prevalence of partly prepared gourmet food has made it easy to serve a classy meal without breaking the bank.

Lectures or talks by prominent people associated with your organization can be another effective technique to build support. These can be of any size, from an intimate discussion with a small group of supporters to an event at a larger venue, perhaps even open to the public. Because you will be inviting people who already contribute to your organization, it's usually best to keep these events free or donation based. For example, the San Francisco Girls Chorus, prior to staging "It Is the Silence," based on the diary of Anne Frank, invited major donors to a lecture by the work's composer, Linda Tutas Haugen. (For more about large lectures as special events, see Chapter 8.)

Another popular type of event, which you can pull together in little over a month, is the house party. It is usually held at the home of a board member, preferably one who has a fair amount of space and is comfortable playing host (and ideally, paying for the food and drink). Between ten and 40 midscale to major supporters are invited (by mail, email, Evite, or whatever feels appropriate). However, you can vary this theme, such as by holding the event at a gallery or private venue that would otherwise be closed to the public. Nevertheless, as Morrie Warshawski points out in his helpful and compact book *The Fundraising Houseparty*, "There is significance and symbolic power to crossing the portal into someone's private home."

Commonly, many of the invitees will be suggested by your development staff. But they should also include friends of the host or of key board members whom you hope to recruit as significant donors. A few representatives of your organization should also attend—some combination of ED, board, and staff members.

The object is to create a mostly social evening, in which supporters connect with old friends (don't be surprised at getting lots of "Who else will be there?" questions), get to know new ones, and learn more about the organization's work. Food (usually hors d'oeuvres or dessert rather than a full meal) and drinks are served. The event should feature remarks by your ED and/or board president about your current programs and why they need more financial support.

CAUTION

The invitation should make the purpose of the event clear. Your guests will resent it if you play a "bait and switch" game, pretending that the party is an ordinary social event when it's actually part fundraiser. Also, you want to make sure that your guests bring their checkbooks or credit cards.

A house party can also include a prominent guest speaker, short video presentation, or similar "extra," but it's not really necessary. Believe it or not, people will be pleased to simply meet the people who run your organization and do its day-to-day work. And because they already care about your cause, it shouldn't be difficult to further inspire them with your enthusiasm, dedication, and stories of struggles and successes. Still, if someone in your organization has a contact with a famous artist, author, or other prominent person whom people would be eager to meet in an intimate setting, don't hesitate to build a house party around this person.

Depending on how much the host will be involved in the food preparation, you may want to do some menu consultation. Food is a powerful symbol. It offers opportunities for your organization to show its personality—whether formal or easygoing, regionally focused, vegetarian, or otherwise. If your organization has an ethnic link, then food prepared in appropriate style is all but essential. The party planners should also make sure the menu doesn't contradict any of the organization's principles. An obvious example would be that a dolphin protection organization probably shouldn't serve tuna.

Plan in advance exactly who will address the group and when this will occur. After the party has gained momentum, but before anyone is thinking of leaving, the host should ask for everyone's attention. If some people are standing, it's often best to ask them to sit in prearranged chairs.

After welcoming everyone and acknowledging the people who helped plan the event, the host should introduce the board chair or ED, who can provide a brief overview of the organization's current plans, upcoming projects, and recent successes. Then someone (usually not the host) whom the partygoers respect and think of as a peer should claim the floor to talk about money.

One effective technique is to mention a specific dollar figure the organization needs to fund the projects the ED discussed. For example, "To buy cages and medicines for the rescued birds we'll need to raise $45,000." If you've already raised some seed money (no pun intended), let people know. This shows that others have confidence in the project.

Another effective technique is for the person making "the ask" to state how much he or she has already given to the project. For example, I attended an alumni event at which a classmate of mine was handed the microphone and said, "My husband and I have been steadily giving to various charities over the years, but this year we've agreed to make the biggest gift we've ever given, period, to the college." You can bet that caused some audience members' eyes to widen. I, for one, was thinking, "Gee, if she can do it…."

Finally, the speaker should make a polite but very direct request, such as, "I'm hoping everyone here can help us with $1,000."

After making the request, make it abundantly clear how people can pay or pledge; or just put a couple of attractive boxes or jars in obvious places in the room. Or, you could have certain people designated to receive checks, pledge cards, or filled-out credit-card payment forms. Those people should wear obvious hats or flowers on their lapels and avoid standing behind any large potted plants. If you'll be accepting credit cards on the spot, whoever swipes the cards should be seated at a table—preferably near the front door.

Creating Donor Recognition Opportunities

Though a few donors wish to remain anonymous, they tend to be in the minority. At the other end of the spectrum are a few donors for whom heightening their reputations as philanthropists, impressing their peers, or being part of a "club" of high-level supporters is a major motivation for giving.

At a minimum, use your annual report to list the names of all major donors, and as many other donors as space will allow. Newsletters or event programs are also good places to thank groups of donors by name, or perhaps to focus on a particular gift and what it helped to fund. Beyond this, talk to individual donors to come up with a way to publicly recognize their contributions (while realizing that not every gift merits a building with the donor's name on it).

Develop options that allow your organization to recognize substantial numbers of donors without having to come up with a fresh and creative approach for each one. A wall of tiles or walkway of bricks at your front entrance, each bearing the name of a donor, is one simple yet effective method—just look around you, at places like the Pike Place Market in Seattle or the beach boardwalk outside Asilomar State Park in California. If a gift went toward a particular use, such as a new piece of playground equipment, a small metal plaque saying "Gift of So-and-So, 20xx" can be affixed to it. For especially large gifts, media coverage may also be a possibility (see Chapter 13).

TIP

A pledge is better than a promise. Some guests will tell you they'll make in a donation soon. This is fine, but to help underline the seriousness of this promise, ask them to fill out a pledge card for your records (and as a basis for subsequent reminders). Also, be sure to give the donor an envelope in which to send their check or a sheet of paper with the URL and instructions for giving online.

One-on-One Meetings

Once you've gained experience with midscale and major supporters and gotten to know some of them personally, you'll be ready to take the next step: asking for a large gift. And you'll also be ready to request gifts from people who haven't previously supported your organization.

Because the techniques for approaching existing and new midlevel and major donors are quite similar, they're discussed together in this section, which covers:

- deciding who to ask
- arranging the meeting
- preparing for the meeting
- assembling materials for the meeting
- the psychology of making a request
- holding the meeting, and
- following up with the donor.

Who to Ask to Meet

For your existing donors, the question of who to ask will be partly answered by their personalities and giving histories. A major donor who gave last year should be asked again, and probably asked for more. An enthusiastic midscale donor who has been giving regular gifts—say, of $100 or $200—should be personally asked to take a step up in giving.

There is no reason to be shy about asking people who already support you. Very few contributors start out as major donors—instead, they work their way up from smaller gifts. Signs that they are ready to make a bigger commitment included repeated gifts of a good size and progressively larger gifts.

Another good sign that someone is ready and able to give more is that they're making large gifts to other organizations. You can find this out by keeping an eye on other organizations' annual reports and other publications, or by doing background research on your midscale donors.

CAUTION

There is no "average supporter." Even when this book cites a general rule—for example, that most donors work their way up to large gifts—there are plenty of people who don't fit this mold. Think of the news stories you hear about people who save their pennies for years and then give a million to their alma maters—or to poetry magazines—in their wills. People have different thresholds at which they feel financially secure, and react to suggestions that they increase their support in different ways. If your donor avoids or resists your efforts to coax him or her to write a bigger check, back off on asking for money, but keep doing appropriate things to build the relationship. You never know—the big check you hope for may show up just when you've given up hope.

Finding potential major donors who aren't current supporters of your organization will require a little more research. The best prospective supporters are people who have a known interest in your cause or a similar one, a financial ability to give, and a history of giving to other organizations. Prospects who match only one of these criteria might not be worth a personal visit, but could be added to your database for a mail appeal. Prospects who match two or three of these criteria are probably worth pursuing in person.

TIP

Your board members may be major-gift prospects. Or some of them, at least. In the words of Tony Poderis, development consultant and author, "... a board that does not have members of sufficient wealth or influence to deliver major gifts is not a well-balanced board." The board president should be the one who approaches other board members for major gifts.

Keep your eyes and ears open to find out who the generous members of your community are. One easy place to find their names is at the back of programs from the theatre, symphony, and special events held by other organizations. You can even read the inscribed bricks on other organizations' walls. (It may feel like spying, but everyone does it.) Though you may not know the person, someone on your board or staff may have a link with them, because they are alumni of the same college or members of the same church or other group, for example.

EXAMPLE: Alan, the development director of a school for autistic children, notices that Tedward Goldstein is listed as a major donor by both a local children's hospital and a homeless shelter that focuses on helping families. After research indicates that Goldstein is a retired family court judge with a long history of personal involvement with children's issues, Alan does some digging and finds out Judge Goldstein's college, temple, and other affiliations. One of the school's board members belongs to the same temple. That weekend, the board member casually approaches Judge Goldstein, describes the school's activities, and asks whether he's interested in more information. The judge is intrigued, they invite him to a lecture event, and through careful cultivation, he eventually becomes a major donor.

Focus your research on people with a history of giving. Though you might dream of finding that quiet rich person who, by some miracle, hasn't been approached by any other group, such dreams rarely come true. For one thing, being rich isn't enough by itself—the wealthy widow who spends half her year shopping and the other half traveling to trendy resorts probably is not going to engage in her first act of generosity as a result of your phone call. Remember, statistics show that it's not the upper strata of U.S. society who give the most; members of the middle class—especially those who have become borderline affluent in middle age—are probably your best bets, even for major gifts.

No matter who you ask, find out whether he or she is part of a couple. If you arrange to meet with someone who doesn't make decisions without his or her other half, then you won't get a decision on the day you meet—and may have to either schedule a second meeting or risk having the partner veto a gift without hearing what you have to say. Be ready to meet on an evening or weekend if that's the only time that works for both.

Arranging the Meeting

Once you've identified a likely prospect, it's time to call him, her, or them and suggest a meeting. (You might also send a letter first, particularly if you're cultivating someone who doesn't know the organization well.) This shouldn't be a stealth mission—simply tell the person that you'd like to discuss the work of your organization and how he or she might support it. Exactly how you phrase this will depend on how well you know the person and how sophisticated he or she is about philanthropy.

For the experienced giver, it's enough to say, "We have a project we'd like to share with you, and we could use your help." For someone who's newer to charitable giving (and might think you're just going to ask for an opinion or a batch of brownies for your bake sale), try something more specific, like, "We're trying to fund scholarships for our kids, and I'd like to talk to you about supporting this effort."

You might worry that such an initial phone call would cause any sane person to laugh or hang up, but you'd be wrong. First, almost no one is offended by such a request—you're paying the person a compliment, implying that you believe he or she has a good heart and is successful enough to be able to share. Second, you've given the person enough information to allow him or her to say no. You've been clear and straightforward, which means no one needs to feel uncomfortable.

To Lunch or Not to Lunch?

Professional fundraisers are of mixed minds about whether to meet with major supporters over lunch. On the plus side, it makes the event seem more social and gives you and the prospect a better chance to get to know each other through small talk before getting to the matter at hand. Also, assuming you make clear that you're hosting the lunch, it allows you to act magnanimous before asking the supporter to do the same—a sort of thanks for past support or thanks in advance for future support.

On the minus side, meeting at a restaurant guarantees not only that you'll use up more of your and the supporter's time, but also that the mechanics of ordering and paying will use up a good portion of that time. And you're leaving more up to chance—what if the food that day is terrible, the people at the next table have a screaming match, and the waiter spills the soup on your prepared materials? All of this helps explain why many fundraisers prefer meetings where food doesn't get in the way—such as your organization's offices or the donor's home or office.

If you invite a potential donor to a restaurant, don't pick the fanciest place in town. That might give the supporter some wrongheaded ideas about where his or her money will be going. This is especially likely to be true if the donor earned his or her own money rather than inheriting it—most wealthy people became wealthy by learning habits of frugality early in life.

Many will say no. But don't assume the relationship is over. Six months or a year from now, the person may be receptive to your call—or may even call you. Remember, you're calling someone whom you've already identified as inclined to give money to a good cause. (Some of the truly wealthy philanthropists say that they'd like to give more money away if only they could find causes good enough!)

A surprising number of people will say yes to your request to meet. With that simple, short phone call, you've taken a huge step forward.

If you're calling someone who has no previous connection with your organization, the initial phone call will have to be slightly longer. Be ready to tell the person where you got his or her name (particularly if it was through a friend) and why you think your organization might be of particular interest. Sum up what your organization stands for and what it does in a few sentences. (Even if you sent an advance letter, it may now reside in the circular file.) It's particularly effective if you have a specific need in mind, something urgent enough to justify meeting soon (and without cultivating the donor more gradually). Here's a sample script:

> Hello Mr. Scarry, this is Ima Edie from the Society for Train Depot Restoration. We're working to restore the beautiful historic train depots in our community. We believe that, because of your interest in train history and in community improvement, you might be interested in supporting these efforts—particularly because the depot in your neighborhood is scheduled for demolition this summer. Could we meet at your convenience to talk this over?

At this point in the call, the prospective supporter will no doubt have questions, which you should take the time to answer in full. There's no harm in giving information that you will later repeat at a meeting (unless you tell the exact same "amusing anecdote" in the exact same words—it pays to have a good memory for these things when fundraising).

If the person agrees to meet, be ready to suggest a location, such as the donor's home or office, your organization's office, or a restaurant. If the person doesn't want to meet one-on-one but is willing to talk the matter over at further length by phone, go ahead and agree to this. In either case, plan on a minimum one-half-hour's meeting time.

After the phone call, quickly send out a confirmation (by email or letter, depending on the person's preferences), mentioning:

- the purpose of the meeting
- the meeting time and location, and
- who will be at the meeting.

And to cover all your bases, contact the prospect a day or two before the meeting to confirm.

Preparing for the Meeting

To prepare for your meeting, start by filling in any gaps in your research about the prospect. Also decide who will attend the meeting. Most development professionals prefer to bring a team of two, including some combination of the ED, development director or other gift officer, and any board members, staff, or volunteers who know the prospect or have mutual interests or backgrounds. Not only are two heads better than one, but if one of you leaves the organization, the personal relationship with that supporter won't be broken. Also keep in mind that the ED or someone on the policy side of the organization may be better able than the development director to speak with conviction about your programs and activities.

Use the results of your background research, along with other considerations such as the scope of the project and who else will be asked to contribute, to decide what to request. You'll want to suggest a specific sum (or item, if you're looking for property). Open-ended requests make donors uncomfortable and lead to lowball offers. Obviously, you'll want to ask for an amount the person can afford.

Also, notice whether the donor has typically made gifts of something other than cash, such as property or stock. And consider the larger social context for the gift. If the donor has friends in your organization, how much do they give? In *Fundraising for the Long Haul,* Kim Klein tells stories of donors who have, after discovering that they gave less than their friends or community peers, expressed annoyance that they were not asked for a higher sum.

Try to choose an amount that challenges the person to give a substantial percentage more than they've given before, but isn't off their personal scale. For example, if a donor has given $1,000 for the last couple of years, you might ask for $1,500 or $2,000 more for a special project.

TIP

Supply payment options. A cash gift need not be made in one lump sum. Many people think of their finances in monthly terms, in which case a monthly pledge might suit them. Or, if your prospective supporter has an entrepreneurial streak, suggest a "staged" gift—one that is given piece by piece, conditioned on your organization's success along the way. If you're starting a new program that looks like an uncertain proposition, this can also allay the supporter's fears of pouring money into a sinkhole.

Here's the big question: Who from your organization is going to make the actual request for money? You can guess the probable result if you leave this vague—or worse yet, if both of you assume that the ask is the other person's job.

TIP

Supporters may inquire whether (and how much) your board members have given. Wealthy people like to know that your board members believe in your efforts—and have backed up this conviction with financial contributions. Be ready with the most up-to-date, positive answer you can muster.

Assembling Materials for the Meeting

You may want to assemble or prepare some relevant written materials. (The exception would be if the supporter has been involved in your organization for years, and prefers to think of the relationship as primarily social, in which case showing up with a stack of brochures and budgets could ruin the atmosphere.) Start with your organization's brochure and annual report.

The more unusual or specific your request for support—for example, if it's around a new project or a capital campaign—the more appropriate it will be to bring additional written materials.

If you plan to ask for support for a particular big-deal purpose—a new transmitter for a public radio station, a new building for a school, or a new outreach program—it's a good idea to prepare a case statement: a two- to five-page document outlining your request. Again, depending on your history with the supporter, this document might also describe your organization's history, mission, clientele and their needs, current goals, money needed to meet those goals, and ability to use the donor's gift effectively.

The statement can be tailored to the donor's prospective giving level, explaining how gifts of particular amounts will meet specified needs—for example, "Every gift of $_____ can fund __ days of research into curing a medical condition," or "It will cost $1,200,000 to build a study annex onto our school's library. To start our campaign, we are seeking 20 founders' gifts of $25,000."

Bring any written materials discussing recognition opportunities for particular major gift levels; it's often easier to motivate donors to make large gifts if a brick, tile, or plaque will commemorate their contributions. And if your organization is lucky enough to have been the subject of any press coverage (positive, of course), bring copies of the articles or transcripts. These are great for adding credibility to your own materials.

Always bring a copy of your organization's budget; a specific project budget; and information about what percentage of every dollar you collect supports your organization's work. (See Chapter 4 for information about the importance of showing that contributions support your cause, not just further fundraising.) Not everyone will read a budget, although your supporter may take a keen interest in it if he or she has a background in business or finance. For those who don't enjoy interpreting balance sheets, be ready to explain the budget in plain English. In particular, note what parts of the budget represent growth or shifts in program focus.

Be sure to point out how much of your budget is made up of individual (as opposed to foundation or corporate) donations. Even if the percentage sounds less than impressive, you can put it in more realistic terms by saying, for example, that, "Without individual donations, we'd have to gut the entire educational portion of our program."

Some or all of your prepared materials should be assembled into a packet that you can leave with the donor after the meeting is over. Put it all together in a glossy folder. The packet shouldn't be overwhelming—the materials should all look professional and factual and be easy to read and understand.

Fundraising Worksheet 5: Meeting Checklist

Here's a summary of things to consider bringing to your donor meeting:

- ☐ Brochure
- ☐ Annual report
- ☐ Historical information
- ☐ Mission description
- ☐ Case statement
- ☐ Budget
- ☐ Plans for the future
- ☐ Publicity materials
- ☐ Copies of any recent newspaper articles
- ☐ Premiums and recognition opportunities
- ☐ Pledge card
- ☐ Return envelope and/or instructions for giving online
- ☐ Credit card swiping device
- ☐ Receipt book

The Psychology of Asking

To get yourself into a frame of mind that will allow you to survive—and even enjoy—the asking process, remember these simple rules:

- Be yourself.
- Be direct.
- Focus on the cause.
- Don't beg.
- Be ready to adjust to opinionated donors.

Be Yourself

Parts of this chapter suggest actual words to use and to avoid when requesting major gifts, so that you won't lie awake at night wondering what the "right" thing to say is. However, no canned script can give you the words to describe what excites you about your organization's work. Although your rehearsed lines may do a good job framing your message, ultimately you'll want to put them aside and speak from the heart.

Be Direct

You'll go a long way toward making yourself and your supporters comfortable by simply being direct. No matter how much you've done to ease into this relationship, there will come a time when you simply have to look the person in the eye and say, "A gift of $50,000 would provide a crucially important launch for this program." You can't back into it and you can't say it in code.

But the wonderful thing is that once the words are out, the air becomes clear. Because you've shown that you're comfortable asking for a specific dollar amount, the prospect has the opportunity to respond with equal directness.

> CAUTION
> **A less direct approach may be appropriate in some cultures.** If you are working with people whose ethnic or cultural background requires or celebrates a more subtle approach, you'll need to adjust your style. In some communities, the potential donor—not you—should mention money first, so as to allow that person to maintain "face" or "honor" if now is not a good time to give. But you should still be ready to suggest an amount.

Focus on the Cause

You'll be more persuasive (and more comfortable) if you can mentally remove yourself from the giver/recipient picture. You're not begging for money for yourself—you're asking the supporter to partner with your organization to achieve a mutually desirable result. Remember, this person has a history of giving either to your organization or others. People don't dip their toes into the major giving waters unless they really do understand that their giving can make a difference in the world.

It will also help if you remember that whether a person writes a big check or doesn't, this isn't about you, your career, or your sinking feeling that you should have signed up for more training seminars. You're simply the intermediary who guides the supporter toward the best path to make a difference.

If you are able to paint a compelling picture of the job that needs to be done—the impoverished people who need AIDS medicine, the inner-city child who can grow via your music program, or the sea turtles endangered by a proposed oil refinery—you've done your job.

 TIP

Ever made a major gift yourself? Then you can mentally picture yourself on the same side of the table as the donor—and if the gift was made to your organization, assure him or her that you've made the same commitment that you're asking for. Also remember what doubts or concerns you had before making the gift and how you overcame them.

Don't Beg

Even with your eye on the cause, it's easy to slip into phrases like, "Could you help us with," "We'd be so grateful if," and "I hope it's not asking too much if …." People who humbly importune a potential donor to make a gift are more likely to get stepped on than they are to get a big check. The supporter may wonder whether you lack other community support or are in such dire straits that the money may just plug a leaking hole and nothing more. The supporter may also buy into your own accidental message and think he or she is being asked to support your organization's need as opposed to a greater good. Better to show your excitement about what results the donor's gift could lead to.

Adjust to the Donor's Interests

Plenty of major donors are just plain opinionated. They may have worked hard for their money, and want to decide exactly how it will be spent. You may hear things like, "No, I won't give one penny to your group to provide extra funding for area public schools—the whole system is a mess—but I might fund a totally different approach, such as a small school demonstration project, focused on parental involvement."

At times like these, you'll have to be quick on your feet. If the donor's suggestion is closer to your proposal than the donor at first realizes, then it may be worth steering his or her attention back to the proposal on the table. If it's not, however, then it is usually best to express sincere interest in the donor's ideas, explain that you will present them to the decision makers in your organization, and get back to the donor afterward.

Holding the Meeting

Now, all you have to do is meet! Some people wonder at first how they'll have enough to say to fill a whole meeting's worth of conversation. But filling the time is rarely a problem, especially if two people from your organization attend. And remember, you've got two fascinating subjects to keep you busy: the supporter (practically everyone likes to yak about their background, interests, opinions, and current activities) and your organization.

If it helps you to think about the meeting sequentially, here's the usual play-by-play: You and your teammate should meet a few minutes in advance to share any last-minute information and, if necessary, discuss what you'll talk about as an icebreaker.

Once you have all assembled, start with introductions. Remind the supporter that you're there to talk about a specific need or new program your organization is embarking upon, the critical importance of financial support, and how long you expect to spend in this meeting. Work in a little fun small talk.

The best fundraisers say that if possible, they like to spend the majority —say, around 75%—of any meeting just listening to the supporter. This isn't idle or phony listening. You'll not only be learning more about the supporter's interests and passions, but also refining your understanding of how and why he or she might give. In fact, if the donor is savvy about your field, you may learn information vital to your organization's successful growth.

Journalists will tell you that the best way to interview someone is to ask open-ended questions—ones that don't show off your expertise or imply a conclusion, but simply invite the other person to educate you. Depending on your nonprofit's work, you might ask such questions as: "What do you think are the most important components of a child's education?" "Which of our shows did you like best this season?" or "How do you think our project could be improved?" Find out about the donor's other interests, hobbies, and work. Ask what other organizations the supporter is actively involved in and what he or she likes about volunteering or other experiences there.

At some point, bring the discussion back to the purpose of the meeting. If you've brought written or visual materials, present these in a well-organized fashion. Lay out what your organization is up to and why its work, or a particular project or program, is worth investing in.

But don't get too buried in your written materials. Always remember the things that get you personally excited about the organization. Draw on these and the inspiring conversations you've had with other staff and volunteers to build the supporter's interest. Your enthusiasm for the cause will usually be more convincing than a briefcase full of budgets and brochures.

Also try to incorporate specific details, to distinguish your organization from the many others doing good work. Which of the following two statements would you find more persuasive?

- "Our program of reading aloud to children in shelters has been shown in statistical studies to make a significant difference to their psychological well-being and produced measurable improvements in their school performance."
- "I'll never forget the first time I participated in our program to teach at-risk kids to read. I was sitting on a mat on the floor at the back of the shelter on 17th Street with a homeless six-year-old whom I had been working with for a month. When one day she picked up a book and read 'Spot saw a cat,' I literally had tears in my eyes."

The first sentence is relevant, and might work (with a little paring down) in a grant proposal, or even as a subpoint in an annual report. But the second one tells your lunch companion what hooks you in, and will probably bring the work alive for him or her as well. It's all in the details.

Before long, it will make perfect sense to start talking dollars. Candidly explain to the prospect exactly how much things will cost and how you arrived at that figure. Mention any in-kind donations that you've received, to show that you're trying to keep costs down, as well as any significant grants or other donations that have come in. This is a great way to tell your meeting companion that he or she isn't the only donor in town, but will join a respectable group of people who believe in your cause.

Learning to Tell Donors About the San Francisco Girls Chorus

Sarah Clark, former development director at the San Francisco Girls Chorus, says she knew upon starting the position that she loved listening to the girls' performances—in fact, they sent chills up her spine. But to really develop her passion for the SFGC's programs, and to help her explain it to donors, the organization encouraged her to get even further involved.

Sarah took the time to attend an array of behind-the-scenes activities from rehearsals to outreach performances (at which the girls perform at schools in order to encourage budding singers to join) to the SFGC's annual summer music camp. She remembers, for example, an experience she had watching the Level 3 girls (ages 10 to 13) being coached by Judaline Swinkles Ryan: "I saw how the teaching emphasized discipline and excellence as well as musicality. Judaline was clear and direct with the girls about things like not coming in late, and paying attention—she'd say, 'Look at me!' And it made a difference. At the beginning of the half hour I spent watching, they sounded okay. But by the end, they were a tight, focused unit—and they sounded great!"

Through these activities, Sarah also got to know some of the girls who participated. She enjoyed seeing how they could be lounging on the stairs, eating junk food, and giggling together offstage, then turn into serious, poised, beautiful singers onstage. This is the stuff of which donor stories are made.

Finally, once the preliminaries are over, and you've built—or reinvigorated—the potential donor's interest in your case, look him or her in the eye and say something like, "We'd like you to consider a gift of $10,000, to bring us within a realistic distance of our goal." Or if you're asking for a slightly raised renewal of a past donation, you might simply say, "Can I put you down for a renewal at the $2,500 level?" or something similarly optimistic.

Then sit quietly and let the person have a chance to think. Try to look hopeful, while you resist the human urge to chatter or even apologize for a bold request. And make sure anyone who accompanies you respects the donor's need for time to think.

If the person agrees, say thank you and be enthusiastic, but keep your wits about you. You'll need to discuss when and how the payment will be made. You'll want to explain various payment methods and ask the donor to commit to one. While few donors will want to pay on the spot, you may meet one who actually pulls out a checkbook or (less often) a credit card. In case of the latter, bring along your organization's credit-card swiping device, if it has one. Offer a pledge card if the donor won't be paying immediately.

Now is also the time to talk about whether the donor is interested in any return gifts or recognition opportunities. Speak in terms of your desire to thank the donor, not the donor's "payback" for giving. If the donor wants no recognition or wishes to remain anonymous, perhaps even in printed materials like your annual report, make a careful note of this and make sure your internal systems are geared to respect this wish. You don't want to be in your office the day someone who made an anonymous donation of $25,000 reads about it on social media.

If the person seems uncertain about whether to give, try to get to the heart of the ambivalence. Would he or she like more information? Need time to think about the purpose for your request or to consult with a key family member? Prefer a slightly smaller gift amount? At this point, your job is to try to learn what the person is thinking. Or put another way, you need to listen to the donor's concerns before you can sensibly respond to them.

Make sure you ultimately get a yes or no answer. As one experienced fundraiser told me, "I like to get to the point of hearing an actual 'yes' or 'no'—in fact, I'll follow up on a vague answer with a question like, 'Does that mean you can't make a donation at this time?' This makes it easier for the other person to respond directly, and allows us all to move on."

If the donor says no, don't take this as a flunking grade on your performance (unless you really did screw up the pitch, which is unlikely). Remember, anyone affluent enough for you to approach has a world of things to consider—how much he or she has given to other causes lately, how his or her own investment portfolio is doing, his or her child's expensive scuba diving hobby, and a recent request for a major donation from another worthy nonprofit.

Also realize that it's not easy for many people to say no, so it's actually part of your long-term development task to make the donor feel better! You might say something like, "I'm sorry this didn't work for you, but I can certainly understand where you're coming from. Of course, we'll keep in touch, and I'll look forward to seeing you at our summer event. Would you mind if I contacted you again next year?"

Some experts recommend trying to negotiate after a "no" answer—for example, by suggesting a lower amount. Obviously, it depends on how the "no" was delivered—sometimes the donor's voice and body language suggest that it was really a maybe, and sometimes you'll get a clear signal that no means no. If you conclude that you really received a flat-out no, it's best not to torture yourself or the donor by trying to turn it around. Thank the person for his or her time, and focus both your attentions on the positive aspects of your time together—you perhaps had an enjoyable lunch or meeting, the other person learned more about your work, and you probably learned something about what ignites or dampens donors' interests. The lessons of that meeting may help you land an even larger gift from this person or someone else further down the road.

> **TIP**
>
> **Is that your final answer?** Take the advice of Sophie Lei Aldrich, Senior Advisor and Specialist in Major Gifts Fundraising at the World Wildlife Fund's Global Development Centre, who says that she never thinks of any "no" as truly final. The "no" is just a reflection of the supporter's inclinations and financial situation on that day. Thinking along those lines gives her the freedom to graciously stop the money part of the conversation, while refocusing on fostering her long-term relationship with the supporter.

In the unlikely event that your meeting experience was truly horrible, just remember this: It will make a great story at your next professional fundraisers' gathering.

Follow Up After the Meeting

As soon as you get back to your office, draft a thank-you letter. And do this whether the answer was yes, no, or maybe. Also, promptly enter the pledge and other information into your database, and follow through on any other promises—for more written information or a meeting with another staff person, for example.

And if a large gift was made, and you have either collected or put the process on automatic, don't forget to gather other staff and board members to celebrate your success.

Setting Up a Focused Major Gifts Campaign

Everything in life gets easier if you can share tribulations and victories with others. That's why many organizations organize major gifts campaigns, in which staff and board members get together and schedule a series of gift solicitations.

The basic task is the same as described in the previous sections: One or two members of your organization invite a prospect to a meeting or lunch, prepare supporting written materials, and ask for the gift. What's different, however, is that the campaign is time limited. While this typically sets you up for an intense fundraising push, it also lets you know in advance when the hard work will be over—something that can be helpful when seeking to involve board and staff members. Most major gifts campaigns last for a few months, with each person going to approximately one solicitation meeting per week.

To organize all this activity, you'll want to:

- **Develop a list of potential donors.** Comb through your existing list of donors and prospects, and meet with board and staff members to identify new prospects, until you have a list of people that's sufficiently large and promising that their reasonably expected donations will meet your financial goal. Only about half of the people on even the most well-developed list are likely to give, so plan your goals accordingly.

- **Start off with a training.** Get all participants together at the beginning for a rousing review of your organization's mission and work, any special goals involved in this campaign, and how to conduct themselves at the meetings. You could photocopy portions of this book for them to review, or bring in an outside trainer. And don't forget that this isn't boot camp—your training should be inspiring enough that it also serves to remind the participants of what is really important about your work and why people will want to fund it. You might bring in a client who's been helped by your organization's work, or a program staff person who can voice how it feels to see the results of the work.

- **Distribute materials.** Give your asking team an internal summary sheet describing the campaign and their roles in it, materials they'll take to meetings with prospective supporters, a contact list of participating volunteers, board, and key staff members, "visit record forms" to be filled out after every meeting for entry into your database and stationery with envelopes to use for thank-you letters.
- **Match askers to donors.** As you plan who will visit each prospect, make sure participants are allowed plenty of input and at least a reasonable degree of choice. Take care that your tracking system will guard against embarrassing mistakes, like more than one participant's contacting the same supporter.
- **Schedule "check-back" meetings over the course of the campaign.** Every few weeks, participants should get together to compare notes, tally results, and exult over or complain about their experiences. This will allow you to fix anything that's impeding the effectiveness of your effort. Check-back meetings also prevent procrastination and are great morale boosters. People who got large pledges help others realize it can be done; and people who had disastrous meetings feel better after turning it into an entertaining story for the group.
- **Tally up your results at the end.** Create a summary of costs and expenses, a list of who participated and who was visited, and any notes about why the campaign succeeded or didn't meet expectations.
- **Celebrate.** Particularly if the campaign went well, have a final meeting or party in which participants hear the final tally, relax with some food or music, and have a last chance to boast about their fundraising prowess.

RESOURCE

Capital campaigns are slightly different. The campaign described above would be part of your annual fundraising program. This book doesn't cover larger-scale campaigns, including capital campaigns, in which your entire organization may mobilize around a particular project or monetary goal—often to fund something on a scale that dwarfs your normal fundraising activities, such as a new building.

What About Those Billionaires?

With many of the rich getting richer, where's the trickle-down to your organization? Or better yet, the fat check? Many new philanthropists say that they'd give away more than they already do if they could only find a worthwhile cause.

But don't get too excited until you hear the catch. If you think that foundations and average individual donors are demanding in terms of accountability and results, you ain't seen nothing yet. The philanthropist of today tends to be:

- highly attuned to business models and success strategies
- focused on personal involvement in a cause, either directly or through his or her foundation, and
- eager to see results within a lifetime.

Wealthy people tend to believe that their own skills and know-how accounted for much of their success. They reckon that the business models they used should be applied to charitable settings, to actually solve problems rather than to bandage them over. They speak of "investing" in programs, not "contributing" to them.

If the work of your organization involves a problem that's just not likely to go away anytime soon—at least, not without a total overhaul of the U.S. or global economic and social structure—you might be hard-pressed to attract the attention of these ambitious philanthropic capitalists. Sadly, feeding the homeless or providing shelters for victims of domestic violence might be seen as programs that don't "solve" an ongoing problem. You'll need to have a vision that's groundbreaking and can be implemented efficiently and effectively.

Still, as time goes by, some philanthropists are confessing to their own naiveté, noting the intractability of certain problems and the importance of experience at working a problem. We may yet see a swing back toward relying on existing organizations.

Funds From the Great Beyond: Bequests and Legacy Gifts

Fundraising efforts with individual donors normally focus on obtaining gifts out of their annual income. However, over the course of a donor's life, he or she may also accrue savings, property, and other assets—and eventually, the donor will have to decide how to dispose of these things at death. While bequests to spouses, children, and other close family members will almost always predominate, some people also plan to leave at least small slices of their estates to good causes. The total accounted for 9% of all charitable donations in 2017 (according to Giving USA). And studies have shown that large numbers of other people, both regular donors to charity and not, would consider doing so if asked. This is where you come in.

By reminding donors about the importance of estate planning, and by explaining how their testamentary gifts can benefit your organization, you help everyone achieve their goals. It's a message that resonates particularly well with fifty-plus-somethings, even if they're not longtime donors. Around half of people age 53 to 71 have planned their estate.

You might start by letting potential donors know that if they fail to plan their estates, state law will direct that their property be distributed under a one-size-fits-all statutory formula (called intestate succession) that's unlikely to fully reflect their wishes. You'll also want to encourage them to include a charitable giving component within their larger estate plan—which you can do not only by demonstrating that your group will put their assets to good use, but also, for your wealthiest donors, by explaining how charitable bequests can reduce (or even eliminate) the amount of estate tax their beneficiaries will owe.

TIP

Those entrepreneurs again! Not only are founders or owners of businesses unusually philanthropic, according to a 2018 report by Fidelity Charitable, but nearly half of them plan to leave a legacy gift to charity.

As your organization grows, and its development efforts become more sophisticated, you might want to offer donors a further giving incentive. Estate planning tools with names like "charitable gift annuities," "charitable remainder unitrusts," or simply "life income gifts" allow people to give assets to your organization for investment, but either continue to derive some income from those investments during their lifetime or give your organization the income but require you to return the principal to the donors or their heirs. (These aren't covered in this book.)

This chapter offers a primer on the rules and methods for making gifts through an estate—commonly called "legacy giving," "planned giving," "gift planning," or "deferred giving." However, because of the complex financial and tax concerns involved, this chapter will stick to the basics. Most organizations that are large and established either hire legacy giving specialists or attend intensive trainings when they're ready to move into this advanced area of fundraising.

Nevertheless, you can start taking important steps right now, especially when it comes to accepting straightforward inheritance gifts. It's a time-efficient way to raise substantial gifts.

 CAUTION

Planned giving programs are rarely a quick fix for financial problems. Although average gifts run between $35,000 and $70,000, according to Blackbaud, most supporters who include your organization in their estate plans will enjoy good health for many years to come. The typical planned giving program doesn't start yielding results for seven to ten years after its inception. And it may take even longer before you receive substantial income from these types of gifts. Once things get going, however, you should find that the return on your investment of time and effort far outweighs the return on any other sort of fundraising.

For some fundraisers, the most difficult part of developing a legacy giving campaign is to overcome the natural reticence to mention the word "death." Until about 20 years ago, fundraisers had a tendency to wait around politely, unwilling to broach the subject but hoping for a surprise call from someone's lawyer. However, the tide has now turned dramatically—requests for legacy gifts have become a normal part of fundraising communications.

But there's still more work to be done and plenty of opportunities to reach potential donors who haven't yet gotten the message. Research typically shows that less than 10% of U.S. residents have included charitable bequests in their wills, while over 30% would consider doing so.

To help you assess long-term legacy giving possibilities, this chapter addresses:

- what kinds of organizations can attract legacy gifts
- how virtually any organization can handle basic inheritance gifts
- how to roll out your legacy giving program smoothly and effectively, and
- the basics of soliciting and handling more complex life-income gifts.

How to Attract Legacy Gifts

Many people's aspirations to do something noteworthy—such as creating a work of art, making a scientific discovery, or helping to bring about peace in the world—are partly motivated by a desire to achieve at least a small measure of immortality. Of course, they know that they won't really live on through such acts. But, regardless of their religious beliefs, they may take comfort in thinking that their impact will be felt on this earth even after their death.

Your organization can play a role here, by becoming the vehicle through which otherwise ordinary folks can make a lasting difference. The emphasis here is on "lasting." Your goal should be to help donors achieve maximum impact (and recognition, if they want it) through their world-improving gifts. For example, bequests that include a plaque or an inscription with the deceased's name are quite popular (though plenty of givers are content to go without such recognition). Planting a tree in one's name has great symbolic significance. And other forms of remembrance—from published thanks to dedicating a building, program, or scholarship to the donor—are equally effective.

To be well positioned to receive bequests, your organization should have some or all of the following characteristics:

- **It will still be around when the donor's last will and testament is pulled out of the file.** This may be difficult for small or new organizations, as well as for those teetering on the edge of financial collapse. It will be impossible for organizations whose sole mission is to accomplish a certain goal and then close up, such as to build a bicycle trail or free a small group of political prisoners.

- **Your organization's mission, goals, and activities are momentous enough to appeal to someone's idea of a legacy.** For example, a donor would presumably rather imagine, "Upon my death, a new stretch of park will be purchased for my home city," than "My legacy will be to buy a year's worth of gasoline for the bowling league van." Most bequest givers choose nature or science, educational institutions, or arts and cultural organizations to leave money to.

- **Your organization can articulate how legacy gifts will be spent.** Most donors prefer to see that your organization has a clear spending plan in place—preferably applying their gifts toward something lasting, such as an endowment or a capital project, rather than toward covering general operating costs. If your organization has thought about how gifts will be used in advance, the donor will know that you won't spend a large gift carelessly.

- **Your organization offers meaningful recognition opportunities,** such as naming a creek, a building, or another long-lasting monument after the donor. Not every donor will want these, of course. As Audrey Yee, Director of Planned Gifts at the Golden Gate National Parks Conservancy (www.parksconservancy.org), puts it, "While many donors appreciate public recognition, others prefer low-key thanks and anonymity. The motivations of those preferring anonymity vary: Some are modest, some don't want other organizations to see their name and solicit them, and a few have delicate family situations— for example, estrangements where a person left out of the will might be upset at seeing that the money had gone to charity."

- **Your organization inspires respect and creates a sufficient sense of personal relationship with its donors,** so that they trust you to use their gifts wisely—even though they won't be around to monitor your actions.

- **Your organization does its homework,** including internal education and discussion, so that relevant staff and board members can competently, confidently, and enthusiastically represent your legacy giving program.

- **When you start to offer more complex legacy giving options, such as gift annuities or charitable remainder trusts,** your financial management system will be in expert hands.

RELATED TOPIC

Don't forget the qualities that bring regular donors to your organization. For more on these—such as a timely and viable mission and a good reputation in the community—see Chapter 4.

To be sure, not every donor places "achieving immortality" as his or her primary motivation to make a legacy gift. Some longtime supporters will simply see a legacy gift as their final way of helping out. Those of more modest means may realize that it will be the first time they can make a gift of a substantial size. However, the characteristics described above are no less important to these people. After all, what donors really want to know is whether your organization can deliver maximum impact for their bucks.

To market your legacy giving options, start by introducing messages into your mailed appeals, newsletter, website or Facebook page, or other communications materials that talk about your organization's long-term goals. An article, for example, on "How Our Work Will Affect Your Children's Lives" might allow you to offer some legacy giving information, in a way that more immediate articles (like "Summer Basketball Camp Opens Soon") don't.

But you'll also want to approach people more directly, through mailings, seminars, and personal meetings, discussed below.

Handling Simple Inheritance Gifts

Here is some good news for small, grassroots organizations not yet ready to handle the likes of annuities, remainder trusts, and other sophisticated estate planning devices: The vast majority of legacy gifts are made the old-fashioned way, through wills and simple probate-avoidance devices such as living trusts and beneficiary designations on IRAs, 401(k)s, and other financial and investment instruments.

Transfers of property through wills and living trusts are known as "bequests." These legal devices are quite simple for a nonprofit to accept. When the will or trust maker dies, the person in charge of handling the estate (usually called an executor, administrator, or successor trustee) simply transfers the appropriate bequest to your organization.

It's perfectly reasonable for an organization to start a legacy giving program by focusing on attracting bequests, and not worry about the more complicated arrangements until later.

In fact, according to Greg Lassonde, owner of Legacy Program Specialists: "My advice to people starting a legacy giving program is to keep it simple. You can start such a program with as little as 5% of your time—that's two hours a week. There's no point in getting too technical too fast."

Estate Tax Reductions Through Charitable Giving

Most of your donors (or, realistically speaking, their estates) probably won't end up owing any estate tax at all. The estate tax must be paid on the portion of a deceased person's estate that exceeds a statutory threshold—often called the estate tax exemption. This exemption amount is very high, making most estates too small to owe estate tax. For deaths in 2019 and beyond, a person can leave up to $11.4 million without owing the tax. Married couples can share their exemptions, leaving a combined estate worth up to $22.8 million tax free.

People with estates large enough to potentially owe estate tax will be eager to find ways to reduce their tax burdens—and all gifts to tax-exempt charitable organizations are exempt from estate tax, period. What's more, any amounts bequeathed or otherwise donated on death to charity are subtracted from the value of the estate to calculate the amount on which the estate will owe tax— and whether the estate will be subject to tax at all.

CAUTION

Don't cross the line into giving legal advice. The information in this section is intended to help you approach donors and explain how gifts can be made to your mutual benefit. Some of them might not know the first thing about estate planning. However, under no circumstances should you help your donors actually write a will or otherwise plan their estates. You could be held liable for practicing law without a license, and the gift could be invalidated if your overreaching looks like coercion. If your donors need specific advice, they should see a lawyer or financial professional. Also, for help writing a will or other essential estate planning documents, Nolo offers highly rated self-help options, including *Quicken® WillMaker* (software with explanatory text); *Nolo's Online Will*; and *Nolo's Online Living Trust*. You and donors can also get free information on wills and estate planning on Nolo's website, at www.nolo.com.

Gifts Made Through a Donor's Will or Living Trust

First, you'll need some basic information about wills and living trusts. A will is a document in which a person both specifies what is to be done with his or her property when he or she dies, and names an "executor" to oversee this process. The person writing a will is usually called a "testator," and those who will receive property are called "beneficiaries." Wills are also useful for taking care of some nonproperty concerns, such as naming a guardian for young children and stating who gets the pets.

A living trust does much the same thing as a will—that is, it allows someone to leave property to chosen beneficiaries. Instead of an executor, the trust maker (called a "trustor") names a "trustee." Usually the trustor chooses him- or herself as trustee until his or her death, when the named "successor trustee" takes over. The successor trustee will oversee transfer of trust property after the trustor's death.

The main technical difference between living trusts and wills is that the legal transfer of property ownership under a will happens only at the donor's death; with a living trust, this transfer happens during the trustor's lifetime. The trustor transfers his or her property into the trust, which technically owns the property, although, as the initial trustee, the trustor generally has the right to use trust property as he or she sees fit; to transfer property into and out of the trust; and even to dissolve the trust altogether.

CAUTION

Bequests via wills can leave your group nothing. A common problem that your group should be aware of occurs when donors leave a percentage of their "estate" to charity via their will—forgetting that hardly any of the estate will actually pass through probate. In other words, they've separately arranged to have so many major assets pass automatically to a named beneficiary (a joint owner of a house, perhaps, or a person designated on a payable-on-death account) that few assets remain within the will's control. If you're in conversation with donors about bequests, encourage them to speak to their lawyers or to separately name your group as a beneficiary of a particular asset. The "nothing's left" problem can be easily avoided once it's been identified.

Living trusts have become quite popular because property left though a living trust avoids probate. Probate is the court process for wrapping up an estate. It can be expensive, time-consuming, and of little benefit to beneficiaries. All property left through a will must go through probate, but property left through a trust skips probate and goes directly to beneficiaries. Even if they have living trusts, however, many people also write wills, to cover any property that they don't get around to transferring into their trusts before they die.

Neither a will nor a living trust needs to be written in legalese, and neither requires the help of a lawyer. Your donor should have no trouble naming your organization as one of the will or trust beneficiaries. The primary issue is simply making sure that whoever is handling the estate can clearly understand which of the world's many charities the deceased person had in mind to receive the property. Whether the donor uses a will or a living trust (or both), all the donor needs to do to leave your organization a gift is to:

- accurately state the full legal name of your charitable organization (for clarity, it helps to include your tax ID number, but this isn't required)
- state your organization's location (again, for clarity, it's good to state the address, but city and state are enough), and
- describe the gift, as well as what the donor expects you to do with it.

To help donors assemble the information listed in the first two bullet points above, prominently display it on your website, your newsletters, and any brochures or other communications related to planned giving. (A donor who is preparing an online will at 11 p.m. and can't find key information on your website may decide to skip the gift.)

CAUTION

Be ready for surprise gifts. The donor can do everything necessary to leave your organization a gift without your involvement—which means that you may not know about the intended bequest, or know how much it is worth, until after the donor has died. Studies show that this is exactly what happens in one out of three cases. I'll explain how to encourage donors to advise you ahead of time.

Progress Report on Berkeley Repertory Theatre's Planned Giving Program

Berkeley Repertory Theatre, a 51-year-old professional resident theatre company based in Berkeley, California (www.berkeleyrep.org), could always count on getting a "surprise" bequest every year or so. However, 12-plus years ago, the theatre decided to institute a more formal planned giving program. Here's how Director of Development Lynn Eve Komaromi describes the program's first steps and subsequent developments:

"We rolled out our program with a brochure and an announcement, containing an invitation to join the Michael Leibert Society (named after our theatre's founder). We sent this package to our longest-time patrons; those who'd been with us for around 30 years. Our reasoning was that this group was not only loyal to the theatre, but likely getting to an age where estate planning was on their minds. A handful of people responded, as did some members of our board. You can't expect people to instantaneously put you into their wills. It's a thoughtful process, which typically requires meeting with an attorney and deciding on issues like which family members to take care of and what organizations to include.

"To acknowledge our Leibert Society members, we host a lunch once a year, at which they meet someone special, such as the artistic director. We also profile one or more members in an article in our playbill at least once a year, in which they describe their decision to include the theatre in their estate plans. And we list each one of their names in every theatre program.

"That list of members keeps growing. Every season, some half dozen more people join. Some are, I think, encouraged by seeing their friends' names on the list. Others respond to the mail and email messages that we send annually to long-time donors and patrons. We also created a video, featuring personal interviews with patrons who've included Berkeley Rep in their estate plans.

"We do our best to find out who should be added to the Society list, by asking them to contact us or sign a letter of intent saying that they either plan to put us in their will or already have. With all of that, we still receive the occasional surprise gift!

"Everyone who has joined so far plans to make a gift through a will or living trust. We haven't engaged directly in any sophisticated planned giving instruments such as CRTs or gift annuities but we have partnered with a local community foundation that's able to offer these."

Types of Gifts

Money is hardly the only asset transferred through wills or living trusts. Most people accumulate copious amounts of other property, far more than they themselves are aware of—everything from clothing to cars to jewelry to childhood journals. Therefore, when a person sits down to draft a will, he or she will have to find a logical way to distribute both the money and the property. The options for types of gifts that the donor might make to you or others include:

- cash of a particular dollar amount (called a "general bequest")
- a percentage of the total value of the donor's estate (a particular type of general bequest called a "percentage bequest")
- a particular item of property, such as real property (land), personal property, such as a car, painting, or refrigerator, or a financial instrument, such as stock certificates (called a "specific bequest")
- a remainder of the donor's estate, after all the other gifts have been made to other beneficiaries, and all debts and taxes have been paid (called a "residual bequest"), or
- a portion of the estate that will go to your organization only if the originally intended beneficiary dies before the donor (called a "contingent bequest").

Restrictions on How Your Organization May Use the Gift

After deciding what type of gift to give your organization, the donor's next task is to specify how the gift must be used. For your purposes, it's best if the donor chooses the broadest possible drafting language, stating, for example, that the gift is "to be used for its [your organization's] general purposes." This is what's called an "unrestricted gift."

Unrestricted gifts can be put toward any uses your organization thinks appropriate, within its mission. But you'll have to respect the fact that many donors will specify purposes toward which the gift must be put (called a "restricted gift"). For example, the donor might state that the gift is to go toward your organization's endowment; that it can be used only for a particular program; or that even more conditions must be met, such as "to be used only for support of hatha-style yoga during the summer children's program."

You're legally bound to follow the restrictions stated in the donor's will to the extent possible and to track the gift funds carefully within your organization's accounting system. I don't need to tell you, however, how frustrated your organization might feel when trying to follow a detailed set of restrictions or conditions, especially if some of them are inappropriate or incoherent. In the yoga example above, for example, suppose you no longer offer yoga? Or, suppose you do offer yoga, but have replaced your hatha program with Iyengar yoga? Although your organization may have some flexibility in cases where carrying out the donor's wishes would truly be impossible, you'll nevertheless need to consult a lawyer about any significant changes in how you use the gift.

If you have a chance to talk to the donor about his or her intention to leave you a restricted gift, it makes sense to remind the donor of the potential difficulties of too narrowly describing the gift's intended purposes. Explain that while you'll do everything possible to respect the donor's wishes, hopefully many years will pass before the gift is actualized, and binding your organization to something that may no longer be important won't honor either your organization's needs or the donor's intentions.

Obviously you can't write the donor's will for him or her, but as an alternative, you might suggest tying the gift to more general purposes that the donor will nevertheless be excited about supporting. Another approach is for the donor to tie a gift to narrowly defined purposes, but ameliorate it by adding a sentence along the lines of, "If the gift cannot be used for these intended purposes, it may be put toward such purposes as the board of directors or trustees decides."

You can also encourage the donor to make a nonspecific gift to your organization while at the same time writing a separate letter, outside the will, in which the donor expresses his or her wishes for how the gift is to be used. While this type of letter isn't legally binding, it should help the donor feel that his or her voice will be heard by your group's board when the gift is received.

CAUTION

Update your database or mailing list when a bequest donor has died.
The last thing you want is for family members, who no doubt know of the donor's generosity to your organization, to receive one of your regular mailings, addressed to the dead person, requesting more funds.

Can You Count on Receiving This Gift?

Even if you have been told that a donor has included your organization in his or her will or living trust, don't forget that—as in those Hollywood scenes, where shocked family members sit around the table while a lawyer delivers the bad news—both wills and living trusts can be, and often are, changed. If, over the course of the donor's long life, the donor becomes bored or disappointed with your group, or simply shifts focus to another group, he or she might rewrite the will or living trust without telling you. Fortunately, such changes are relatively rare, especially because many donors make bequests to more than one charity in the first place.

Another concern often expressed by nonprofit fundraisers is that disgruntled family members might go to court and contest the will. Rest assured that contested wills are also rare, particularly because the family member would probably have to prove either that the donor was mentally incompetent when writing the will or living trust, or that your organization used fraud or exerted "undue influence" on the donor. Both of these are presumably unlikely scenarios.

While chances are reasonably good that you'll get any legacy gifts that donors have told you about, you can't count on them until they are sitting on your desk (or in your parking lot). Above all, don't enter such gifts into your organization's budget, break ground for the intended new building, or otherwise change your organization's plans in anticipation of a particular legacy gift.

Gifts Made Outside a Donor's Will or Living Trust

Wills and living trusts are not the only methods by which estate gifts can be transferred. The simplest probate-avoidance technique is to name a person or an organization as the beneficiary, upon death, of specified property, such as a bank account, life insurance policy, or retirement plan. These financial instruments usually require the naming of a beneficiary, so the donor doesn't have to take any extra steps—except perhaps to fill out a change of beneficiary form—to choose your organization.

Another transfer possibility is use of a donor-advised fund (a charitable account set up by a public charity, which makes it easy for donors to give in a systematic way). While these are primarily designed to arrange for gifts during the donor's lifetime, many donors nearing retirement age set up a DAF in order to set aside funds for a charitable legacy.

First Steps Toward Attracting Inheritance Gifts

Your organization could just go about its business, never planning for the certainty that key donors will eventually die, and hoping for surprise windfalls. Although you may receive the occasional gift this way, you'll be much more successful if you ask donors to actually consider including your organization in their estate plans.

Get Your Legacy Giving House in Order

Your first step is to create a plan to attract bequests. Hold a meeting among your board, ED, and development staff to reach agreement on the following issues:

- **Your organization's ability to attract significant amounts of inheritance gifts.** Determine whether your organization has the characteristics that legacy donors are seeking.

- **Your organization's ability to actively solicit and appropriately handle inheritance gifts.** Consider how far you want to go with your program: Will it be limited to simple inheritance gifts, or is your eventual goal to offer your donors more complex giving arrangements, such as life income gifts?
- **The types of gifts you're willing to accept.** Cash gifts are a no-brainer, but what about gifts of stock in a private corporation, interests in a limited partnership, or other financial instruments? Unless you have a board member or staff person competent to deal with these types of arrangements, you could end up squandering a potentially valuable gift. Gifts of property are an even iffier proposition. Real property (land or houses) can certainly be valuable—but such gifts can also create problems and even substantial liabilities if they come with environmental messes, long-term tenants, or other baggage that makes a quick sale impractical. (Some nonprofits attempt to reduce their risk by limiting gifts to "marketable" property, but remember that donors may not realize the potential liability problems.) And, gifts of personal property can simply be a hassle, if you have to arrange for the property to be sold or hold an estate sale yourself.
- **How your organization will use inheritance gifts.** Donors will be eager to hear that their gifts will have a deep and lasting impact.
- **Initial budget for staff time and training, explanatory brochures, volunteer mobilization.** Consider these and other costs of instituting the program and communicating with donors.

Plant a Seed in Your Donors' Minds

Step Two is communicating your bequest giving plan to your donors. Some of them might need a reminder to plan their estates (though probably not your older donors—a whole industry exists to remind them). But you do need to remind your donors how satisfying it will feel to leave a world-improving legacy, via your organization.

You should be conveying this message to all of your donors, not just the affluent ones; and to your board members and other volunteers. As Audrey Yee of the Golden Gate National Parks Conservancy explains it, "I think of planned giving as a hybrid of the other individual giving models. You have your annual gifts, your major gifts, and your planned gifts, and you can view each in some respects as a subset of the other, or all of them as intersecting circles. For example, an annual giver might become a planned giver without ever becoming a major donor. This is especially common when an annual giver needs the money during his or her lifetime, but is sufficiently interested in your organization to want to help as soon as he or she can."

Greg Lassonde echoes this analysis: "I'd estimate that only about 10% to 20% of legacy gifts come from major donors. That makes legacy gifts special—so much thought goes into them, by people who may have never before had the means or opportunity to make a substantial gift."

The simplest way to start conveying estate planning information is within your existing newsletter, brochure, website, or social media pages. Make sure that any section that discusses general giving also mentions inheritance gifts. Many organizations simply insert a shaded box into every newsletter, containing the central message and key information, including:

- a reminder of the importance of estate planning
- a suggestion that supporters consider planned gifts
- the great uses to which their gifts would be put
- any recognition or naming programs
- your organization's legal name, and
- who to contact for more information.

Others add a checkbox to their donation reply cards, saying something on the order of "Please send me information on how I can make a bequest gift to your organization through my will or living trust," or "I have included your organization in my will or living trust."

Separate email blasts can also work, particularly if you have relevant news to share, such as new legislation concerning an IRA-rollover opportunity. Or, you could email donors an online survey asking about their planned giving intentions.

A Commitment as Great as the Redwoods

Debra and Rich Whitall fell for the redwoods — and each other — as students at Humboldt State University in Arcata, California. They love redwoods so much that Debra changed her major to forest hydrology so she could help protect the forests, and Rich worked his way through college as a forest firefighter throughout the redwoods' range. They were even married in a redwood grove before they graduated in 1984. Fifteen years later, they showed their commitment to the redwoods again, by including Save the Redwoods League in their estate plan.

"It just made sense to start considering who is really doing the kind of long-term work that we value," said Rich, referring to their estate beneficiaries.

Debra and Rich Whitall made a commitment to include the League in their estate plan.

"The ancient groves are such a powerful reminder that we humans have a huge responsibility to honor and preserve the remaining wild places," said Debra, a social scientist with the U.S. Forest Service in Washington, DC.

For information on including the League in your estate plan, visit savetheredwoods.org/development/planned-giving.shtml, or contact Sharon Rabichow, Major and Planned Gifts Associate, at (888) 836-0005 ext. 828 or srabichow@SaveTheRedwoods.org

Reprinted with permission

CAUTION

Terms like "legacy giving" and "planned giving" may mean little to your donors. Therefore, your communications materials should avoid headings like, "Have you considered a planned gift?" Better to stick to plain English, with headings like, "You can leave a living legacy," or "Please consider including [*name of your organization*] in your will or living trust."

Another great form of encouragement is to tell stories of other donors. Save the Redwoods League uses this strategy nicely, as shown in the example from its newsletter above. Sharon Rabichow at Save the Redwoods League, says, "Our work really comes alive when it's told through people. The stories about why our members make planned gifts stir similar emotions in our other donors, motivating them to leave a legacy as well." And, notes Lynn Eve Komaromi from Berkeley Repertory Theatre: "It helps to put a human face on this potentially daunting process. By seeing the satisfaction others gain from planning their legacy, donors come to feel that, 'I'm ready to do that, too.'"

Again, such stories—in either written or video form—could go in your newsletter, on your website or blog with links from your Facebook page, or even in your annual report. They can be anything from lengthy profiles to small boxes with photos and mentions of the intended gift (particularly appropriate for your website, in the section describing donation possibilities). You'll need the donor's permission, of course, or that of his or her family if the donor has already died. But there's no need to wait until the donor is gone to celebrate a planned posthumous gift—many donors will be pleased to get credit for their generosity while they're still around to appreciate it.

Your anecdotes should briefly highlight each donor's personality, special interests, and values during his or her lifetime, and explain how the gift allowed, or will allow, these interests and values to be furthered. Describe how your organization has made excellent use of the gift (if it has already been received), and its lasting impact. Positive quotes from family members are also reassuring to donors fearful of disappointing rightful heirs.

Be Ready to Respond to Interested Donors

After you start putting the word out, you're bound to get some responses from interested donors. This is where some organizations fall down on the job. Perhaps because they never believed in the possibility of success, they fail to put together materials or a plan in advance. The result is that donors may feel alienated and/or lose interest in the whole enterprise.

The appropriate plan for your organization depends partly on the types of overtures you made in your marketing materials. For example, if people checked a box saying "Please send me more information," then of course you'll want to have an explanatory brochure or other information at the ready. (The same information should be available on your website.)

If you've asked people to check a box saying they'd like to be contacted to discuss this matter, then you'll want to call right away to offer more information—whether it be immediate details over the phone, written materials, or a sit-down meeting to further explore the possibilities. Try to make personal contact if at all possible.

Approach Prospective Legacy Donors Who Haven't Expressed Interest

Consider how and whether to approach the topic of inheritance gifts with appropriate long-term or major donors who haven't spoken up. Perhaps your newsletter and other messages haven't made an impression on them. As with any major gift request, scheduling a personal meeting may be appropriate. (See Chapter 6 for more on arranging and holding personal meetings with donors.)

No need to schedule a separate meeting with every donor, or even with every major donor. Ideally, you should approach donors whom you, or one of your board members, know well enough to comfortably offer this giving option. Keep your ears open; Berkeley Repertory Theatre's Lynn Eve Komaromi remembers talking to a donor who lightheartedly said of her annual gift, "Well, I guess I'll keep doing this for as long as I live!" That gave Lynn Eve an opening to suggest that the donor think about giving even after she is gone—and they immediately scheduled a meeting to discuss it further.

Beyond the donors whom you're close to personally, the most likely ones to approach are those who fall into at least one of the following categories:

- **Committed supporters of your organization.** These may be major donors, with whom your organization has built a solid and warm relationship. Also look for longtime volunteers and donors who've been making gifts for years, even if only $10 a year.
- **Donors age 45 and older.** This is the age at which most people write at least a basic will or living trust. And the younger they are, the more likely they are to include a charitable donation. (But not everyone will be ready for will writing; statistically, people at age 45 can expect to live from 40 to 45 more years, and many won't yet be interested.)
- **Donors of any age who are childless or widowed.** Such folks are more likely to have considered their lack of natural heirs and the prospect of a planned gift.
- **Donors with wealthy children.** The reason is obvious.
- **Younger donors who work in a field like law, accounting, or medicine.** These professionals are conditioned to be realistic about preparing for their death (although they may still be procrastinating).

- **Homeowners.** Something about buying a house spurs people to write a will. And longtime homeowners in urban areas may be living in an appreciated asset, and so have a good-sized estate to plan around, regardless of their current income level.

As with all donor interactions, success in attracting legacy gifts comes down to doing your research and understanding each donor's individual interests.

> TIP
> **Meeting with prospective planned givers may jump-start their annual giving.** According to planned giving professional Linda Solow Bouwer, "I've had many experiences where I've helped a donor who had never once made a major gift look into our planned giving options—and, as a result of the conversation, the donor's level of excitement about our organization rose so much that he or she began increasing the level of his or her annual gifts, as well! The lesson is to make every donor aware of your planned giving program, if only through a mention in your newsletter or website."

Before meeting with a potential legacy donor, write up a statement explaining how your organization will use a significant gift. Be specific about how the gift will go toward an important, lasting goal (such as opening a new wing to your clinic or saving a beach from development) or support the donor's favorite programs and activities (such as a literacy program that will help bring reading to future generations). Your written statement should also briefly explain what sorts of gifts your organization is in a position to accept (or can't accept, such as real property). If your organization offers more complicated giving vehicles, explain these possibilities.

The end of a conversation about a posthumous gift is quite different from one about a current major donation, since the donor won't open up a checkbook on the spot. A good way to close, assuming the response was positive, is to ask the donor to stay in touch as he or she takes the various practical steps required, so that your organization can appropriately recognize the planned bequest. To be even more proactive, ask whether you can follow up with any program material tailored to the person's interests (particularly if he or she seems inclined to make a directed gift), and offer to send your nonprofit's IRS exemption letter and other tax-related information for the donor's lawyer or estate planner.

And, after your program has a significant number of participants, you may also want to invite them to join in events or groups geared toward honoring planned gift donors.

> **TIP**
>
> **Get your board on board.** As committed members of your organization, your board members are good prospects for planned gifts. One effective way to enlist them is for one member to take the floor at a meeting, and say, "I've included this organization in my will—who else is willing to commit to this?" Ask these board members to help recruit others. After all, a pitch that begins with the fundraiser's own story of setting up a planned gift to your organization stands a better chance of success.

Develop Meaningful Ways to Recognize Legacy Donors

Finding ways to thank legacy donors is interesting, because the gift hasn't been made yet. You may not know for sure how large it will be. Yet waiting until the donor's death to recognize his or her generosity would be nonsensical.

First, you need to find out what inheritance gifts lie in store for your organization (whether from major donors or others). The only way to get this information is to actively solicit it. (A minority of donors proactively advise the nonprofit of their planned gifts.) For example, your reply cards for fundraising appeals might include a box to check, saying, "I have included your organization in my will or estate planning arrangements."

Follow up on those who check "yes," by calling to thank them and ask whether they'd like to discuss the uses to which their gift might be put and recognition opportunities. Your newsletter or website might also ask your donors to advise you if they've named your organization in their will or other estate planning arrangements.

Next, you need to find special ways to thank your bequest donors. Many of the familiar ways remain appropriate, including a thank-you letter or lunch invitation after you first hear about the bequest and a mention in your annual report or event program. (Names can be removed a year or two after the gift is actually made.) However, you should also consider how to give unique recognition to this group. After all, they haven't merely given you a slice of their income; they've promised you a potentially substantial amount of their worldly goods, as one of their last acts on this earth.

Be Ready for Memorial or Tribute Gifts

If a donor who cared deeply about your organization dies, marries, has a birthday, or something similar, family members may be asked to make a charitable memorial gift in lieu of sending flowers or material objects. Memorial gifts not only require special handling, but fast action. Be prepared to:

- Provide the donors a specially designed card that they or you can immediately mail to family members or the honoree, offering condolences or congratulations and advising that they have made a gift in honor of their loved one.
- On your website, for those wishing to donate online, add a box for donors to check indicating a memorial or tribute gift, followed by a space where they can fill in the person's name.
- In addition to sending the usual thank-you letters to the actual donors, notify family members or honorees of the amount of each gift made.
- List these gifts under the name of the honoree in your annual report, newsletter, and website, as appropriate.
- If the person was well-known and the gift pool may be large, be ready to establish an ongoing special fund in the person's name.

You might send memorial and tribute gift donors a brochure with your acknowledgment letter and add them to your mailing list, at least for a year or two. Even if they weren't interested in your cause before, their friend's commitment to it may inspire their interest. And they'd probably be interested in seeing how their gift was spent. But don't be surprised if the gift was just a one-time deal—and be sure to remove donors from your mailing list if they show no interest after a reasonable period of time.

TIP

How should you treat contingent bequests? Some donors—for example, married persons with no children—may name your organization as a "backup" beneficiary in case their spouse or another primary beneficiary dies before or at the same time they do. It's wonderful that they're doing so, but given the unlikelihood that you'll ever receive the gift, do they really deserve a place at your legacy luncheon table? According to Greg Lassonde, "You'll obviously want to thank the donor if you find out about such a contingent bequest, but most organizations don't go beyond this when it comes to recognition."

CAUTION

Distinguish the living from the dead when creating your recognition lists. If your annual report, newsletter, program, or website lists legacy donors by name, be sure to asterisk those who are already deceased, and explain this in a footnote. (Otherwise, some people may assume everyone on the list is dead, a potentially very disturbing miscommunication.)

For gifts that are particularly large and might inspire future gifts, you might create a fund bearing the donor's name, dedicated to a particular purpose—the Warner Scholarship or the Guerin Endowment, for example. To ensure the posterity of the gift, it's possible (after some internal planning and policy decisions) to make it an "endowed gift." With an endowed gift, your organization invests the gift, and uses only a portion of the interest earned to carry out the gift's purposes. Creating a named fund or endowment not only gives posterity to the donor's name, but also allows you to leverage the donor's gift, by using it to attract others.

For the larger pool of more modest gifts, some organizations create a special "society," with an honorary name.

Once you have your society in place—and even if you don't institute an actual society—consider these additional ways to honor your legacy gift donors:

- Invite them to an annual thank-you lunch, tea, or dinner, just for them (the San Francisco Symphony, for example, holds an annual lunch at which the members listen to chamber music, meet the musicians, and receive a small gift such as a chocolate musical note).
- Invite them to volunteer events (the Golden Gate National Parks Conservancy, for example, has invited its legacy donors to spend a morning at one of their native plant nurseries in the parks, and serves them an organic box lunch).
- Create bonding opportunities (the Golden Gate National Parks Conservancy holds fireside chats, evenings around a campfire, and invites legacy as well as major donors to watch Fourth of July fireworks together from a local park).
- Establish a walkway, a wall, or another place where society members' names can be inscribed.
- Have your ED or a board member visit society members occasionally, especially those whose health doesn't permit them to attend events.

- Send regular letter reports or greeting cards with news of your organization's doings, and perhaps a small gift, such as a pin commemorating their society membership.

What Should You Name Your Society?

For the unimaginative, a host of generic names are possible, like "legacy society" or "heritage club." It's far more compelling, however, if you follow the lead of those organizations that name their group after an honored person, such as one of the organization's founders, like Berkeley Repertory Theatre's "Michael Leibert Society." (This so-called "society" isn't a separate legal entity; it's just a way to name a segment of your donors.) An added advantage to naming your group after a known person is that some people treat this as akin to a memorial gift, and make bequests in the named person's honor.

Other organizations choose a name that's inspiring for other reasons: as with the Golden Gate National Parks Conservancy's "Silver Lupine Circle," named after its successful efforts to replant the silver lupine in order to create a habitat for the endangered Mission blue butterfly.

You should also, of course, include your legacy society donors in the same activities and opportunities as your other donors, such as tours of your facilities and holiday parties. If, however, certain donors have made restricted gifts, try to tailor your efforts to their interests. For example, if the donor has promised a bequest for the free meals portion of your homeless services, make sure he or she is invited to attend during one of these meals.

Preview of Other Legacy Giving Arrangements

As you've seen, gifts made via wills or living trusts require very little action from your organization. Most of the hard work is done by the donor, possibly (but not necessarily) with the help of a lawyer. After the donor's death, the estate's executor, administrator, or successor trustee will ensure that your organization receives its due.

Life income gifts are another matter. Most of them are designed to take advantage of favorable but complicated tax laws. Typically, they involve a donor gifting money or property to your group in exchange for your commitment to pay the donor regular interest income for life. You'll need the help of a professional, either an in-house staff person, or an outside consultant or bank, to set up and run this kind of program. For this reason, this section will simply give you a taste of the possibilities.

TIP

Your local community foundation may be willing to handle life income funds on your behalf. Many are already accustomed to creating pools of donor funds and handling complex financial arrangements for small nonprofits. Talk to the larger foundations in your area to find out what they have to offer.

Below are the main types of life income arrangements and their close cousins. Which one is best for any particular donor depends on the donor's current level of assets, need for predictable future income, and various income tax and capital gains tax considerations.

Charitable gift annuity. During his or her lifetime, the donor gives the nonprofit either cash or another asset (often stock shares or real property), and the nonprofit in return gives the donor (or another beneficiary) fixed payouts (an "annuity") on a monthy or quarterly basis, for life. For the initial contribution, there's like;y to be a minimum (say, $10,000). To hopefully cover the amount of the annuity, the nonprofit invests the assets or proceeds from the sale of property (or, in the case of real property with tenants, may manage and continue to rent out the space). When the donor (or another beneficiary) dies, the nonprofit becomes sole owner of the assets and can use them for its charitable purposes.

Deferred payment gift annuity. This is much like the charitable gift annuity described above, except that the donor decides not to start receiving annual annuity payments until a later date, usually at a specified age. This option is most often chosen for tax reasons, particularly by younger donors (who can claim a tax deduction in the year the gift is made, but don't have to worry about paying tax on the annuity payments until they are older— and presumably in a lower tax bracket). The payout amounts are typically higher than with a regular gift annuity, too.

Charitable remainder annuity trust. The donor gives assets over to a trust, and a trustee manages and invests the assets, then makes payments to the donor (or another beneficiary or beneficiaries) out of the trust's income and, if necessary, out of its assets. This continues for either a specified number of years or for the rest of the donor's life. When the term of years ends or the donor dies, the nonprofit gets what's left in the trust. Though very similar to the charitable gift annuity, the charitable remainder annuity trust is preferred by some donors for capital gains tax reasons. (In particular, with gifts of securities or other property that a donor purchased a year or more ago and that have appreciated in value, transferring them to a trust completely bypasses the capital gains tax system. Contrast this with a donor who transfers appreciated securities to a nonprofit for a charitable gift annuity and will still have to pay tax on a portion of their value.)

Charitable remainder unitrust. A donor gives assets over to a trust, and the trustee manages and invests the assets, then pays the donor an annual percentage of the trust's current value (meaning that the amount the donor receives may go up and down over the years, depending on how the investments are doing). After the donor dies, remaining assets go to the nonprofit. This has capital gains tax advantages similar to the charitable remainder annuity trust. The unitrust is also good for donors who aren't as interested in a fixed income, but are willing to gamble that the value of the trust will go up, and that their payments will therefore increase.

Charitable lead trust. This is sometimes called a reverse charitable remainder trust, and for good reason. The donor creates a trust, out of which payments are made to the nonprofit for a specified number of years or until the donor's death. When those years are up or the donor dies, the principal assets are returned to the donor or whoever else the donor has named as a beneficiary. Donors enjoy the same capital gains benefits as with other trusts, as well as estate tax benefits when the property is transferred to their heirs. A charitable lead trust is especially appealing to those donors who want to leave a particular piece of property to their heirs, but also want to put it to use both philanthropically and for tax purposes in the meantime.

Pooled income fund. A group of donors contributes assets to a particular fund at a nonprofit, and the nonprofit invests the pooled assets and pays out the earnings to the donors. When each donor dies, the nonprofit may withdraw that donor's share of the fund for its own charitable use. This is a good option for schools, hospitals, and other nonprofits whose donor base doesn't include many people with enough money to warrant setting up an individual charitable gift annuity.

Retained life interest. The donor transfers ownership of a piece of real property, such as a home or farm, to the nonprofit, but retains the right to live there for life.

RESOURCE

Need updates and other help with your legacy giving program? See the following resources:

- the website of the National Association of Charitable Gift Planners, at https://charitablegiftplanners.org. This is the standard-setting organization in this field, and it holds seminars and publishes educational materials.
- the website of consultant Phil Murphy, at www.plannedgivingcoach.com. This site contains free information, including sample letters to prospects regarding both bequests and life income gifts.
- *Planned Giving Today,* a monthly newsletter written in plain English with a marketing focus, available by subscription at www.liebertpub.com/pgt.
- Crescendo, at www.crescendointeractive.com. This popular group arranges conferences and sells planned giving software.
- PG Calc, at www.pgcalc.com, offering software designed to help you calculate, explain, compare, and promote planned gifts.

Special Events

Ask any professional fundraiser to name best or worst fundraising memories, and you're likely to hear about special events. Special events can be the highlight of your fundraising year—grand occasions that mobilize volunteers, bring you into direct contact with your friends and supporters, and create a festive atmosphere for everyone involved. Unfortunately, special events can also set the stage for huge public embarrassments and spectacular losses of money. I know one fundraiser who still shudders when she thinks about the 600-person picnic where the person with the one and only restroom key disappeared.

By definition, special events are occasions outside your nonprofit's usual activities, where your membership and/or the public is invited to attend and support your work, usually by paying an admission fee or buying things once they get there. Dinners, auctions, fairs and festivals, lectures, benefit concerts, home and garden tours, tournaments, contests, sporting events, walkathons, garage sales, and bake sales are common examples. Whole books have been dedicated to exploring the array of possible special events—and they still don't cover everything that an innovative mind might envision.

Rather than attempting to describe how to plan and put on every possible type of special event, this chapter focuses on how to make your special event serve the focus of this book: raising money. This is an important distinction: One of the first questions that experienced development pros ask when considering a potential special event is, "Will this be a fundraiser or a friendraiser?" It's an especially legitimate question given a report by Charity Navigator, a watchdog group, finding that special events are an inefficient way to raise money, bringing in an average of $1 for every $1.33 spent on them, and generating only 15% of total individual contributions. The exceptions are often large groups with well-connected boards and compelling causes.

Events that don't bring in any actual profits can still be valuable, particularly if they bring visibility to your organization, mobilize and expand its donor base, or highlight a particular issue of special importance to your members and/or clients. An open house, for example, when you invite your membership—and possibly a few prospective new members—to come see what you do and meet your staff, might serve important purposes beyond raising money for your group.

Be clear on your goals, and rethink or even drop events that absorb too much valuable staff time and energy. With careful budgeting and planning, however, you may be able to turn a break-even event into a true fundraiser.

This chapter covers:

- types of special events and their fundraising potential
- choosing an event that suits your organization
- planning the event with respect for the climate and environment
- creating a realistic budget
- creating a schedule of activities before and during the event
- protecting your organization from legal and financial liability
- tips for making your event go smoothly, and
- following up after the event.

TIP

Get attendees' names. No matter what type of special event you choose, you'll have an opportunity to put your organization's name and work in front of new eyes—which means you'll want to be organized about capturing names and addresses (including email) for your mailing list. If you won't know in advance who will be attending, create a sign-in sheet. But to make sure people don't breeze right past your registration table, professional events planner Laurie J. Earp (based in Oakland, California) suggests an even more effective tactic: "I like to create a door prize, requiring people to fill out their name and contact information or provide a business card. I've found that this brings in not just a few more names, but many times more names than I'd get with just a sign-in sheet." Also, be sure to have a table or another location featuring brochures, photos, and other demonstrations of your organization's work, so that new people realize that the event serves goals beyond their own pleasure.

Other Reasons to Hold a Special Event

Although this chapter focuses on the fundraising potential of special events, there are a number of other good reasons to hold one, such as to:

- **raise visibility**—the promotional activities surrounding the event, as well as the new contacts you make with people who attend, will be of lasting benefit
- **improve your organization's relationship with the public,** such as the residential neighbors around your shelter, or with a particular group of influential people (if you're a children's education group, for example, you might hold a reception for faculty members of the education departments of local colleges)
- **mobilize volunteers**—and bring in new ones
- **celebrate milestones and achievements,** such as your organization's anniversary, approval for a large grant, a staff or board member's departure, or the graduation of a group of students or trainees (though these can easily be turned into effective fundraisers)
- **thank dedicated people who have helped your organization,** or
- **kick off a membership or fundraising campaign** (although the larger purpose here is to raise money, the event itself may be primarily a consciousness raiser).

Survey of Special Events

This section takes a quick ride through the special events landscape, looking at the most common types, the major costs associated with them, and the keys to making yours a financial success. Bear in mind that the biggest predictor of any event's success is the quality and energy of the people who work on it, as well as the size and dedication of your group's core roster of supporters.

> **TIP**
>
> **Watch the calendar.** Keep tabs on events being held by other organizations in your area. This is important both to collect creative ideas and to make sure you don't duplicate something already happening nearby or at the same time. Also, keep an eye on important dates—you don't want to schedule an event on a Jewish or Muslim holiday, for example, particularly if you have members from these faiths.

Lunches, Dinners, and Other Food Events

The most common special event is the annual or special celebratory dinner (or luncheon, tea, or cocktail hour). There are numerous variations on the meal theme—your basic hotel or restaurant sitdown meal (most often with your organization paying the costs, though some restaurants will cut you a discount as a donation); a small food or drink event at the home of a supporter; a meal for which your clients or supporters make the food, such as a themed or an ethnic buffet; a staged event where participants go to different houses or restaurants for drinks, appetizers, a main meal, and dessert; and a "tasting," where you arrange for local vendors, such as restaurants, wineries, or ice cream manufacturers, to send a representative offering samples (free advertising for them, free food for you).

Most meal events also try to incorporate some sort of entertainment or education, such as a speaker, musical performance, video presentation, or showcase of clients' talents or activities. If your organization doesn't regularly hold an annual dinner, then other effective event themes might include its anniversary or the retirement of a longtime ED or board member—especially because such occasions tend to bring back long-lost supporters who want to share memories or honor a favorite person.

The key to making a dinner event profitable is to understand that its main proceeds won't come from ticket sales. (In fact, "banquet fatigue" is a common complaint among philanthropic types.) Instead, you must make the event serve as a rallying point for a broader effort to collect individual and corporate donations. For example, a local business that might not give you a cash donation to support your programs might instead be willing to donate in-kind to your annual dinner, especially with your assurances that the event will receive press coverage and that the business will be appropriately (and prominently) thanked in the printed event program.

Many dinner events also incorporate another moneymaking activity, such as an auction, a raffle, or a series of booths with items for sale. Involving a well-liked celebrity is also a good way to boost your dinner's fundraising potential—it will both elevate ticket sales and allow you to charge more for the tickets. Or, how about a signature drink? If you're planning an event with a no-host bar, you can ask the bartender to create a special mixed drink, which you name for something thematic to the group or season. Then you mark up the price a bit beyond the usual.

> ### TIP
> **Seek donations of necessary items.** There's no limit on what you can request—flowers, balloons, other decorations, costumes for the waitstaff, music or other entertainment, a sound system, printing services, transportation for your keynote speaker, and more. With these covered, you can more confidently approach potential donors about your surefire-success event.

On the expense side of the ledger, prepare for venue, food, and catering costs to add up fast.

One option is to have volunteers prepare the meal, but you'll probably have to bring down your ticket prices for a more homespun event like this. Also, you'll find that feeding large numbers of people requires special equipment, such as warming trays and coffee urns, not to mention space, tables, and chairs, that you may have to rent. After adding up all the extras, some organizations find it more cost-effective to hire professionals.

Renting a private hall and hiring a caterer is usually cheaper than contracting with a hotel—the latter are famous for charging five bucks for a mediocre cup of coffee. If a hotel seems like your best option, you can bring down the costs by asking to include some separately donated items on the menu, such as wine or chocolates.

> ### CAUTION
> **Serving homemade food?** Check your local health department regulations, which may prohibit serving food from noncertified kitchens at ticketed events. Sometimes you can get around this with a "suggested donation."

CAUTION

Watch out for corkage fees. As nonprofit consultant Sue Hall explains, "Most hotels and venues charge an outrageous corkage fee—that is, a fee for opening and serving each bottle of wine or liquor you bring in from elsewhere. But it's in your interest to get wine donated, as we do for the Friends of the Saint Paul Public Library annual event that I'm involved with. Luckily, we've negotiated a very good corkage rate."

The Virtues of Combo-Platter Events

To maximize both fun and profits, always consider whether mini-events can be dovetailed into the main one—combining, for example, a raffle with an open house, an auction with a dinner, or booths of food vendors at a sports tournament. As long as you're mobilizing your volunteers anyway, you may as well offer them alternative directions in which to channel their energies.

You'll be surprised, too, at how many donors are willing to spend money on a variety of things, even if they wouldn't have been willing to write one big check. (No one who arrived at your event willing to spend more should leave unsatisfied! At the very least, a booth where you sell your organization's T-shirts might be profitable.)

Combining activities can increase participants' enjoyment. At a dinner, for example, many people will be too shy to mingle with strangers on the open floor, but will happily chat as they view the silent auction tables.

There are, however, two potential drawbacks to consider when combining events. First, if your event is already complex, and your pool of volunteers stretched thin, you can easily overdo it by piling on more responsibilities. (In any case, make sure your various activities don't get into one another's way—keep them to a strict schedule, and make sure, for example, that a silent auction ends before dinner starts.)

A second possible drawback is that combining fundraising activities might exclude potential donors. For example, a friend of mine volunteers at her children's school, where a gala fundraising dinner was formerly combined with a raffle. However, the development committee realized that, because many of the parents are low-income, they couldn't afford the relatively expensive dinner tickets—but would have been quite willing to buy raffle tickets. So, the two events were split apart, and overall parental donations increased as a result.

TIP

Good food is critical. Participants will remember overcooked pasta or tiny portions years later. I heard of one event where a group tried to cook dinner for 500 people—who waited hungrily until 10:45 pm to be fed. If you're doing your own cooking, at least consult with a professional about how to pull it off. If not, ask the hotel, restaurant, or other food preparer to make you a sample meal—the same one your guests will be served. Make sure it's filling and tasty, but isn't so decadent that health-conscious diners will stick to the parsley garnish. Also be ready for people with special diet needs, such as vegetarian, gluten-free, or kosher. It's usually easiest just to give your guests the name of a chef or another food-planning person to contact directly, and let them work out the details.

Auctions

An auction, whether silent or live, can be a stand-alone event or a part of another event, such as an annual dinner. (Even online auctions, discussed under "How to Hold an Online Auction," below, can be incorporated into live events.) A silent auction is one where people write their bids on a sheet of paper, usually in an area where the items up for auction are displayed, with little time pressure. People can go back to see whether they've been outbid, and then write in a higher bid if they wish. At an appointed time, you close the bidding, and later announce the winners or let people check for their names on the bidding sheets.

A live auction, of course, is one where an auctioneer (preferably a professional) is at the helm, and people call out (or otherwise indicate) their bids. Which one you choose may simply be a matter of practicality—an important advantage to a silent auction, for example, is that it can be conducted quietly, without disturbing any other simultaneous activities (such as speakers or cocktail hour conversation).

If your choice between a silent or live auction will be based on which is more profitable, go with a live auction. Silent auctions usually bring in about half the market value of the items auctioned, while live auctions tend to bring in bids closer to or exceeding an item's market value. The reason may be that more excitement, or even frenzy, develops as people compete out loud. People may start out looking for a bargain, but end up saying, "Well, at least it was for a good cause."

How to Hold an Online Auction

An online auction is one in which the nonprofit displays photographs of items up for bidding on an auction website such as BiddingForGood.com, BiddingOwl.com, and Charity.ebay.com. Would-be bidders register, enter credit card information (to guarantee payment from the winning bidders), and then place their bids within a set period of time, typically one to three weeks, after which your nonprofit sends the winners the goods.

Online auctions offer many advantages over live events. You don't have to fill a room with people, they're open to members who are spread out geographically (or to the whole world if you wish), bidders can participate at any time of the day or night without leaving home, you won't need volunteers for setup (though you will need some for the shipping or delivery), and you won't have to deal with the risk of displaying fragile or high-value items.

The online auction method isn't free; you'll have to pay the hosting website or auction service provider. Someone will also need to pay for shipping, but you can specify ahead of time whether it's the buyer or the organization.

The preparatory steps to holding an online fundraising auction are much like those for a regular auction. You'll solicit goods, set starting bids, and present goods in an attractive light to bidders—which in this case, means taking high-quality photos and/or writing up enticing yet accurate descriptions.

An online auction can also be combined with a live auction. You'd allow online bidding to begin first, with the highest online bid serving as the live auction starting bid. Or, you let online bidders enter a maximum dollar amount for an item ahead of time, which is told only to a volunteer proxy who bids on that person's behalf. Another option is to hold an online auction after your live or silent auction, to deal with items you didn't have room for or that didn't sell.

No matter which kind of auction you hold, your overall profits will also depend on your audience. In the words of events planner Laurie Earp, "You have to know who your guests are going to be. Are they looking for a good bargain, or are they looking for a good bidding war, and willing to pay more than the retail value of the items? It's best to have a combination of both." Part of this will depend on whether your guests are existing organization members or donors, or are simply members of the community who attend for their own pleasure. If it's the latter, try reminding them of the purpose of the event—and set minimum bids higher than bargain-basement levels.

TIP
Numerical rules of thumb for auctions. Experienced fundraisers suggest making sure you'll have a minimum of 25 people in the bidding audience, with at least two people for every item to be auctioned. And, to reach a certain dollar goal—for example, if you're hoping to raise $8,000—get donated items whose worth is at least double that amount, or $16,000.

Auctions can be highly profitable fundraisers because, of course, you'll be auctioning off donated goods. Many businesses understand that donating something to an auction brings them publicity. They probably paid wholesale prices for the goods, while you will bring in something closer to their retail cost. You can also minimize how much you ask of any one business (and have fun to boot) by creating packages—the classic one being plane tickets to a holiday destination like Hawaii, with a week's stay at a hotel (or supporter's home), and meals at nice restaurants. Package deals don't have to be on such a grand scale, however—you could also create an auction package offering "A Day on the Avenue," and ask merchants along a popular commercial street to donate certificates for a spa visit or massage, lunch, movie tickets, and a latte. Or, you might create a food basket, with every item carrying a tag from its donor.

Some of the best donations come from your own board members or other supporters—for example, a ride on someone's sailboat, dinner at someone's home, a foursome at a private golf club, use of a vacation home, or use of professional services from chiropractic to accounting to hairdressing. A friend of mine who happens to be a highly ranked chess player offered a free chess lesson as an auction donation. The most interesting auction I've attended was one selling paintings made by elephants—abstract paintings, of course. These particular elephants were on an animal preserve in Thailand, and the auction helped to raise money for their care. See the website of the Asian Elephant Art and Conservation Project, at www.elephantart.com.

The drawback to auctions is that they take an enormous amount of time to prepare. Every merchant or other donor needs to be approached, the items need to be picked up, certificates may need to be created for the winners of intangible items such as dinner at a board member's house, packages need to be put together, and thank-you letters need to be sent out to every gift giver. Obviously, these tasks are ideal for board members and other volunteers—but you'll need to set some parameters first, on the types of items you want and the potential sponsors or donors who should be approached. Otherwise, volunteers may show up at your office with donated kittens or carloads of used goods.

Coordinate your volunteers so that the same donor isn't approached twice. Also make sure that all volunteers are armed with brochures describing your organization and a "Dear Friend" letter explaining the event and the recognition the donor will receive for making a contribution.

> **TIP**
> **Raffles are a close cousin to auctions.** Though they're not really "events," raffles are a great way to earn between $2,000 and $10,000. The principles of lining up donated goods are the same. You simply set a raffle ticket price that seems fair (and sufficient to make it worth your investment of time), create tickets with a stub for the buyer and a portion for you where the buyer fills in his or her name, address, and email, and then sell the tickets. I have a friend who says, "All you need is three kids and a mountain bike." The concept is that you arrange with a sports store to buy the bike at cost, then post the kids (and the bike) outside the store or at another popular location, such as a coffee shop. They sell raffle tickets until they've earned enough to cover the bike plus a healthy profit, then some lucky ticket holder pedals off into the sunset.
>
> The names and addresses you collect from your raffle tickets are yet another source of potential new members for your mailing and email lists. A caution, however: Some states separately regulate raffles—for example, by limiting the number you can have per year or the value or type of items you can raffle, or by requiring you to file a report when you're holding a raffle. Check with your state nonprofit-regulating agency for more information.

Fairs and Festivals

This category encompasses events like crafts fairs, carnivals, Renaissance fairs, music festivals, and other occasions that showcase a variety of vendors or talents. Some organizations invent their own theme festivals—for example, the International Crane Foundation, a Wisconsin-based group that works worldwide to conserve cranes (www.savingcranes.org) holds Crane Festivals in various locations. These feature bird-related activities like guided hikes, origami crane folding, bird-feeder building, and lectures on nature photography and more. The key is to create an occasion where people can access things that they might not ordinarily find all in one place—or attract people who are simply looking for something to do.

Don't try to undertake a large-scale fair or festival until you've had experience with other or smaller special events. For example, if you hold an ethnic culture fair at a local church, no one is going to expect miles and miles of booths. You might increase profits by combining it with a silent auction. Make sure your publicity materials don't exaggerate what you'll be offering, of course. If you feel you must start on a larger scale, it may be worth hiring a professional—not only an events coordinator, but perhaps also someone with experience in the particular industry you'll be featuring, such as music or arts. If you work with a professional outside the nonprofit world, be prepared for him or her to charge a substantial fee, or to take a percentage of the proceeds.

As the scale of your event gets larger, you can charge rent to the exhibitors and sell tickets to the people who attend. Also, because a fair or festival is already a variety program, it offers you great opportunity to mix in other fundraising methods, such as raffles, bake sales, and the like. And, although costs start to go up as you look at larger venues and more equipment, the greater community benefit you'll be providing increases your chances of getting help from sources such as your city government (for example, with waived parking fees) or local businesses (for example, with loans of equipment).

Benefit Concerts, Lectures, and Other Presentations

Here's where your organization's personal contacts come in handy. If you know a celebrity, author, expert, or musical group that will offer to perform or speak for free or at a discount, and if the public would be interested enough to pay money for it, you've got yourself an event. It's crucial, of course, that the person or group be interesting or high profile enough to inspire high tickets sales. This is worth some research—at least ask your friends, or kids, to find out which names generate excitement. Someone you've never heard of may pack the house, while a famous old warhorse may barely fill the first five rows. (See Chapter 11 for suggestions on getting media publicity before the event.) Depending on how many seats you have to fill, however, realize that you may not have to look for someone of national interest. If a local band, for example, has a devoted following—even if it's mostly family and friends—it may be enough to pack a coffee shop that donates its space for the evening. Or, a well-regarded local pianist could perform in a board member's living room.

You can also approach people with whom you have no personal connection, although it's harder. Most celebrities and groups have publicists who handle their bookings. The publicists are very experienced at diplomatically saying "no" to the many charitable organizations that approach them. Your job is to convince the publicist that your event will be good publicity for the entertainer(s), that they will be well taken care of, and that they may even enjoy themselves.

If you don't have any personal contacts, the celebrities who are most likely to be interested in participating are those with something to sell—in particular, authors. Upon publishing a new book, a big-name author may go on a multicity publicity tour to visit bookstores, give media interviews, and make other public appearances. If there are any open spots in the author's calendar, the publicist will be eager to fill them—particularly if you can promise some time for the author to sit at a table and sell and sign books. By watching the local bookstores' speakers schedules, you may be able to figure out who's coming. Or, simply contact a publishing company whose works would be appreciated by your audience and ask to speak with one of its publicists. Explain your needs and approximate time frame and see what he or she can suggest.

> **TIP**
>
> **Avoid canned and rehashed speeches.** "I try to create an event that otherwise wouldn't have happened, and preferably won't ever happen again," says Bob Baldock, events coordinator at KPFA radio in Berkeley, California. "For example, I ask authors to not simply read from their book, but to talk about how they're apprehending the world at this time. Or, I'll try to put together an interesting pair— or even a small group—of people. With enough ingenuity, you can create an event that will basically promote itself."

To protect your organization's interests, consider signing a contract. This is particularly true if you'll be covering a number of costs, such as transportation, hotel, room service, and the like. Your contract should clearly specify and limit the costs you'll cover, so that you won't be surprised by a bill for your celebrity's personal assistant's three-hour massage at the hotel spa after the event.

Benefit events can be reasonably good moneymakers, because you can control your expenses, including the cost of space, promotion and publicity, a sound system (always expensive, but not something you should compromise on), and refreshments. Expenses can mount quickly, however, if you're bringing in out-of-town performers—the cost of transportation and accommodations for your performers and their entourage can be especially high.

Walkathons, Tournaments, Contests, and Sporting Events

Events that get people out sweating or competing are particularly appropriate for organizations with young memberships or concerned with health issues. The various "a-thons" (walkathons, bike-a-thons, swim-a-thons, 10Ks) are among the simplest ways to fundraise, because your primary needs include only a route or pool, sponsor sign-up software (see Techsoup for the latest recommendations), refreshments to hand out along the way, and a few prizes for those who finish first and/or collect the most in sponsorship money. Of course, larger events will need to incorporate more, including medical assistance, bike mechanics, and other support goods or services.

Also try to solicit corporate sponsors (months ahead of time). Fortunately, people are so accustomed to seeing corporate logos associated with sports events that you can prominently exhibit these without fearing that folks will think your nonprofit has sold out. The sponsors will probably ask for their logo to be displayed on your promotional brochure and Web ads, on banners at the event, and possibly on participant T-shirts.

One problem with these various "a-thons" is their very popularity. The public can get tired of participating. Some really do lack imagination— I remember participating in a walkathon as a teenager, and thinking at approximately Mile 16 that they couldn't have chosen a less interesting stretch of paved-over Seattle suburb for us to drag our feet through. Our energy would have been better spent volunteering for the cause—and in fact, some groups now organize volunteer-a-thons, along those very lines. For example, the Nakomis Healthy Seniors Program, in Minneapolis, Minnesota, holds a Clean-a-Thon, in which volunteers spend a weekend morning doing yard work and heavy scrubbing at the homes of neighborhood seniors.

However, there are times when a walkathon can be just the right fundraiser for an organization. Schools and other organizations with lots of kids and families, for example, find that they are a good way to tap into this donor group (with the added benefit that you start children on a tradition of philanthropy). Walkathons and their ilk are also a good fit for organizations in low-income areas, where small amounts can be solicited from a large number of donors.

Organizations that do best with these events make it an inspiring experience for participants, as described in "How Project Bread Keeps Its Walkathons Exciting," below.

A close cousin to walkathons are sports tournaments and contests, in which you raise funds either by charging an entry fee, relying on individual and corporate sponsorships, or both. Groups that successfully organize such specialized events are usually already associated with the activity, such as a horse, vintage car, or motorcycle club might be. Be sure to involve someone in the planning process who truly knows and loves the sport or activity. You wouldn't want to plan a Scrabble tournament only to discover you'd brought the wrong kind of dictionary, for example, or plan a foot race on a route with significant air pollution.

How Project Bread Keeps Its Fundraising Walks Exciting

Boston-based Project Bread, which works to prevent and end hunger in Massachusetts, founded one of the first U.S. fundraising walks—now an annual event, the proceeds of which are used to make grants to anti-hunger organizations across the state. In fact, long before becoming Communications Coordinator there, Anna Spack regularly took part in the 20-mile walk; starting in first grade and continuing through 12th. Anna remembers: "You're walking down Commonwealth Ave with masses of people from all over; they're incredibly diverse, yet they're all united in one cause."

With that kind of history, Project Bread can count on a dedicated core of walkers. But the organization can't be complacent. As Anna acknowledges, "Many other groups now hold fundraising walks, and we've seen a dip in walker participation in the past decade or so. This may also have to do with the political climate and the fact that prospective donors are feeling pulled in many directions."

So, Project Bread has taken steps to ensure that its event continues to stand out. Anna says, "For starters, we never forget that 20 miles is a long walk! We arrange for music to be played along the route, and for entertainment groups to perform—dance, step, a cappella, drummers, and more. We line up vendors to give out free snacks, especially at the halfway point. We offer games and other activities—yoga, corn hole, hula hooping—to make the Walk even more fun and interactive. This year, we also added a three-mile route option, as a way to make the Walk more family-friendly and accessible.

"Another thing we've recently added is called the 'Hunger Solutions Village,' at the end of the Walk. We invited a number of our partner organizations (to whom we made grants from previous years' Walk proceeds) to set up tables offering interactive demonstrations. During last year's Walk, for instance, a farm and garden organization offered people a chance to plant a seed. Another organization talked about soil health. And one called Fresh Truck, a mobile market in a converted school bus, invited participants to walk in and see their produce. This helped engage people in our mission—in the cause we're raising money for."

For a relatively small, grassroots organization to pull off an event of this scale would obviously be a lot of work. Anna notes, "We have several staff people dedicated to planning this year round." Still, it's worth considering whether a smaller-scale fundraising walk might work for your organization, and—following Project Bread's lead—how you might set it apart and include a tie-in to your mission.

TIP

Contests make good media fodder. There's always a winner and, particularly if you've got cute kids involved, some good photo opportunities. For example, a kids' pet show is almost sure to be covered by local media. See Chapter 13 for details on how to access and notify the appropriate media outlets.

Home and Garden Tours

Organizing a successful home or garden tour usually involves convincing a group of private home or garden owners to open their space to members of the public—who then buy tickets for the privilege of wandering through these (hopefully) gorgeous inner sanctums. The themes can be refined almost infinitely, from kitchen tours to Victorian home tours, sculpture garden tours, or whatever else might fit the interests of your nonprofit—and sell tickets.

Tours are a wonderful way to make money from something you get for free. The main costs are promotion (printing and advertising), supplies for the day of the tour (such as banners and ticket tables outside the various stopping points, and brochures describing the homes or gardens) and anything else you add to the process (such as refreshments).

Tours also afford an opportunity to charge for extras, particularly if people will spend any time at a central location. For example, Park Day School in Oakland, California, holds an annual garden tour. Ticket holders start on the school campus, where they (as well as the general public) can browse and buy garden-related items, such as ceramic pots, tools, and starter plants, from booths operated by local vendors. For an additional fee, participants may buy box lunches.

The challenging part of putting on a home or garden tour is the massive amount of organizing required. You've got to start well in advance to find appropriate homes or gardens and negotiate with the owners to make them available on the appropriate day. You'll also have to politely say no to some eager people whose homes and gardens just aren't worthy of a tour stop.

After identifying a set of homes or gardens, you'll need to gather information about them and write up descriptions for a brochure that visitors can carry with them on the tour. Unless you're lucky enough to identify homes and gardens within walking distance of each other, one of your volunteers should drive to every destination and write up any tips on directions, such as landmarks to look for along the way and suggested parking areas).

Also, you'll need to organize a large group of volunteers for the day of the tour, to handle tasks like checking tickets at each stop and standing at key points to answer questions and make sure visitors don't step on the tulips or pocket the silverware.

⓪ CAUTION

Stay in touch with homeowners. There's nothing worse than having someone withdraw a week before your event because they must jet off to Rome, Italy, or attend their grandson's kindergarten graduation. Checking in with homeowners in the months and weeks before your tour will demonstrate how seriously you take their participation and help discourage last-minute defections.

Garage Sales, Bake Sales, Used Book Sales, and More

There's a reason why garage sales, bake sales, used book sales, car washes, and the like never go out of style. They don't require much time, money, or expertise to set up, and loads of people are happy to buy something at a reasonable price while simultaneously supporting a good cause. As a classic example, events planner Laurie Earp told me, "The third grade at our school spontaneously put together a garage sale in just over a week and made about $1,100. This was with incredibly minimal effort—imagine if they'd started earlier!" And, if you also hand out pamphlets and collect interested participants' names, you may also get some long-term donors out of the event.

Anyone who has been involved in one of these types of events knows how crazy things can get, with goods, cookies, or soap suds flying. The key to making it all work is organization, before, during, and after. Even if your event is small scale, it will probably take at least twice the volunteer time that you imagine. In addition, you'll always want to have an extra person on hand during the event to deal with unexpected questions or requests. ("Can someone help me count these puzzle pieces to make sure they're all here?" or "Would you please load this into my truck?")

Used goods sales: Here are some tips on making used goods or book sales profitable. For starters, every item should have a price tag on it, so that buyers don't have to find someone to ask. Pricing is an art unto itself. Karen Garrison, whose years of garage sale experience are described in "Hill-Wide Garage Sale in San Francisco," below, says, "You have to designate someone as a pricing czar. Otherwise, you'll have your various volunteers coming around and saying, 'Oh no, I think it should be more,' or 'You're nuts, no one will pay that,' or unilaterally dropping prices."

Ideally, all donated merchandise for garage or used book sales should be reviewed in advance by an expert, who can help you figure out which items might be antiques or first editions and worth setting aside in a special area at a higher price. If you know an antiques dealer, a used clothing expert, or a used-book seller who will volunteer to take a quick look, you're in luck. Failing that, pick the most knowledgeable people available. After all, you don't want to sell a pair of once-worn Prada shoes for $3.50.

Your experts can also help you identify which items are junk and should either be sold at a very low price or disposed of immediately. If you don't recognize and deal with the junk well in advance, two bad things happen. First, the worthless items tend to pull down the prices of the more valuable property. Second, your trip to Goodwill or the nearest thrift store at the end of the day—an inevitable part of the event—will be an even bigger endeavor than you'd anticipated.

> CAUTION
>
> **Accepting old clothing, household goods, or furniture?** If so, the IRS says that they must be in "good or better" condition for the donor to take a tax deduction. You can help donors by providing filled-out receipts stating the products' condition, though few organizations have time for this. Experts also advise the donors themselves to take photographs of the goods in case of an audit.

Assuming you've priced things well, you'll probably want to hold fairly firm to those prices for at least the first half of your sale. Reminding people that this is a fundraiser will help deflect persistent bargainers. Also decide in advance when to start dropping prices, to make sure you aren't left with too many unsold goods. For an all-day sale, late afternoon is usually an appropriate time to offer some bargains (allowing some discretion by your pricing czar, depending on how sales are going).

! CAUTION

Decide how you'll deal with earlybirds. First, you'll have to consider whether to sell particular items to a professional antiques dealer or bookseller, particularly those who helped set your prices, and to your other volunteers who've no doubt been eyeing things they'd like, in advance of your sale—this might bring in guaranteed profits, but it also diminishes the public's perception of the quality of your sale. Next, you'll need to be ready to deal with the semiprofessional bargain-hunting community. They're likely to show up at your sale well before it is open, demand to start shopping, and scarf up all the good stuff before you've even begun (goodbye Prada shoes). The aggressive response is to put up ropes and post no-nonsense volunteers until you're ready to open; the lower-conflict but somewhat unsatisfying alternative is to warn your volunteers that they should plan to start the sale around 30 minutes before it's officially open!

Bake sales: Bake sales or other food sales are almost guaranteed to please a crowd. Even so, you've probably seen some of the problems that can reduce profitability—such as stingy or overgenerous portions or badly labeled items that are hard to identify. Also, with allergies and vegetarian or vegan diets increasingly on the minds of the American public, you need to be prepared for probing questions about what your food items contain. Ideally, have each of your food preparers list the ingredients in every item. Also, be sure to stock at least some items without common allergens (nuts, eggs, peanuts, wheat, gluten, and milk products).

Car washes: A standby of grassroots nonprofit efforts, car washes can be particularly effective if you can put a hose or towel in the hands of a celebrity or two. One perennial tension, however, is that it takes a fair amount of time to wash a car well. This can mean either that the nonprofit doesn't make much money, or that the customers end up dissatisfied, as the soap bubbles dry into spots on their windshields. To keep things moving along, it's essential to use an appropriate space, preferably one loaned by a gas station or another place with lots of hose hookups. (In many areas, these are also environmentally friendlier, since they drain to the sewage treatment system rather than through the storm drains to local waterways.) To ensure some quality control, practice car-washing techniques with your volunteers, and explain to everyone what you expect. Volunteers should work in teams of four or five so cars move in and out quickly.

Choose the Right Event for Your Organization

The first step in deciding what type of special event to hold is the same as the first step in planning your annual fundraising strategy—examine your organization's assets. (Review Chapter 3 for a reminder of how this is done.)

If you've got a large physical facility, think about events that might attract a crowd. If you've got an unusually large volunteer corps, consider events that require large numbers of people to prepare or run, such as an auction, fair, festival, or home tour. If you've got access to celebrities or experts, consider lectures, benefit concerts, or major donor parties (see Chapter 6 for details).

CAUTION

Any special event should be grounded in your annual fundraising plan. When a volunteer in a good mood offers up a beautiful house for a party or proposes some other unplanned event, it's easy to say "yes" without considering all the consequences. Unless you can truly mobilize volunteers who weren't serving any other fundraising purpose—a rare situation, and one that should cause you to question why those volunteers weren't otherwise occupied—your special event is likely to divert time and attention away from potentially more profitable fundraising activities. This doesn't mean that you should never seize an unexpected fundraising opportunity, but do so only if it doesn't unduly disrupt your plan.

After figuring out what types of events you could offer, think about who is likely to show up. Although "paying customers" are your first priority, remember that your event is also an opportunity to pick up new support, which means that you'll want to attract people who fit your donor profile. For example, I once spoke with members of a suicide prevention group who started an annual golf tournament simply because one of the founders liked golf and could mobilize his friends—but its effectiveness sputtered out after a few years, as they realized that participants weren't interested in other donations or involvement.

Once you've got a brilliant event idea in mind, do some research to find out whether people will pay to attend (or pay for items once they're there). For a small event, this may require no more than talking informally to your major donors and other supporters. For events designed to bring in more members

Hill-Wide Garage Sale in San Francisco

Years ago, the senior services department of the Bernal Heights Neighborhood Center (www.bhnc.org) decided to try a fairly traditional fundraising strategy: a garage sale. BHNC was already working to build community in this somewhat remote part of San Francisco, and had willing volunteers among the seniors it served (with classes, congregate meals, and outings). This event grew into an award-winning community tradition, involving as many as 120 registered garage sale sites at locations spread throughout Bernal Heights, and attracting thousands of customers, some from many miles away.

Karen Garrison, former director of senior services with BHNC, described this event: "Normally we have a large garage sale here at the Neighborhood Center, so we're sort of the epicenter. Our volunteers also set up some food booths. People come to the center and buy things at our sale, but they also pick up event maps, telling them where other sales are being held throughout the neighborhood. This gives us a few seconds—because people are eager to get going—to tell the visitors about BHNC's work, and suggest a donation for the maps. The map is a surprisingly important piece of the picture. People who want their garage sale included on our map pay us $30. The reverse side of the map contains narrative information, including a reminder that the event is a fundraiser. Of course, some people don't stop for maps, and just drive around looking. The energy on the street is unbelievable—lots of people, lots of cars.

"We start planning about two months in advance, but once we get going, it's very labor-intensive, about 200 staff hours, and many more volunteer hours. Aside from sending out invitations to potential participants (and guidelines, after they sign up), coordinating volunteers, and creating the map, promotion is a big part of our preparation. We make use of all the community media outlets' opportunities for free announcements, do outreach within our own service network and at churches, and our volunteers place around 2,000 fliers in local store windows, coffee shops, and the like." The catch, as Garrison acknowledges, is that the event doesn't make a lot of money—a little over $2,000 is typical, most of that from the on-site garage sale (in addition to map fees and percentages of proceeds from other sales, which some people voluntarily pledge). BHNC has tried to attract corporate sponsors, but hasn't had much luck. But, Garrison adds, "What makes the event truly worthwhile is both the increased visibility for BHNC and the fact that it creates wonderful community feeling."

of the general public, however, you may have to find experts in the relevant area—such as the music business—to quiz about attendance estimates. Also talk to folks at other nonprofits that have done similar events (contact groups in comparable cities, if you're worried about being in competition with local nonprofits).

How much time will an event take to organize and put on? Because you should be conceptualizing the event as part of your overall fundraising planning, answering this question—with regard to both staff and volunteer time—is critical. It's hard to exaggerate how much time a good-sized special event can take to organize! Multiply your initial estimate by three.

WORLD's Fashion Show Develops from HIV+ Clients' Personal Interests

WORLD (Women Organized to Respond to Life-Threatening Diseases) is an Oakland, California–based information and support network by, for, and about women living with HIV/AIDS (www.womenhiv.org). You might not think a fashion show put on by HIV-positive women and their children would have been the most obvious special event for the group to try, but the women, many of whom are low-income and dealing with AIDS-related illnesses or the side effects of medication, conceived of the event as a way to celebrate their lives and their bodies.

This fashion show provided an excellent example of planning an event around existing resources. As then-board co-chair Sonja Mackenzie told it, "Not only did the idea of the fashion show start organically within this group of HIV-positive women, but it so happened that in its first year at WORLD, our organization had a useful connection—one of our donors had friends within the fashion industry. She was able to line up loans of some incredibly fancy outfits for the women and children to wear, from notable designers such as Jessica McClintock. The women (and children) looked and felt beautiful.

"Audience reaction to the show was indescribable, incredibly powerful. I think the show really hit on the core elements around HIV and being a woman with HIV. The audience included medical providers, family members, and members of the pharmaceutical industry. They were both moved and impressed by seeing their family members/patients in a new, powerful role."

For a big event, hiring an outside consultant or events planner can be an efficient way of ensuring that your staff's daily work isn't greatly disrupted. Although this is likely to cost you several thousand dollars, a good, experienced events planner can often earn back his or her fee and then some, simply by drawing on longstanding relationships with graphic designers, printers, musicians, local businesses that are proven donors, and others, to keep costs down and minimize delays. They can also help you make informed decisions about what works to draw in and satisfy the public, and how to maximize profits overall.

Just don't expect the events planner to do everything—in particular, soliciting donations from your own donors or even some local businesses is a task that should stay within your own staff and board, as part of your relationship-building efforts. In fact, you might want to aim for eventually bringing the event back in-house (after the consultant has helped you learn the ropes and get it streamlined). In that case, the worst thing would be for everyone to have fallen out of practice with these tasks.

Keep It Green

Whether your group's mission relates to preserving the natural environment or not, your upcoming special event shouldn't present an example of waste and excess. With some prioritizing, budgeting, and consideration of your nonprofit's core values, you may be able to choose and use many of the tips below.

Choose a Green Location

A country inn or your board member's vacation home may be a beautiful setting for a gala event—but is it the best choice from an environmental standpoint? Your choice of venue will literally set the stage for whether you can achieve a number of other green goals.

First, think about how many people will be driving many miles, and therefore consuming gas and emitting pollutants, to get to your chosen venue. If public transport is an option, one way to ameliorate the distance issue is to provide alternate directions to the event using public transport and bicycles (and then ensure the availability of safe bike racks or storage). Send this message loud and clear, or you'll find that most guests hop into their cars without thinking twice. If public transport is not a realistic option, you might coordinate and encourage (or even sponsor) carpools or shuttle services. Or perhaps a more centrally located facility (such as a downtown museum, hotel, or art gallery) will be your best bet.

Next, look into the venue's history of attention to and cooperation with environmental goals—and its willingness to sign a contract stating it will comply with your agreement regarding environmental matters. For example, a venue that agrees to use compostable plateware, but whose staff hasn't been trained to separate the bags of garbage when throwing them out, won't help your goals at all. Along with this, consider whether the place has ready access to a waste management server providing recycling. Some signs that a venue is already committed to environmental protection include that it uses energy-efficient lighting, low-flow toilets, and recycled paper materials, and places recycle bins next to the trash cans.

Many venues are taking the initiative and getting LEED certification (Leadership in Energy and Environmental Design) from the nonprofit U.S. Green Building Council, Inc. This certification means they've proven that their facility has been built, designed, and operated for improved environmental and human health performance.

Create Environmentally Friendly Invitations

Sending "save the date" notifications by email is now completely appropriate and will save a lot of paper. For the invitations themselves, you (and your donors) may prefer traditional paper—but talk to a printer about how to minimize the size of the invitation and amount of paper used. One possibility is to issue a small invitation, or even a postcard, and then direct people to a page on your website for detailed program information and registration.

Also look into using recycled paper and soy-based inks (made from a renewable resource and far less toxic than regular inks, plus easier to wash off during the recycling process). The costs are close to comparable.

Avoid Creating Mountains of Wasted Paper Plates

If you'll be serving food, consider what you'll buy or use in the way of cups, plates, and serving ware. "Real" or reusable china and forks and knives, as well as cloth napkins, are obviously best. If these are impractical, a quick online search will bring up an array of environmentally conscious suppliers of serving products, so that you can comparison shop—but don't forget to prefer local vendors, so that the goods don't have to consume energy making one last trip across the country. Note that "compostable" is better than "biodegradable": It refers to something that breaks down as easily as paper and is nontoxic.

CAUTION
There's nothing worse than buying a "recyclable" product, then discovering it's not recyclable in your community. Check in with your local trash/recycling company. They work on this every day, and can tell you exactly what's recyclable, what's compostable, and what's not.

You can both save money and make an important environmental impact by the simple step of not serving water in individual plastic bottles. Instead, put out pitchers and reusable, or at least recycled-material cups.

If you'll be serving mainly appetizers or snacks, making sure that every bite can be eaten with one's fingers will save having to put out forks.

Don't Go Overboard on the Decorations

When planning flowers, decorations, and gifts, realize that less can be more. Now is not the time, for example, to plan a theme party with lots of plastic leis, disposable hats, and so forth. With a little creativity, you can save both money and the environment.

For example, how many of your board members have beautiful flowers or shrubs growing in their own garden that they'd be willing to clip from and bring to an event—even if you hire a professional to do the arranging? (And while your board members are at it, ask them to check their houses for spare vases. Almost everyone has a cheap one taking up space from their last floral delivery.) Another option for centerpieces is potted native plants, which can be reused or raffled off.

Other nonprofits may also have bought decorative items for events that you can borrow or swap for something from your last event.

Reduce Use of Other Materials

Start by investing in reusable nametag holders. You'll need to create paper inserts with people's names, then collect the badges at the end of the event for reuse.

Consider also how many handouts you need to provide. For disseminating general information, such as a map, can you post a few in highly visible places rather than putting a copy in everyone's folder? When handouts are necessary, create double-sided printouts when possible.

And don't feel you need to provide a tote bag! People have plenty of those already.

Serve Green Food

Your food choices for the event, and the way that the food is served, make an important statement about your environmental commitment.

Organic, seasonal, locally grown, and sustainable food sources should be your first choice whenever economically possible. Many caterers and restaurants specialize in such menus—and, as you know, some may be willing to offer you a nonprofit discount, particularly if you give them lots of good publicity. You'll probably encounter demand for vegetarian, vegan, and gluten-free options.

Buffet service rather than individually boxed or served meals can reduce both food and packaging waste. Even when it comes to snacks, avoid individually packaged items in favor of trays of fruit, crackers, or trail mix. The same goes for condiments, cream, and sugar (to go with your fair-trade coffee).

What about the leftovers? Either arrange for guests to be able to take home doggie bags or contact a shelter ahead of time to set up a donation.

Develop a Realistic Budget

There's no great mystery to creating a special events budget: You list all your anticipated expenses in one column, then enumerate what you expect to bring in from various intended activities in the second. Finally, you subtract your expected revenues from your anticipated expenses to give you a total.

The trick, of course, is accurately projecting your expenses and income. Part of this involves taking your analysis to a micro level, so that you don't forget to budget for, say, paper napkins and microphone rentals. Another critical factor is how faithfully your volunteers follow through on certain activities. In other words, if you plan to keep expenses down by getting donated food and chairs, and to keep income high by getting corporate sponsorships, you've got to communicate this to whoever is in charge of doing these things, and make sure the tasks get done.

Every fundraising event creates financial risk. You'll have to cover most of your expenses before you know how much the event will bring in—or whether an unexpected snowstorm or other disaster will soak your balance in red ink. One great way to minimize risk is to stick to events that don't cost a lot to stage. Then, if anticipated revenues don't materialize for some reason, you haven't dug yourself a huge financial hole.

Estimate Expenses

There's no better way to understand the event budgeting process than to grab a pencil and paper. To make this easier, use the expense worksheet below (and on www.nolo.com; see the appendix for the exact URL). As you start to fill it out, you'll inevitably learn more about what you can afford, what key decisions need to be made (for example, how much you're willing to spend on advertising and promotion), and how many guests you'll need to attract. You'll also hopefully think up a few special items to add to the worksheet, based on whatever is unique about your event. And be sure to consider which needed items can be obtained through donations, or rented as opposed to purchased.

If you're new at this, assume that your final figure will be on the low side—some suggest adding at least 20% for unanticipated costs or occurrences. And always remember that staff time is a hidden cost—although it doesn't show up in the budget, it's a very important consideration. Staff can too easily get pulled away from important development or program responsibilities by the whirl of activity leading up to a special event.

> **CAUTION**
> **A cheap sound system can ruin your event.** We've all been at events where the electronic feedback made our fillings ache or the speaker equipment was diabolically positioned to blast the VIP table. This isn't random bad luck—it can be overcome by paying a little more for your sound system. For example, in a large hall, it's best to connect speakers at points around the room rather than just line them up on the stage. Though paying more seems hard to justify at the abstract, budget-planning level, think of it as an investment against audience irritation or inattention.

Estimate Income

Correctly anticipating income is difficult, particularly in the first year or years of an event. Your crystal ball rarely reveals how many people will show up at an event, how much they'll buy, or how high their auction bids will go. Fill out the worksheet as best you can (available online; see the appendix for the link), but protect yourself from risk by starting small and getting lots of advance support from major donors and corporate sponsors. If the event becomes a tradition for your organization, your projections will become more accurate, aided by your experience and by last year's records.

Compare Projected Expenses and Income

For a successful event, your income should exceed your expenses by a healthy margin. This is hard to quantify, but aim to earn at least five times your expenses—for example, kids selling a mountain bike worth $500 should attempt to bring in $2,500. Using this approach, even if you collect only $2,000 you're still doing pretty well. The actual dollar amount that you'll hope to earn depends, of course, on the size of your organization's budget and the size of the event. But if it's only a couple thousand dollars, think hard about how much staff time will be going into the event. Again, I didn't work this hidden cost into the budget worksheet, but when profits will already be low, staff time can make the difference between making and losing money.

Fundraising Worksheet 6: Projected Special Event Expenses

Expense Category	Projected Cost	Description of Reasoning or Assumptions, Particularly for Discount or Donated Items
Physical Space		
Room, building, outdoor space	$ _____	_____
Chairs, tables, performance platform	$ _____	_____
Site manager and other staff fees	$ _____	_____
Heating or air conditioning	$ _____	_____
Sound system, projector, screen, other equipment	$ _____	_____
Municipal permits (traffic, etc.)	$ _____	_____
Subtotal:	$ _____	_____
Decorations		
Banners	$ _____	_____
Lighting	$ _____	_____
Flowers	$ _____	_____
Candles	$ _____	_____
Balloons	$ _____	_____
Party favors, gifts, award plaques, and certificates	$ _____	_____
Other	$ _____	_____
Subtotal:	$ _____	_____
Food and Drink		
Snacks or appetizers (for participants and volunteers)	$ _____	_____
Main meal	$ _____	_____
Extra catering or corkage fees	$ _____	_____
Alcohol, other drinks, ice	$ _____	_____
Plates, cups, napkins, cutlery	$ _____	_____
Waiters and bar staff	$ _____	_____
Subtotal:	$ _____	_____

Fundraising Worksheet 6: Projected Special Event Expenses

Expense Category	Projected Cost	Description of Reasoning or Assumptions, Particularly for Discount or Donated Items
Performers/Speakers		
Performers' or auctioneer's fee or honorarium	$_____	_____
Transportation and parking (airfare, shuttle, rental car, cabs, or limousine)	$_____	_____
Hotel	$_____	_____
Meals	$_____	_____
Telephone and other extras	$_____	_____
Subtotal:	$_____	
Publicity		
Graphic designer and/or artist	$_____	_____
Printing (posters, programs, ad books, auction catalogs)	$_____	_____
Stationery, envelopes	$_____	_____
Postage (invitations, press releases, thank-yous)	$_____	_____
Professional mailing services	$_____	_____
Event website	$_____	_____
Event photographer	$_____	_____
Subtotal:	$_____	
Miscellaneous		
Taxes on goods sold	$_____	_____
Photocopying	$_____	_____
Supplies for volunteer meetings and information packets	$_____	_____
Reimbursement of volunteers' expenses (i.e., gasoline, telephone)	$_____	_____
Name badges	$_____	_____
Insurance	$_____	_____
Unexpected or emergency expenses	$_____	_____
Subtotal:	$_____	
Total:	$_____	

Fundraising Worksheet 7: Projected Special Event Income

Income Category	Projected Amount	Description of Reasoning or Assumptions
Tickets	$_____	____ of guests at $_____ per ticket
Ad books or ad space in program	$_____	____ of advertisers at $_____ per _____
Exhibitors' or vendors' rental fees	$_____	____ of exhibitors/vendors at $_____ per booth
Corporate sponsorships	$_____	_____
Sales of food or goods	$_____	_____
Silent auction or raffle proceeds	$_____	_____
Other	$_____	_____
Total:	$_____	

Make sure your projected budget still shows a profit if things go wrong. For example, try running the numbers with a third of the attendees showing up, and see what happens to your income. Once you've swallowed that bitter pill, think about which of your expenses you can put off incurring until you're sure of attendance figures. Hotels, for example, will generally ask for a deposit up front, then require that you confirm attendance and pay for a set number of meals by a certain date. Make sure to set your ticket sales deadline before that date!

CAUTION

Tell donors exactly how much of their ticket price or other payments to your organization during an event are tax deductible. You and they must subtract the value of actual goods or services they received. For more information on tax deductibility of donations, see Chapter 4.

Plan and Pace Event Activities

The success of your event depends in large part on what goes on behind the scenes in the months or weeks leading up to it. Allow plenty of lead time—the "classic" special event, such as an annual dinner, a gala ball, or a benefit concert, normally takes between six months to a year to prepare. Giving yourself a realistic amount of time will not only save your sanity, but also save your organization money. For example, the costs of design and printing will go down if you give your designers and printers ample time to work the tasks into their schedules—and will go up just as easily if you ask for a rush job.

It's also important to get a head start on corporate sponsorships. Most companies make their decisions about sponsorships in either the last quarter of the preceding year or the first quarter of the year when the event will be held. This means that even for some fall events, you'll need to have gotten your sponsorship requests out in the previous year.

If you're working primarily with volunteers, however, it is often better not to really launch into preparations until six months before the event. If you give more lead time, people won't feel any time pressure—and some of them won't get over this feeling until a few weeks before the event. Be warned, too, that volunteers may be heavy on the good intentions and somewhat lighter on the follow-through, so having leaders who can motivate them (as well as do a little friendly monitoring) will help make sure tasks get done on time.

TIP

Motivate participants by creatively announcing your progress. For example, the Bernal Heights Neighborhood Center marks its progress toward its community-wide garage sale (see "Hill-Wide Garage Sale in San Francisco," above) in terms of how many neighborhood residents have signed up to participate. They create a huge sign with the latest number and prominently hang the sign at the center for staff, volunteers, and passersby to see.

Some of the main preparatory tasks are covered below. However, when you've identified your event and outlined your goals regarding promotion and publicity, sponsorship, and the like, you may want to consult some more specialized resources. You'll find some listed at the end of this chapter.

Create a Calendar of Activities

The time-tested way to figure out what needs to be done by when is to work backward from the day of the event. What are the final steps—such as picking up rental chairs and flowers? By when do these need to be ordered? By when do decisions need to be made about how many chairs and what type of flowers? Who will be responsible for the decisions? When should this committee meet? Similarly, if you'll have a featured entertainer, when must you choose this person to make sure that his or her name will be announced in promotional materials? How much time before this should you allow to negotiate and sign a contract for this person's services? How many weeks in advance should be allotted for approaching different performers? When will the committee meet to select potential performers' names? You get the drift.

Create a calendar, whether online or on a giant poster (or both). Write in the dates on which you or one of your volunteers must start the various activities, not the dates by which they must be completed. For example, "Last day to choose menu" is not a helpful calendar entry unless it was preceded by one advising you to begin the selection process.

Working with the dates entered on the calendar, create checklists for yourself and your committees, itemizing every task that needs to be done. You or your committee leaders should review these checklists regularly, ticking off items as they are completed, and calling people to confirm that they have completed their assigned tasks by the required dates.

Define Committees and Assign Leaders

Every special event needs a central point person to coordinate volunteers and keep things moving according to schedule. But one person can't pull off an event alone. By looking at your budget and other planning materials, you should be able to identify all of the activities that need to be attended to. Then, create subject committees to match. For example, depending on the type of event you're planning, your committees might include some combination of the following:

- site planning
- meals or refreshments

- choosing exhibitors, performers, vendors, or home or garden tour destinations
- decorations
- transportation
- awards
- gathering auction or raffle donations
- obtaining corporate sponsorships
- event staffing and registration
- keeping it green
- promotion and publicity (including graphics and printing), and
- cleanup.

Some of these activities are discrete enough that they may require only a single person, or a committee of two or three. In fact, at times it's best not to assign too many people to a task, lest the abundance of people give committee members the idea that little is expected of them. The two most important considerations are these: First, everyone must understand his or her responsibilities, including what needs to be done, by what deadline, with what special considerations in mind (such as keeping the event green), and with whom to communicate about progress (or the lack thereof).

Committee members should also understand the limits of their responsibilities. For example, if you want the food committee to come up with a potential menu, but the ED will actually have the final say on what is served, this needs to be made clear from the beginning.

CAUTION

Communication between committees and other leaders is key. The more committees you've got, the greater the risks of miscommunication. As Sonja Mackenzie, then WORLD board co-chair, put it: "I'm a strong proponent of open group process, but you still need to be clear about who the point person is, and keep the communication channels open to that person. If you've got a lot going on— for example, in WORLD's case, we combined a fundraising dinner with a fashion show—you'll find that the questions start multiplying, such as who picks up the microphone, and whether the dinner planners remembered to rent a venue that will accommodate a fashion show stage."

Your chosen point person should plan to be in regular contact with all committee leaders. Depending on the timeline and number of people involved, scheduling regular meetings or conference calls, where everyone will report on their progress and any difficulties they're facing, may be worthwhile. To save on unnecessary meetings, periodic email check-ins are useful—perhaps once a week early on, moving up to daily in the last week.

In the name of good record keeping, the point person should ask for documentation of certain accomplishments, such as names of committed corporate sponsors or copies of press releases. Excessive politeness has been known to lead to situations where volunteers assert that everything is going great, when in fact little or nothing has actually been done.

> **TIP**
> **Time to get organized.** Your event point person should create a notebook or an equivalent system to help track important pieces of information and to ensure that nothing gets forgotten. This should include your checklists, a month-by-month planning calendar, budgeting and finances, subject matter sections for each committee (containing important documents such as contracts or notes on decisions and accomplishments), a master contact list of all vendors, volunteers, and other participants, and anything else relevant to the particular event. The leader should also work with the committee heads to help them get similarly organized.

Plan Promotion and Publicity

If you're hoping to attract members of the public to your event, especially members who are not on your organization's mailing list, you'll need to pay particular attention to promotion and publicity. (Loosely speaking, promotion is advertising that you arrange or pay for yourself, such as posters and invitations; publicity is media reporting, usually in response to your press releases or other contacts.) In fact, because the success of an event like a garage sale or street fair rides upon people's hearing about and attending it, plan for promotional and publicity activities to consume the vast majority of your and your volunteers' prep time. It's helpful if you can enlist the services (preferably volunteer) of a professional public relations or marketing person.

Of course, Step One in promoting your event is to tell your members and supporters about it. Your social media feeds, newsletter, and website should start generating excitement months in advance, mentioning the date, location, and contact person for more information or volunteer opportunities. Send a "save the date" postcard or email approximately three to five months before the event. For large events that take on a life of their own, you might create a separate website.

Invitations, or opportunities to buy tickets, should be sent or announced six weeks before the event. In addition to contacting your supporters, you might rent a mailing list of potentially interested people—for example, members of a musical society if you'll be holding a concert. (See Chapter 4 for more information on the process of acquiring mailing lists.)

Collecting additional names is a separate and important task, one which you might assign to a committee. For example, all volunteers who get involved in the event should be given a piece of paper and asked to write the names, addresses, email addresses, and telephone numbers of any of their friends who they think might be interested in attending. Similarly, any featured speakers or honorees should be asked for the contact information of friends or relatives who might wish to attend. (You'll need to develop a policy in advance regarding how many complimentary tickets your speakers or honorees will be given—normally tickets for a spouse or significant other and minor children should do it.)

TIP

Each one bring ten. Sometimes the simplest and cheapest promotional methods work the best. If you have a good-sized local membership, you might charge each member with recruiting ten friends. Especially if you include a fun contest (the winning recruiter gets a weekend at a donated vacation home, for example), this can be an incredibly cost-effective way to spread the word.

Event posters should be created for any event to which the public at large will be invited. If pressed for cash, this is something you can do in black and white with your own photocopying machine, but don't try this if you plan to charge high ticket prices or attract high-income attendees. Usually the help of a graphic designer is required, unless you have particularly artistic folks involved in your effort. An attractive poster can be a sought-after item, so that coffee shops, stores, and other public places will be more than happy to display it. Putting up posters is a good task to assign to a large number of volunteers, making sure that each is assigned a separate geographical area. Watch out for local ordinances concerning placing posters in public spaces or on telephone poles.

Your promotion and publicity committee should also consider which newspapers, magazines, or websites are most likely to be seen by your potential ticket buyers. (Eventful.com, for example, provides a special page for "Fundraisers.") Look for media outlets that offer free community calendars, and arrange for announcements within the newsletters of local churches or potentially interested groups, such as a bicycling or garden club.

The best advertising, however, is a positive media write-up or in-depth coverage by electronic media. See Chapter 11 on how to generate media attention for your event.

> **TIP**
> **Take photos of this year's event for next year's promotion.** Even if your event won't be highly photogenic, good-quality pictures of key speakers or people enjoying themselves are great for your website and promotional materials. If you'll be sending out a press release immediately after the event, photos will also increase the chances that your story will be picked up. Be sure to let your photographer know who any important personages in attendance are, and send their photos to the relevant society columnists.

Create Corporate Sponsorship Opportunities

Despite the fact that many events charge admission fees, event profitability often depends on garnering money from outside sources, such as corporate sponsors. Sometimes, getting corporate sponsorship can be as simple as encouraging your board members to ask their employers to buy a table's worth of tickets for an annual dinner event. Other times, you will want to look for more major sponsorship—for example, by asking a company to be the lead name on your 10K run or whale-watching tour, with its logo prominently displayed on your banners and publicity materials, in return for underwriting costs or supplying space, food, or other event necessities.

Either way, the important thing to remember is that a business doesn't ordinarily sponsor an organization unless it feels assured of gaining good publicity. Be prepared to explain to any businesses that you approach:

- the nature of the event
- why it will suit its interests to be affiliated with the event
- how many people you expect to attend, and
- what sort of publicity you're willing to give their businesses.

> **TIP**
>
> **Set up a system to display sponsors' logos.** Although it's fine to have a lead sponsor pay for this prominent position, you'll rarely want to depend on one sponsor alone, unless that business is truly willing to make a major financial commitment. Instead, set aside space for a number of corporate sponsors—and let them know that their names will be front and center at your event.

Advertisements in your event program or an ad book are other popular ways of getting corporate sponsorship. I know of one organization that earned $125,000 on its ad book alone, which was prepared in conjunction with an annual dinner.

An ad book is just what it sounds like—a small brochure that displays either traditional advertisements or small testimonials to the organization on behalf of the business or person buying the ad, such as "Bronze Medal Athletic Gear wishes to congratulate KidsClub for its 25 years of helping inner-city youth excel through physical activity and teamwork." Some sole proprietor or professional ad buyers, such as lawyers, accountants, or music teachers, will simply want a copies of their business cards in your ad book. Your graphic designer or printer should be able to help you set guidelines for planning and selling ad space.

Deal With Risks and Liability Issues

Because making your event profitable will require keeping costs down, you must consider any minor or major disasters that might occur—such as a child getting injured on the site, a donor drinking too much and causing an accident driving home, or a thief taking your cash box or goods for sale. Because a special event is outside your usual course of business and may involve large numbers of people, you'll have to adjust your thinking to expect the unexpected—and plan to deal with the consequences.

There are three important steps you can take to forestall mishaps and disasters: First, make sure you've complied with all applicable laws and permit requirements; second, put your own sensible safety measures into place; and third, consider buying special insurance for the event.

For smaller events, accomplishing Steps One and Two would probably be enough, but for large-scale events attended by many people you don't know, buying insurance may also make sense. And some event sites may require you to carry a specified type and amount of coverage as a condition of using their facilities.

Comply With Laws and Permit Requirements

Whether your event is on your organization's own site or elsewhere, unusual attendance or activities may bring up legal issues. Large numbers of people impeding traffic flow or parking in one area may require advance discussions with your local police department. If you'll be serving liquor, you may be required to obtain a license or permit, usually from your city. Whoever will be serving the alcohol may also be required to go through special training (to make sure they understand how to check IDs and when to cut someone off). Auctions (particularly of luxury items) and gambling activities may also require licenses or permits.

As appropriate, talk to other nonprofits, your police department, or to a city official before proceeding with your plans or finalizing your budget. (Permit fees can be several hundred dollars.) And, if you still have legal questions, look for a lawyer (perhaps a volunteer) to help you find the answers.

Implement Appropriate Safety Measures

The best way to minimize damage is to avoid it in the first place, then create backup measures to deal with whatever can't be predicted or avoided. For starters, make sure that your event is well staffed and that every volunteer knows who to go to with a problem. The person in charge should carry a cell phone, and give every volunteer the number. Volunteers should wear something distinctive, so that members of the public know who to alert when the food has run out or they observe a burst pipe leaking in the direction of your sound system.

Also consider whether there are any rules that you want members of the public to observe. For example, if it wouldn't be appropriate to allow children below a certain age to participate, make this clear in your publicity materials, and be prepared to enforce it at the door. Similarly, if people shouldn't bring certain materials like alcoholic beverages or firearms, warn them in advance and be prepared to check for violations. This may require hiring a security person who is trained in dealing with such matters. I also suggest saying no to dogs, as well as to more exotic creatures—the cleanup problems are immense, and there's no upside unless it's an animal-centered event. (Working dogs, such as seeing-eye dogs, are of course an exception.)

Think carefully about who you're going to trust with sensitive tasks, such as handling money (never leave one person alone with it), serving alcohol, or transporting people by car or van. Don't forget that these people will need to take breaks or spend some time enjoying the event themselves, so schedule additional people to spell them from time to time. Ask to see the license of every driver. If someone will be driving a large truck or bus, make sure he or she is specially licensed for this as well.

All volunteers carrying out sensitive tasks such as cashiering should be told that they can't just hand their responsibilities over to someone else; by the same token, other volunteers should understand the limits of their roles and responsibilities.

If you anticipate large amounts of cash changing hands, make sure to have a foolproof system in place for tracking it and keeping it secure. For starters, tell your cash handlers to put all large bills, as well as all bills in excess of what are needed to make change, into a special place—either under a plate in the cash register or, better yet, into a locked and hard-to-move box. It is also sensible to schedule a two-person team to pick up cash at periodic points during the event. That team should keep records of exactly how much cash is taken from every cashier or box, in case questions arise later.

💡 **TIP**

Take it to the bank. Picking up cash every hour or two solves one big problem, but creates another. Now you've got wads of money just waiting to be stolen or misplaced. Instead of devising an elaborate security system, it's usually easier to simply deposit cash after every pickup.

Serving alcohol creates its own set of issues. You don't want to serve drinks to minors, you don't want people who've had too much to create a scene or a medical emergency, and you certainly don't want a drunk guest to injure someone driving home—who can then sue your organization for the damages you "caused." Even if your area doesn't require alcohol servers to be specially trained, servers should be ready to check IDs and tell patrons when they've had enough (or start mixing their drinks with nine parts soda).

As the event winds down, someone should be stationed at the door to wish people farewell—and to offer a cab or other ride to anyone who seems to be staggering toward his or her car. To be extra cautious, you could arrange with a cab company to have a couple of taxis waiting for this purpose, though they'd probably charge you for this service. One way to deal with all the above issues is to restrict alcohol events to restaurants, hotels, and other venues with experienced staff on hand.

Disability access is an important consideration, too—and one to consider before contracting to use a particular physical space. Some buildings claim to have wheelchair accessibility, but it turns out to be a makeshift ramp at a precarious angle. Restroom accessibility is also an area where many physical spaces fall short. The last thing you want is a situation where helpful volunteers try to carry a disabled person up a set of stairs or into a bathroom.

These are just a few of the safety measures you can put into place. You may need to develop others based on the type of event, the number of people and type of activities people will be engaging in, any special needs that your guests are likely to have, and your own common sense.

Purchase Insurance

Ask your insurance broker or company to go over your policy with you, to explain how many of your activities will be covered. Chances are, there will be a number of gaps in your coverage. For example, someone who slips and falls while at your organization's office will probably be covered—but not if they slip while at a picnic in your local park. And injuries caused by staff members—for example, if your ED accidentally drops a case of wine on someone's foot—may be covered, while injuries caused by your volunteers may not be.

Fortunately, event-specific insurance is available at a reasonable cost. Events in private homes may well be covered by homeowners' insurance. Realize, however, that almost no insurance policy is a substitute for detailed planning, and most won't cover harm caused by reckless or intentional acts (for example, if one of your volunteers drives a car filled with balloons at 90 m.p.h. and crashes or if a staff member punches a guest).

Last-Minute Tasks and Tips

The last days and hours leading up to the event are usually whirling-dervish time for even the most organized events planner or leader. Review your checklists frequently and carefully. Double-check that all of your committee leaders are communicating with one another as needed. Here are some other things no event planner should forget:

- **If you are the event leader, delegate shamelessly to make sure that your list of assignments for the actual day of the event is blank.** As Jan Etre, who organized crafts fairs for KPFA Radio for many years, says, "You should be completely available for answering questions and putting out fires. Someone will tap you on the shoulder, and you never know what's coming next—perhaps a lost child, or a parking problem." Sometimes just walking around your event can be important. One year, Karen Garrison took time out during the BHNC community-wide garage sale to walk the neighborhood, and discovered a number of "renegade" sites that hadn't paid for inclusion. After gently reminding them that this was organized as a fundraiser, she collected more fees.

- **Take a last look through your notebook, to make sure nothing got lost in the shuffle.** Make confirmation calls to any important speakers or vendors. See that all money owed to you has been paid, and that you have paid all the appropriate vendors. You don't want to be signing checks and working out small disputes over financial matters during the event itself.

- **If you're having a sit-down lunch or dinner, take your final list of ticket buyers and draft a seating chart.** Create an easy way for people to find their way to their tables, such as a number on a flag in the centerpieces. And be sure the registration staff know what to do if someone shows up without a ticket.
- **Pack any items that could possibly be useful in a pinch, such as adhesive tape, petty cash, a stapler, trashbags, paper towels, and first aid supplies.** Of course, you should also have created a checklist of—and started packing—those items you know you will need for the event, such as food and equipment.
- **Buy snacks and goodies for your volunteers and water for everyone.**
- **If using rented space, make sure you'll be allowed in with enough advance time to set up, decorate, arrange silent auction items, and so on.** These tasks always take longer than you expect—three to four hours is usually considered the minimum for a "typical" event.
- **Double-check that your registration tables will be adequately staffed and provided for.** A whole book could be written about the event registration process alone. Your goal is to have people registered and into the event within a few minutes of arriving. Depending on how many attendees you anticipate, this may require a whole bank of registration tables, with easily visible letters of the alphabet to divide people by name. Make sure all your volunteers know your policies on issues such as check acceptance and dealing with lost tickets.
- **Create contact lists of key people and vendors for you and other lead staff or volunteers.** This will help reach someone in case he or she has forgotten something or you need emergency help or a security guard.
- **Create a final list of who needs to be publicly thanked (hopefully, you kept a running list and will compare your final list against those of other event leaders).** At some point during the day, a key staff member or volunteer may have an opportunity to address the crowd. If so, that person should start by effusively thanking the people who did the most to bring about the event. Relying on memory has obvious dangers. If the names are too many to list one by one, refer to committees or groups, and make clear that there were many helpers who must remain unnamed.

> TIP
>
> **You can't prepare for everything.** Some final thoughts from events planner Laurie Earp: "Life happens, and you've just got to be ready for surprises—the caterer who doesn't show up, entertainers who bring lighting that's not bright enough to see them by, or equipment cables too short to reach electrical outlets. If you think on your feet, you'll find a way around the problem, and the event will be great in the end."

After the Event: Assessment and Follow-Up

A day or two after the event, you'll probably be dying to return to the other tasks you've been ignoring—all those unreturned voice messages and emails. However, if you don't tie up loose ends now and follow up with your new contacts, you may never get to these crucial tasks.

Send thank-you letters. You already know the importance of thank-you letters when dealing with individual donors, but after a special event, you'll have whole new lists of people to thank—and each one is critical. Send personalized thank-yous to every committee head, volunteer, sponsor, individual donor (including donors who bought things at auctions, because part of their payment was a contribution—but not including people who purchased items from independent vendors at craft or art fairs), and business donors. Note within these letters the amount of any financial contribution, minus the value of anything received in return, for IRS purposes.

Issue press releases. If the story of what happened at your event is media worthy, then immediately send out a separate press release—for example, describing and quoting the contents of your famous speaker's presentation, complete with photo, or announcing the winners of your bicycle race.

Reach out to participants. This step is one that too many nonprofit organizations skip. But with your organization fresh in the minds of everyone who came to your event—some of whom may be entirely new contacts—you'll be squandering some of your hard work if you don't implement some strategic follow-through.

For starters, you must immediately enter information on every person in the room into your database, so that they receive any emails, newsletters, or other communications that you're already preparing. Next, take a close look at the list of new contacts and consider (based on anything you know about them, such as who brought them), whether they are prospects for more targeted follow-up. If possible, have a board member or another volunteer call and thank everyone who isn't already closely affiliated with your organization for attending, find out more about what brought them to the event, and then discuss how they might get further involved.

Collect committee members' thoughts. Even if your event was a roaring success, there are no doubt lessons to be learned from it. Assemble committee leaders, and potentially the entire committees, to collect impressions. Alternatively, you can simply send out surveys. Keep the focus positive. Although there will undoubtedly be touchy areas where people would love to shift or assign blame, the important thing is to constructively figure out how similar problems can be prevented in the future.

Prepare a final budget. Compare this to the original budget, to see how well your projections ultimately matched up with reality. After you've collected all your information, write up all of your narrative and budgetary conclusions, and put them into your event folder for future reference.

Update your notebook. Finally, imagine that this time next year, you and all your committee leaders will be enjoying Brie and baguettes at an undisclosed Parisian location. Meanwhile, back at the nonprofit, some poor soul will be trying to recreate your smashingly successful event. Will your notes and files be enough to tell the whole story of how the event was done, who helped out (or flaked out), who was invited, who did the graphic design and printing, where to advertise, which media outlets were responsive, what other vendors to contract with, and the rest?

This is not an idle exercise—nonprofit turnover rates being what they are, you really could be somewhere else next year, or you might have simply forgotten all the details that seem so deeply burned into your brain right now. Add in any documents that are floating around elsewhere, making sure every section is complete and writing memos to explain important issues that aren't otherwise covered.

The Importance of Recognizing People's Special Efforts

Dr. H was a successful businessman with a comfortable cushion of inherited wealth. His family had a tradition of philanthropy, and he gave generously to a number of causes. When a local charity hosted a fundraising dinner, Dr. H bought tickets for an entire table, filled it with his friends, and made sure that his table set the evening's record for spending the most at the auction.

After the event was over, Dr. H promptly received a thank-you letter—but it was the same letter that everyone else involved in the event received. A form letter. It made no mention of the special efforts he'd made or the amount he and his friends had given. He felt sufficiently let down that he cut his contributions to that organization and has not attended any further events. He doesn't even return their phone calls—and they're still scratching their heads about it.

Raising Money Through Business or Sales Activities

There have been times—usually late at night, when struggling over a grant proposal—when I've wondered whether it wouldn't be easier to just stand by the nearest bus stop and sell cookies.

Of course, my idea isn't an original one. There is a time-honored nonprofit tradition of hawking cookies, T-shirts, and tote bags, as well as conducting raffles, garage sales, and even car washes to augment other fundraising activities. Sometimes the only thing that stops a nonprofit from going into one of these or similar businesses is fear of the unknown—or of the IRS, which can investigate and ultimately shut down nonprofits that stray too far into the profit-seeking world.

On the other side of the coin, many nonprofits take a full plunge into commercial enterprise, by starting major side businesses, such as restaurants or retail shops, in some cases enlisting their clients' help, or entering into relationships with for-profit business ventures. Although some of these businesses have prospered or been spun off into successful subsidiaries, a daunting number have failed miserably, and a few have indeed dragged the nonprofits into trouble with the IRS.

TIP

Business is business, whatever the terminology. A lot of highfalutin terms have been coined to describe profit-making efforts by nonprofits, including "social entrepreneurship," "social-purpose enterprises," and "social enterprise." The trouble is, there is little agreement as to what these terms really mean. To steer clear of semantic confusion, I'll simply refer to all of these activities as business ventures run by nonprofits.

It's impossible to draw a firm conclusion as to whether small-business ventures make sense for a particular nonprofit. There are just too many variables, and much depends on the skills, interests, and energy of the people involved—you might as well ask whether an ordinary person who wants to make money should open a business. Even nonprofits that enjoy significant success in the business realm have to overcome major challenges, some of which inevitably take time and energy away from their altruistic concerns. But one generalization seems to hold true—starting a business is not a good strategy for a nonprofit that's desperate for cash, because a significant return on initial investment usually doesn't come for a few years at best.

On the other hand, for those nonprofits able to find a profitable market niche, their ability to draw funds from outside the usual donor pool can contribute mightily to their growth and long-term survival. The YMCA, for example, whose central mission remains to nurture young people, typically earns about 70% of its revenues from health club membership and other program fees—many paid by affluent adults who just want a good place to work out.

Business revenues offer entrepreneurial nonprofits a way to break out of heavy reliance on grant funding. And they can simultaneously make funders more excited about your operation's long-term growth prospects. In fact, the prevailing belief among many funders is that the very process of starting and running a business venture can transform a nonprofit into a more effective and efficient operation.

So, the question becomes, would marketing goods or services to the general public give your nonprofit a fresh way to bring in significant dollars from sources outside your donor base—better yet, funds with no strings attached? Or would it drag your staff into spending precious time on activities outside your core mission that end up producing little return—and may even lose money or jeopardize your tax-exempt status? This chapter will help you answer these questions, by considering:

- how much business activity the IRS permits without penalty
- lessons that can be learned from other nonprofits' business successes and failures
- how to come up with a business idea that's a good match for your nonprofit
- how to compare your business ideas with market realities
- how to create a business plan, and
- whether partnering with an existing business makes sense.

CAUTION

Is your accounting house in order? Unless and until you've got a good in-house bookkeeper and an outside accountant, who have together successfully implemented a system for efficiently tracking your existing costs and cash flow, don't even think of launching a small business. The dollars will be flying around a lot faster once you start a business, and you'll need to be ready to keep up.

Tax Rules for Business Activities

Your organization was granted its 501(c)(3) status—and therefore allowed to avoid paying taxes—because its founders said that it would engage in charitable activities, not in for-profit business like the rest of the corporate sector. And the IRS will hold you to your promise, by taxing certain business activities and even revoking your tax-exempt status if you start to look more like a for-profit business than a charitable organization.

But the prohibition against nonprofits' engaging in business is far from absolute. As long as a nonprofit stays away from ongoing profit-making activities that don't further its purposes and don't personally benefit any individual (other than a client), it's usually not at risk of losing its 501(c)(3) status. This means that a nonprofit can engage in one-time or irregular business activities, or business activities that fall squarely within its mission, as long as all profits go to the nonprofit and don't benefit insiders, such as staff or directors.

Sounds simple enough. But what understandably confuses many nonprofit managers about the federal tax law is the large gray area that exists between those activities that are absolutely prohibited and those that are clearly permissible. Much of this confusion stems from the fact that a nonprofit can, in some circumstances, engage in business activities beyond the limits of its tax-exempt mission or that are ongoing, without risking its existence as a nonprofit, as long as it pays corporate income tax on the business profits.

To understand how IRS rules might apply to your nonprofit's possible business ventures, it's helpful to separate business activities into the following categories:
- clearly allowable activities
- activities that raise income on which tax is assessed, but that nevertheless do not endanger the nonprofit's 501(c)(3) status, and
- business activities that the IRS considers excessive or inappropriate, and therefore undermine the group's very 501(c)(3) status.

CAUTION

Never use nonprofit income for noncharitable purposes. Though there's a lot of gray area in the tax rules regarding how money comes into your nonprofit, there's very little ambiguity about how it's supposed to be spent. Profits generated by a nonprofit business may not, repeat *not*, be used for the private benefit of any person or organization outside the charitable organization.

Activities That Will Never Raise IRS Eyebrows

Take a look around you—plenty of nonprofits are selling goods and services without so much as a peep from the IRS. Chances are that in storefronts near you, you'll find the Goodwill, Salvation Army, and perhaps a local church-run thrift shop. Your local museum or hospital may run both a cafeteria and gift shop. And, of course, you have the Girl Scouts selling cookies, your local public TV station peddling calendars and coffee cups, and dozens of environmental groups offering calendars, T-shirts, and tote bags.

What makes these and similar merchandising activities legally acceptable? For the most part, they're viewed by the IRS as falling into one or more of the following allowable categories:

- activities within an organization's mission
- activities that are not part of an ongoing business, or
- income or activities that are subject to a special IRS exception.

Activities Within Your Nonprofit's Mission

If your sales of goods or services are in some way tied to your organization's mission, you're probably on safe ground, tax-wise. Museum gift shops, for example, stay within their mission by selling items to educate or interest people in the subject on display—such as animal magnets at a wildlife museum or art reproductions at an art museum. Even so, these shops may be required to pay tax on some of the items they sell. For example, the IRS says that an art museum shop that sells souvenirs of the city in which it is located will have to pay tax on those items.

Organizations such as Goodwill further their mission of employing needy people, through selling used goods. Goodwill uses its shops as a training and employment center, as do many other nonprofits that run businesses such as bakeries, bicycle repair shops, and more.

Activities That Are Not Part of an Ongoing Business

A normal, for-profit business needs to keep its doors open on a fairly regular basis, or risk having customers go elsewhere. To maintain a clear separation between these businesses and nonprofits, the IRS allows nonprofits to make sales that occur irregularly or a few times a year. For example, the Girl Scouts sell cookies only once a year (to the frustration of many a sweet-toothed consumer), so their cookie sales are not part of an ongoing business. They could probably sell cookies more often than once a year and still be fine—as long as the sales aren't as frequent as those a commercial business would conduct in order to survive and prosper.

Other examples of irregular nonprofit sales abound—such as auctions, bake sales, benefit concerts, car washes, garage sales, and calendar sales. Most of these tend to be specially scheduled activities, outside the nonprofit's usual day-to-day work.

The one area where you need to be careful, however, is with activities that are sporadic by nature—for example, if you run a catering business that is hired only every few weeks or so, you may look very much like an ordinary catering business—although not a wildly successful one.

Activities That Fall Within IRS Exceptions

You might be encouraged to learn that the IRS has created numerous exceptions and exclusions: Activities or income that fall within these categories are automatically considered nontaxable. Smaller groups that sell the occasional T-shirt or coffee mug (as much to encourage organizational solidarity as to raise money) will be delighted to learn that they needn't report annual earned income amounts less than $1,000. Such small amounts don't even require the nonprofit to file a tax return, even if the business activities were clearly outside or unrelated to the group's mission. The other major exceptions include business activities in which:

- Substantially all of the work of providing the services or creating the products is done by volunteers (for example, if you sell volunteer-created baked goods or crafts, or your volunteers can be hired as translators).

- The product or services are primarily for the convenience of the group's members, students, patients, officers, or employees (for example, an on-site cafeteria or pharmacy).

- The nonprofit accepts money from a company that sponsors its educational, fundraising, or other event and displays the company's name or logo on its premises or publications in return. But it's not okay for the nonprofit to provide the company with advertising or allow it to use the nonprofit's logo in company periodicals. (For example, you can't devote a page of your newsletter to a company ad, or accept payment for having your logo appear in company materials, without paying tax on any income you receive.)

- The nonprofit sells merchandise that was donated to it (an important exception that allows for the many thrift shops, donated-goods auctions, and used-car resale businesses run by nonprofits).

- Bingo games are used as fundraisers (as long as bingo is legal in the nonprofit's area, and is not played in a hall that's also used for commercial bingo gaming).

- A nonprofit exchanges or rents its membership list with another nonprofit.

- Entertainment is provided to attract people to a fair or exposition that promotes agriculture or education.

The IRS also excludes from tax any income that comes from:

- dividends, interest, annuities, and other investment income

- royalties earned from allowing use of the nonprofit's trademark, trade name, copyrighted material, or other valuable rights (but not personal appearances or services)

- rents from real property (such as land or buildings; but see IRS Publication 598, *Tax on Unrelated Business Income of Exempt Organizations* for the various exceptions, for example if you're also providing personal services to the renters, or if you've got a mixture of real and personal property, such as equipment)

- income from research grants or contracts, and

- gains and losses from selling property.

If you can think of an activity that would both serve your mission and bring in funds, you're in great shape. For starters, any fees that you charge for special events or client services are no problem—you don't need to worry about the federal tax implications, and you can even charge market rates.

If there aren't any natural ways to raise funds within your mission, then your next step is to consider raising revenues on an occasional basis, or starting up an activity that fits within an IRS exception. Any revenues you earn from any of these ventures will not only be safely within the rules of your tax-exempt status, but will also be tax-free.

> **SEE AN EXPERT**
>
> **Get answers to your questions about unrelated business income.** This section summarizes the IRS's definitions, exclusions, and exceptions dealing with unrelated business income. However, before you make any final business decisions, you'll want to read IRS Publication 598, *Tax on Unrelated Business Income of Exempt Organizations*, available on the IRS website at www.irs.gov. Consult an attorney if anything remains less than completely clear.

Activities That Will Be Taxed

What happens if your nonprofit's business activities don't fit within one of the permitted categories just discussed and, instead, constitute an "unrelated trade or business"? As long as you're churning 100% of the profits back into your charitable activities, they are still permitted, with one big catch. You'll have to pay corporate income tax (21%)—to both the feds and possibly your state government—on any profits ("unrelated business income" or UBI) of more than $1,000 per year. The 2018 changes made by the TCJA added a twist: Nonprofits engaged in more than one, unrelated business can no longer offset income from one with losses from another. This could mean that, for instance, profits from ads placed in your group's newsletter can't be offset by losses in its gift shop. Unused losses can, however, be carried forward to future years for the same business activity. You pay the tax using IRS Form 990-T; if you earn less than $1,000 in total, there's no need to file the form. But if it looks like your total tax payment (not income, but the amount you'll owe) will be $500 or more, you'll have to pay quarterly, estimated taxes even before the usual April tax time rolls around.

The IRS definition of income from an unrelated trade or business is remarkably free of gobbledygook. They call it: … *income from a trade or business that is regularly carried on by an exempt organization and that is not substantially related to the performance by the organization of its exempt purpose or function, except that the organization uses the profits derived from this activity.*

Of course, it wouldn't be the Internal Revenue Code if there weren't a couple of terms that need defining:

- **"Trade or business"** means selling goods or services in order to produce income. If you think you're in a trade or business, you probably are. For example, if your organization charges nonclients for consultations on organic landscaping, you owe tax on the profits. And the IRS is quick to point out that you can't hide a trade or business by burying it within your exempt activities—for example, a nonprofit hospital pharmacy that sells drugs to its patients (within its charitable purpose) would still have to pay taxes on drugs it sells to the general public.

- **"Regularly carried on"** is another term that has been the subject of much discussion by nonprofit tax experts and the IRS. Whether your business is "regularly carried on" (or, hopefully, is only occasional and, therefore, exempt from tax) depends on whether it's run with the same frequency and continuity as a typical profit-making business. Like any business, however, your own commercial viability may depend on running a continuous operation. So, for example, if you're planning to run a bakeshop, there's no point in closing it on odd days and times in an effort to make it "irregular"—you're better off just paying the taxes. And note that you can't necessarily get around the requirements by choosing a business with "irregular" operations, such as a catering company. If your company caters functions with the same frequency as a commercial catering company, your income will be taxable.

- **"Substantially related"** business activities—those that contribute importantly to your nonprofit purpose—are entirely tax exempt. If you're thinking that any fundraising helps you accomplish your charitable purposes, I'm sorry to report that the IRS is one step ahead of you—and specifically rules out this line of reasoning. The IRS appears to grant tax exemption when the products or services being sold are a spinoff of the nonprofit's existing activities or a direct result of its charitable activities. For example, if your organic agricultural research nonprofit sells milk produced by your herd of experimental dairy cows, the profits are not taxable—but once you start turning that milk into ice cream and the like, it stops being an activity that contributes to your charitable purposes, and you would have to pay tax on any profits.

Here are some of the IRS's examples of activities that are taxable because they constitute trades or businesses that are not substantially related to charitable purposes:

- selling a nonprofit membership list to a for-profit business
- using a school facility to run a summertime tennis club open to the general public
- selling handicrafts made by local members of the public (even if they're sold alongside handicrafts produced by the nonprofit's clients)
- renting studio apartments with dining room services to artists even though the organization's main purpose is to sponsor art events
- offering pet boarding and grooming to the public (even if it's by an organization dedicated to preventing cruelty to animals)
- offering travel tours that don't include an educational component related to the group's purpose, or
- charging for the use of an organization's name on product endorsements.

 SEE AN EXPERT

Congress made more UBIT-related changes in 2018, which aren't covered in detail here. The TJCA included various provisions that don't concern fundraising per se. For instance, some private colleges and universities will need to pay a 1.4% excise tax on net investment income; nonprofits offering salaries of $1 million or more per year will have to pay a 21% excise tax on what their five highest-compensated employees received; and certain employee benefits are now taxable, such as transportation fringe benefits, on-site parking, and an on-premises athletic facility. See an accountant for help.

Activities That Risk a Nonprofit's 501(c)(3) Status

Paying tax on your unrelated business activities is not as good as paying no tax at all, but it's greatly preferable to engaging in activities that call into question your nonprofit's 501(c)(3) tax status. Unfortunately, you can face this unhappy situation if doing business becomes the focal point of your nonprofit's activities. This is doubtless one reason your local YMCA works so hard to raise money for its charitable programs, despite all the profits it is likely to make from fitness centers.

Unfortunately, there's neither a bright line nor a numeric amount (such as a percentage of total income or a flat dollar figure) at which the IRS automatically finds that your profit-making business is too large in comparison to your tax-exempt activities. However, if your programs are shrinking but your business is growing, it's time to take a closer look. And even if both your business and nonprofit activities are growing, if you're lucky enough to enjoy substantial business profits, it may be time to spend some of that money on a nonprofit lawyer who can evaluate the situation for you.

 TIP

Consider creating a separate tax-paying organization. If your business activities threaten to overwhelm your nonprofit purpose, you might want to make the business a separate, for-profit venture. For example, if your education-centered nonprofit publishes calendars and books that become hugely popular and profitable, it might make sense to spin those activities off into their own publishing company. This way, the business could channel its profits in your direction, without threatening your 501(c)(3) status. You'll need a lawyer's help for this.

Learn From Other Nonprofits' Experiences

Although only a minority of nonprofits engage in any significant business activities, the creativity and range among those that do is inspiring. Nevertheless, a number of hard lessons have been learned along the way—which gives you an opportunity to avoid relearning them.

As a broad generalization, nonprofit businesses fall into two categories:

- enterprises centered on client training and employment, and
- sales of goods and services produced by nonclients or outside sources, sometimes but not always with a thematic connection to a nonprofit's mission and work.

Although hybrids of the two models certainly exist, each is covered separately below, so as best to highlight its advantages and challenges.

Client-Based Businesses

The ultimate in mission-based enterprises is to involve your clients in some part of the business. Sometimes called "social-purpose enterprise," this strategy has been utilized by numerous nonprofits to teach business, vocational, or life skills to low-income, disadvantaged, homeless, recovering, or disabled clients. Instead of training the clients and then sending them elsewhere to get "real" experience, such organizations bring the world of business in-house.

The clients use their newly acquired commercial skills to do everything from selling Christmas trees and moving furniture to woodworking, mechanics, cooking, landscaping, and computing. Typically, they either create things for sale or operate businesses serving the general public. As a result, consumers can now purchase everything from coffins to salad dressing to Web design services for good causes.

Ideally, social-purpose businesses will earn enough to be able to pay the client-employees salaries or stipends, thus reinforcing the larger point that work is rewarding. In rare cases, it might even bring in profits to the organization. And if your customers are satisfied with what you sell them, they might turn into donors.

 CAUTION

Operating a client-based business is probably not the most efficient way to raise funds. While businesses that use clients as workers may provide the clients with excellent training and life skills opportunities, such businesses' chances of doing much better than breaking even are slim. They're a fine idea if your main goal is to create a setting where clients can gain real business experience, but a poor choice if you need to raise extra funds to cover other programs.

Organizations with experience in running client-based businesses—even successful ones—have identified the following unique challenges:

- low worker efficiency and high turnover, as compared to for-profit businesses
- difficulty in finding professional-level managers to oversee operations
- conflicts between mission-related goals and business goals, and
- heightened risk that business failure will harm the lives of client workers.

Worker efficiency and turnover issues. Let's start with the most hopeful scenario: Your new client-based business has been well planned and managed and breaks even almost from the start. Best of all, your clients are learning a new skill—perhaps baking or bicycle repair. Customers appreciate the quality of what they're receiving and are returning for more and sending their friends. Your client workers enthusiastically complete their training in a matter of months and find better-paying jobs in the private sector. But unfortunately, you now have a new problem—you've just lost valuable, trained workers, while you must continue pleasing your growing customer base.

Even with good planning, this problem doesn't always have an easy solution. Assuming that part of your goal is to help your clients develop job skills, you certainly don't want to discourage them from moving on, both to better themselves and to make room for new clients. But the inevitable result is that unless you can carefully phase your "graduations" so as to always have a decent number of experienced workers, you'll always be trying to run a business with new or only minimally trained workers.

Of course, quick success probably won't be your biggest problem. If you honestly consider who your clients are, you may also have to face the very real reasons that they're not already in the workforce. Sometimes a second chance is all someone needs, but often it's not that easy. As worthy of help and respect as they are, your clients may lack not only tangible work skills, but other personal qualities customers have come to expect.

Basic things like showing up regularly or on time and interacting appropriately with others can sometimes be significant problems, depending on a client's personal background and ongoing medical, family, or other needs. For clients with cognitive difficulties, completing tasks will obviously take longer—which can become frustrating to the clients if they're put under pressure. And clients with criminal backgrounds may even fall into old habits around your inventory or cash register.

To some extent, you can factor these issues into your business planning by choosing a type of business that is easy to run, doubling up on personnel on any given shift, and providing extra supervision and separate counseling, for example. But no matter which way you slice it, your business efficiency will be reduced.

Finding qualified managers. If extra supervision is required, you may need some luck to find it. Your existing staffers may be highly skilled in client training and support, but not necessarily in the business aspects of supervising a staff, much less in other business management techniques. You may well have to hire additional staff—but finding a person who has the full plate of business and client interaction skills may not be easy, especially at a salary you can afford.

Once again, high turnover isn't going to help a fledgling business. There is some hope on the horizon, though: As more and more business schools establish nonprofit management programs, the field is receiving growing attention and interest, so the pool of applicants may expand. And when you do find a skilled person, he or she will probably have knowledge and talents to lend to other aspects of running your nonprofit.

Conflicts between serving clients and serving customers. If your client-based business doesn't turn a decent profit—and it probably won't in the first few years—conflicts may arise between your organization's goals and needs and the business's requirements. For example, what if you're attempting to pay your clients a salary—but having trouble paying them the minimum amount that will allow them to stick with the program? If neither your business profits nor your agency's budget can accommodate such expenditures, you've got a conflict. Or what if one of your client workers is going through a personal crisis, and others feel that the first priority should be to listen to and support him or her—even if it means setting the work aside? A steely-eyed businessperson might take a more draconian approach to these issues than you can—or should. But you may find yourself choosing whether the organization as a whole or the business suffers—with the added frustration that the business may have been budgeted to be self-supporting.

Impact of failure on client workers. In the worst case, your business may head toward failure. While this is a reality that every business faces—and it does not mean the end of the world—failure of a nonprofit-run business may nevertheless spell unusual rupture and economic difficulty for its client workers. If your business provides the sole source of support for clients who are already on the economic margins, layoffs may, in an instant, push them back toward homelessness, substance abuse, personal crises, or precisely the traps that the program was meant to help them out of. Even if the business merely reduces hours, such cuts can dampen your client workers' morale— and lower their paychecks—at a time when they're vulnerable. You might need to plan ahead for the extra client support that such a scenario would require. You might also find yourself scrambling to find other funding to plug the holes in the failing business.

RESOURCE

Want to learn more about client-run enterprises? Check out the Roberts Enterprise Development Fund (REDF), at www.redf.org.

Other Sales of Goods and Services

Another option is to create a small business that sells goods or services created by your own staff or by others. Nonprofits operate small businesses at nearly every scale imaginable, from selling the occasional mug, to retail shops and website sales.

On the plus side, a business project can energize people who are tired of feeling like they're begging for money. Your venture may be just the place to direct the skills or energies of particular board members—like the entrepreneurs or those who drag their feet when asked to do other types of fundraising. You may be able to tap into the artistic, culinary, or other skills of existing staff members or volunteers. Also, selling goods and services lets you reach out to people beyond your usual donor base. Everything that you sell with a tag or label on it should loudly proclaim what your organization is about and how the buyer is helping an important cause. Interested buyers may eventually turn into donors as well.

On the minus side, you're launching into an area that is probably outside the expertise of most of your staff or board. Enthusiasm may flag when it comes time for the real work—or they receive the first customer complaint (complaints being inevitable), or don't see profits coming in at the rate you'd anticipated.

As with client-based operations, another inevitable disadvantage comes up when conflicts arise with your mission-based activities. In fact, these conflicts can look even starker when you're selling something that has little immediate benefit for your mission, because it doesn't employ or train a client. For example, what if the business needs a cash investment in order to get past a difficult period or produce some inventory, but cash is tight, funding has been cut for one of your other programs, and you're already deeply in debt? Or, what if you're counting on a staffer to write a book for sale, but a pressing environmental or social concern makes it urgent for everyone to spend their time mobilizing your membership instead? If everything is happening under the same roof—or with the same people—tugs-of-war are inevitable.

Fortunately, there is a wide variety of business types and models for you to consider. At the most minimal end of the scale, many nonprofits offer souvenir-like products (e.g., T-shirts or mugs) showing their logos or something thematically related to the work that they do, such as wild animals for an environmental group. (Scads of companies will quickly print your organization's logo, a photo, or another design on just about anything you want.) Many nonprofits make such items available as small thank-you gifts for donations, but in part because the unit costs for these items are far cheaper when they are purchased in large numbers, nonprofits often end up with a garage full of items they need to sell separately. Most fundraising staffers will tell you that these small-scale sales are not a good way to raise money, but they keep the sales going for other reasons, such as getting the organization's name into the public eye and increasing membership. Nevertheless, with the right kind of sales strategy and perhaps volunteer commitment, you can turn anything into a moneymaker if you sell it for significantly more than you paid for it.

Another common nonprofit enterprise is small-scale publishing of books, reports, or classroom materials produced by the groups' own staff or supporters. The tricky parts are not so much the writing and publishing—although, done well, these are harder than most people credit—but the marketing. A huge amount of material makes it into print but very little of it finds a sufficient audience to be profitable.

Yet another significant niche is selling products that you've sought out or commissioned in order to serve the particular interests of your clients or the larger community. For example, SightConnection, in Seattle, Washington, (www.sightconnection.com), sells products that help the blind and partially sighted. It offers everything from magnifiers to eye patches to talking clocks. SightConnection's revenues support its programs to help vision-impaired people maintain their independence and well being.

SightConnection Store

Reprinted with permission

And let's not forget the variety of cards and posters sold by museums and arts and environmental groups—the Sierra Club calendar is a famous example. Take a lesson from the Sierra Club's closure of its retail stores, though. They found it more cost-efficient to sell online or through bookstores. You're not likely to achieve large sales unless you're either a national group with a large audience or have a killer marketing plan.

Marketing is the area where most nonprofit businesses fall down. I learned that lesson the hard way myself, while I was a legal staffer at an immigration nonprofit. I got involved in a project to create greeting cards that featured photos from the four continents, with a regional recipe on the back. I and other staffers had a wonderful time collecting the photos, trying out the recipes, and admiring the cards once we'd spent a few thousand dollars having them professionally printed. The trouble was, we didn't have a solid marketing plan in place, and at a certain point, we could no longer spare time from our client service work to pound the pavement in search of buyers or distributors. I still think the cards look beautiful—and I get to see them often, when my mother-in-law, who kindly bought several packs, uses them to write to me!

Rosie's Place Holiday Card Sales

Rosie's Place is a Boston, Massachusetts, sanctuary for poor and homeless women, offering emergency and long-term assistance with the help of private (nongovernment) funding and numerous committed volunteers. (See www.rosiesplace.org.) Since 2001, the organization has annually offered an attractive selection of nondenominational holiday cards, containing local artists' images of winter, particularly in Boston. The cards have had impressive fundraising years and slow years, as Vice President of External Relations Leemarie Mosca describes:

"From the beginning, we were able to keep production costs down in various ways. The artists—who are well-known in our area—allowed us to use images of their works at no cost, and a local printer, with whom we've built an ongoing relationship, gave us a discount. Before long, we were earning around $15,000 on the card sales. As the project evolved, we began offering organizations and companies the opportunity to buy customized cards (with their name and message inside) in bulk. That took our sales up to a record $90,000 in 2007. But our proceeds plummeted in 2008, and stayed low for the next few years. The recession caused companies to slash their marketing budgets at the very same time that people began shifting to use of personal photo cards and e-cards.

Sample Holiday Card

Reprinted with permission

"So, we reevaluated. We realized that these cards were more than a fundraiser for Rosie's Place—they are an important marketing and PR tool. Whenever someone sends out one of our cards (which has our mission statement on the back), they're demonstrating support for, and spreading the word about the services that Rosie's Place provides to women.

Rosie's Place Holiday Card Sales (continued)

"We called up the companies that had bought from us before, and said, 'We understand you aren't able to buy at the same volume; would you consider buying less as a way to share our mission with people in your network?' Then we asked our constituents (via our website and e-newsletters, print ads donated by local newspapers, bloggers, Facebook, Twitter, and the website CardsThatGive.org), to buy cards and send them to their network as a way of supporting our mission. To further attract buyers, we've made sure to offer a variety of images, so that they can send our cards out year after year without repeating the same one. And, on our order form, we added an opportunity for people to send in additional donations, which resulted in many people who were spending, say, $18, rounding up to $20.

"These efforts have brought our revenue back up to $40,000 (representing an approximately 50/50 split between companies and individuals). Not only is that good news by itself, but we feel the cards give us a springboard to promote other types of giving and engagement. Building relationships with bloggers, for instance, means they'll write about Rosie's Place's other initiatives. And people who come to our website to buy cards then notice that we also sell handcrafted jewelry (and vice versa). In redirecting our focus, we've rebuilt our card program's fundraising potential."

Develop Your Own Great—And Low-Risk—Business Idea

Your best starting point for a business or sales idea is the very asset list you drafted to create your fundraising plan in Chapter 3. Many of the items on your asset list will be relevant to planning a business as well—don't stray too far from what you or your inner circle knows best. Good examples are all around—every hospital that opens its cafeteria to the public, every museum that sells reproductions of its artworks, and every public radio station that sells tapes and CDs of its programs makes use of assets it already has or owns as part of its mission.

Similarly, some organizations identify a good or service already being offered to their clients—such as a seminar on recovering from addiction or learning how to budget—and make it available to the general public for a price. You can get even more creative, as the Red Cross did in designing First Aid Emergency Preparedness Kits for sale (see www.redcross.org). Similarly, various environmental organizations offer test kits for radon, arsenic, and other home and garden toxins.

Once you're serious about considering a business or sales venture, pull together a small working group (under ten people) of staff and board members to generate ideas. You might also ask people from outside the "usual suspects" list to join the group—perhaps donors or vendors with experience in the type of business you're contemplating, or in sales or marketing. (This type of short-term commitment is ideal for many volunteers.) Ask the group to come together for a brainstorming meeting, modeled on the type of panning you did based on Chapter 3.

What Customers Want or Need

Customers can be fickle, but you can stay in the safety zone by focusing on goods or services that you know are already needed or wanted. (Especially if your organization is dedicated to protecting the environment, it should avoid selling unneeded junk that will further deplete world resources and quickly end up in a landfill.)

Some of the most successful, as well as socially responsible businesses, were not begun with the primary motive of making money. For example, the founder of Patagonia, Yvon Chouinard, was a blacksmith and mountain climber who was disturbed that the very steel pitons he was creating were contributing to damage to the wilderness. He started by creating alternate, aluminum gear, then branched into clothing and other supplies, and Patagonia was born.

And finally, let's not forget Nolo, the publisher of this book, begun by legal-aid lawyers who saw that sky-high legal fees meant ordinary people were going without basic legal services and protections when getting a divorce or writing a will. They published a pamphlet explaining how to do your own divorce, and the rest is Nolo history.

If you aren't poised to fill a gap like this, your next best bet is to identify goods or services that people already need or are buying, and that they'd be willing to buy from a different source. Food is the classic example here; the salad dressings, popcorn, and spaghetti sauces sold by Newman's Own (which donates all profits to charity) are the stuff of fundraising legend, having earned over $500 million for good causes since the company began in the early 1980s. As Paul Newman once said, "If you can make people aware that things are going to charity, and if there are two competing products on the shelf, maybe people will grab the one where some good will actually come of it" ("Newman's Own: Two Friends and a Canoe Paddle," by Jon Gertner, *The New York Times*, November 16, 2003).

Food is not your only possibility, of course. People also need clothing, though perhaps not a T-shirt or baseball cap from every nonprofit they support. Be cautious, however, in considering the potential profit margins— you'll essentially be reselling something that someone else has put all the labor and materials into, which means that they'll have to charge you a reasonable amount unless they're exploiting someone. If the only thing that makes the clothes that you're selling unique is a logo from your nonprofit, you'd better have a large and enthusiastic membership. You might have better luck, if one of your volunteers is willing, for example, to produce hand-dyed scarves for sale.

People may not "need" recreation, but they are willing to pay for it. This accounts for the many tours run by nonprofits, in particular colleges, environmental groups, or groups with an international focus. You don't have to plan an overnight, or an international tour—a simple day trip, on a bus, boat, or on foot, can be a great way to start. One advantage you have as a nonprofit is that many travelers are actually searching for something more meaningful than a margarita-on-the-beach outing. If you can offer a combination of scenery and education, you may attract people who are genuinely interested in your nonprofit's work and will pay to get involved in it.

CAUTION

The IRS closely scrutinizes travel tours. In the IRS's view, tours by nonprofits compete closely with those offered by for-profit businesses and may be required to pay tax accordingly. Still, if you introduce a unique educational component, you should be able to operate tax free. Consult a lawyer for information and advice specific to your tour idea.

The lesson here is that the most solid business ideas begin close to home. Winning ideas should have many "yes" answers to the questions below.

- ☐ Does your organization have special assets, expertise, or potential partners that can be used in this business?
- ☐ Can the up-front costs be kept to a minimum?
- ☐ Can the business be started relatively quickly—preferably in less than six months?
- ☐ Is the business likely to generate enough profit to support other program activities, or, alternately, is your organization content to start a social purpose enterprise that will be self-supporting while it achieves an important mission-related purpose?
- ☐ Is there one person within your organization who can enthusiastically dedicate most of his or her time, thought, and energy to this project (a factor widely cited as vital to a nonprofit business venture's success)?
- ☐ Will you be able to deliver a product of high enough quality to compete in the marketplace?
- ☐ Does the business steer clear of high-risk, potentially high-liability activities, such as working with hazardous materials or caring for children?
- ☐ Will your intended customers be able to find your product and be willing to pay for it? (For example, starting a fancy sit-down restaurant in a fast-food neighborhood is probably a bad idea.)
- ☐ Can your existing staff spare enough time to help launch and run the business? How else could they be deployed to raise money if you didn't start a business?
- ☐ Will the activities involved in starting and running the business be meaningful—or, hopefully, even enjoyable—for the participants and affected staff and board members?
- ☐ Can the business be started on a small scale, so you won't be forced into higher overhead costs or production runs than you can necessarily handle?
- ☐ Is the business likely to stand the test of time, rather than fade due to changes in fads or technology?
- ☐ Can your organization survive if the business doesn't live up to expectations?

☐ When all is said and done, could you make more money with a simple auction or raffle? The expenses and effort of running a small business often cancel out many of its profits, while mobilizing your volunteers and collecting donated goods will often reliably produce a one-time major cash influx.

You'll want to consider the financial questions on this list with the help of your core group of leaders and accountants. (And don't forget, there's no shame in deciding that your organization isn't in a position to launch any sort of business at all.)

Measure Your Ideas Against Reality

An estimated three out of four new businesses close in the first five years. Let's look at some realistic ways of measuring your chances of success in the world of small business generally, including customer research, price research, and competition research.

Customer Research

By now, you should have identified a product or service that you reasonably believe your customers could benefit from. But the big question remains: Will they buy it? For example, many of us need funeral plots, but how many of us plan to shop for one in the near future? And if your business sells something new or innovative, its existence may be so far from any customers' imaginations that they don't think to look for it. Fortunately, multitudes of business and marketing experts who've gone before you have turned customer research into a science. Use as many of the methods below as it takes to get you a set of consistent, logical answers.

Talk to owners of similar businesses. Look for businesses that do what you'll do, in a similar locale. To avoid future competitive problems, focus on those outside your own neighborhood or city. If you can find a business being run by a nonprofit, all the better. Be open about who you are and what your goals include, and ask them to spend a few minutes telling you about what's worked, what lessons they've learned, who their best customers are, what kind of marketing has been most successful, and how long it took their business to get on its feet. You'll be surprised at how eager some businesspeople are to talk. Even local business owners may reveal more than you'd expect if you stop by, as a customer, and simply ask, "How's business?"

Observe customers of similar businesses. Let's say you'll be opening a bagel bakery. If you stop by a bagel bakery in a nearby city and munch slowly on your cream cheese and lox for an hour or two, you should be able to pick up scads of relevant information: the going prices, number of customers, number of employees, favorite flavors, number of people who buy sandwiches versus a dozen to take home, discounts the bakery offers in order to boost sales, sources of customer complaints (check their Yelp reviews, too), and amount of leftover inventory at the end of the day. (Remember that if you visit during lunch hour or a busy time, it doesn't represent the entire business day.) An even more effective approach is for someone in your organization to volunteer in the business for a week or two. Yes, it's time consuming, but there is no better way to learn a lot quickly.

Talk to, or survey, your most likely customers. It may be that your customers are people already known to you—for example, patients at your clinic, patrons of your museum, or participants in your classes. You can either talk to them informally or ask them to fill out a survey containing simple questions like, "Would you be interested if we made (a café, gift shop, etc.) available?" "Would $_____ be a reasonable price to pay?" "How often would you be likely to purchase this?" "Is there a related product or service that you wish we'd offer instead?" Also talk, or send surveys to, any sympathetic friends, family, or supporters of your organization.

If your customers are not likely to be people with whom you're already in contact, you'll need to start by defining who you think your customers are most likely to be, such as "middle-income teens involved in sports and living in the nearby suburbs" or "wealthy urban vegetarians with pets." Likely characteristics around which to define your customers include (depending on your business type) age, gender, income level, profession, family size or composition, ethnic background, geographic location, education level, media preferences, buying habits, and hobbies or activities.

Once you've created your customer profile, you can—probably by going through friends and friends of friends—pull together a group of people who fit that profile and are willing to serve as a focus group. Ask them to test your product (if you have it available already) or to offer their opinions as prospective customers. If possible, try to offer choices—would they rather you located your service here or there, do they prefer doughnuts or pancakes, what kind of people do they think would buy your product, and the like. Although commercial operations pay people to serve on focus groups, you have every right to ask for volunteers—but you should treat them well and probably serve snacks!

Research demographic data. Using your developing sense of who your customers are most likely to be, research how many of them are around. If your likely customers are clients or visitors to your nonprofit's office, counting them up should be easy. If, however, you're seeking a new customer base, you'll probably need to rely on sources such as the U.S. census (www.census.gov).

Price Research

If you'll be selling goods or services, a basic question you'll need to answer is whether you can sell enough of them, at a hefty enough markup, to make a profit. Once you add the costs of purchasing or producing the goods or services, plus an adequate profit margin, you may be shocked at how much you have to charge. The low prices consumers expect to pay for many items are based on low-wage overseas workers, highly automated supply chains, and high-volume discounts at the wholesale level, none of which are available to you.

Be sure the price you plan to charge is at least within the realm of reasonableness. Compare prices on the Internet, or by calling the merchants you find in your local yellow pages.

Also plan to have all your advertising and other materials clearly explain that by buying your product or service, the customer is supporting a good cause. See "Stand By Your Price," below, for an example of how one nonprofit learned this lesson.

Competition Research

Even if you think you know who your likely competition is, double-check this with some research. The purpose is to discover how many other similar businesses there are in the area you plan to serve. (If you'll be selling online, then that area is nationwide and potentially worldwide.)

CAUTION

Don't ignore businesses that have recently closed their doors. It does you no good to be the only business of your type if your predecessors tested the waters and drowned. See if you can contact the proprietors to find out what went wrong—people love to share a tale of woe.

Stand by Your Price

The DAMAYAN Migrant Workers Association came up with a fundraising idea that its volunteers and new members were excited about: to set out a table at the Asia Pacific American Festival in Union Square Park, New York City, and sell homecooked Filipino treats. (DAMAYAN is a nonprofit membership organization that organizes Filipino domestic workers in the New York area to fight for their rights and welfare; www.damayanmigrants.org.) Here's how Amanda Vender, then board member, describes the event:

"It was a beautiful, sunny day. We unfurled our newly painted green banner, propped up the photo display of recent events, and put out stacks of brochures. Most of the table was filled with trays of cassava cake, biko rice cakes, and empanadas—$2 each. Festivalgoers flocked to our table.

"When the time came to pack up, the organizers found the food trays empty and the brochure stack mostly full. And when all of the cooks were reimbursed for the ingredients, we found that we had only broken even. What happened?

"It turned out that a few festivalgoers were more resourceful than we were. They negotiated down the price of our sweets and empanadas, saying that they were cheaper at other tables. And as the day went on, our volunteer salespeople rushed to get rid of the perishable goods. Two dollars apiece became $1.50, then $1.00, then 50 cents, then three for a dollar, and finally four for a dollar!

"We had obviously forgotten an important element: to sell our organization, not just the empanadas. With the help of a fundraising consultant, we learned that we should have been telling customers: 'Your donation of two dollars helps to support our organization. We organize Filipino domestic workers—some of the most isolated and exploited workers in the city—to know their rights and to fight for better conditions.'

"Before our next fundraising event, we resolved that everyone involved would practice and roleplay our fundraising pitch, and hand out a DAMAYAN flyer to every customer."

What is a "similar" business? For the most accurate research, you'll want to look not only for businesses that provide the exact same thing, but for those that satisfy the same market segment. For example, if you plan to open a bagel bakery, and there's no bagel bakery nearby, that's good so far—unless there happens to be a bread store on the same block.

Research the competition using your telephone book, the Internet, and your local Chamber of Commerce. If your business will have a storefront and will rely on walk-in traffic, also drive around the area to get a sense of where else potential customers might go.

Create a Meaningful Business Plan

Up to this point, you've been conceptualizing your business and researching its prospects for success. Now it's time to sit down and plot out its future, for approximately the next three years. (Don't bother projecting further— too much guesswork is involved.) This may or may not involve preparing a written business plan.

Although some MBAs and consultants will warn you that few businesses can succeed without a written plan, including an extensive narrative, charts, budgets, and projections, the truth is that for many small nonprofit enterprises, such plans consume more energy than they're worth. Worse yet, they may produce an artificially rosy picture of the future. ("How can we fail, when we've got two inches of paper saying all will be well?")

What your organization needs to arrive at through planning is a deep understanding of what your business is about. In other words, you must think through every element of starting and running your business. Even if you don't plan to write it up in a fancy document, you should be able to summarize it in a succinct report. To do this, you and the other wise heads in your organization should consider the following:

- What will the business sell or do, and for what types of customers?
- Who will your most likely customers be, and what's your basis for believing they'll be interested in buying?
- Who will be responsible for what tasks, using how much of their time?
- How closely connected will the people who do the work be to your nonprofit "mother ship"?
- How much initial investment will be required to start the business?

- How much will it cost to run the business and produce the goods or services on an ongoing basis?
- What's your break-even point—how much will you need to bring in to cover your running costs and pay back the initial investment?
- At what price will you need to sell your product in order to not only cover your costs but to make a profit?
- How will you deal with any significant foreseeable legal, insurance, or tax concerns?
- How will you market (tell the world about) your goods or services?
- What's your profit timeline—how many months will you go without a profit, when should you expect to see profits, and at what levels?
- After your start-up investment is spent, will your incoming cash flow be enough to cover your costs month by month, or are you likely to require loans or other cash infusions?

Take the time to write up a brief planning document covering these issues. Include the specific research sources or bases upon which you projected any financial figures, market demand levels, or other external facts and figures that may affect the business's success.

Next, bring your marketing and accounting experts into the process. Ask them to help you create forecast budgets for three scenarios:

- **Best case:** if everything goes right, you keep your costs down, and your customers respond as well as can reasonably expected
- **Break-even scenario:** often best calculated backwards, to see how much you'd need to purchase or produce and sell just to cover your costs. (For more information on how to calculate this, see the article entitled "Will My Business Make Money?" free at www.nolo.com.)
- **Worst case:** what will happen in the case of such foreseeable problems as product cost increases, failure to obtain donated equipment or labor, and, most important, a disappointing customer response.

If the best-case scenario doesn't look too exciting, your business idea may not be worth the effort. Same story if the worst-case scenario would result in losses that would cripple your organization. The break-even scenario should help you determine whether the business is realistic—and hopefully lead you to further planning of how to push it to true profitability.

CAUTION

Never hand the entire business planning process over to a consultant. It's your business and only you can determine whether it will be viable. Business consultants can help you make this decision, but don't turn the whole job over to them: Chances are that all you'll get in return is a long and expensive document that you don't really understand.

You can, of course, develop a much more detailed business plan. In fact, if you plan a large business that will require either major support from donors or foundations or commercial (most likely bank) loans, you'll surely have to do so. Such a business plan should include narratives and formal financial reports, including a break-even analysis, a profit-and-loss forecast, a cash-flow projection, and a start-up cost estimate. Also contact local business schools; many sponsor classroom projects in which students evaluate potential new businesses. You can bring a great deal of free, personalized, and expert attention to your business planning process this way.

RESOURCE

Need help drafting a business plan? For a quick introduction to what belongs in it, see the free article "The Essentials of a Business Plan," at www.nolo. com. For in-depth information, *How to Write a Business Plan*, by Mike McKeever (Nolo), offers easily digested, plain-English guidance on general business plans.

Minimize Risk by Starting Small

Before attempting a high dive into full-scale production, it's worth dipping your toes into—and testing—the business waters first. Three good ways to do this include:

- starting with borrowed or temporary resources
- running a test version of the business, and
- lining up customers before you create the product.

As a nonprofit, you have a huge advantage when it comes to minimizing your risk: You're accustomed to getting by with less and being creative about filling your daily needs. For example, the file folders that a corporate office might recycle after one use probably have, in your office, been relabeled so often that you could perform an archaeological dig on the layers. Don't drop these thrifty habits once you enter the business world. A surprising number of new businesses spend far too much, far too soon.

If you can't use existing resources, think about how to avoid expensive investments. A surprising amount of equipment can be borrowed or leased short-term, rather than purchased outright. You may be able to line up donated facilities, at least for the short term—for example, a restaurant's kitchen on a day when it's closed for business, a church's basement for initial product assembly, or an undeveloped lot for purposes of starting a garden.

If you'll need to purchase products or inventory, see whether the most expensive items can be donated. Talk to local businesses, especially those that you or your clients already patronize. As discussed in Chapter 2, many businesses see charitable donations of goods or services as a normal part of their annual financial cycles—though you may need to catch them early in their fiscal years.

There are limits, of course, to this "just getting by" philosophy. The two most important are that you shouldn't compromise the quality of your goods and services, and the process of soliciting donations shouldn't take more time than it's worth. For example, customers might not mind a hand-printed label on your jar of homemade applesauce, but the applesauce itself should be of top quality. Fortunately, no one expects your nonprofit to look like the corporation next door.

It's usually best to start small, which can include beginning with mini, test versions of your business. If, for example, you're thinking of opening a crafts business, why not try setting up booths at a few fairs first? Or better yet, avoid the costs of retail altogether and sell by mail order or online. This will not only keep your costs down (opening storefronts is notoriously expensive) but will also tell you a lot about whether your staff and/or clients can handle the production and service end of the business. You'll also be learning what your customers like and respond to—or don't. You may even decide that a small-scale operation is all you want to pursue for the moment.

Women's Studio Workshop Summer Arts Institute

For most of the year, the Women's Studio Workshop (WSW, at www.wsworkshop. org) in Rosendale, New York, focuses on providing arts residencies to people making careers out of art. During the summer, however, they use their 6,500 square feet of professional studios (for printmaking, papermaking, photography, book arts, and ceramics) to offer classes in traditional and experimental studio techniques. Practicing artists and the arts-interested public from across the country participate in classes, private instruction, and intensive workshops.

The institute's classes are a good example of building a small business using existing resources. According to Anita Wetzel, retired development director and cofounder, "Part of the reason this works for us is that we already have the facilities. We are known in the field and have established connections to artists who teach. Also, we keep our plans small scale, while being flexible enough to expand on short notice. A full class is about six to eight people, allowing participants a lot of hands-on time in the studios and one-on-one interaction with the instructors. We make sure that, at a minimum, we have enough people to pay for the teacher's salary and transportation to get her here. Then, if more than the maximum number of students sign up, we do our best to create an additional class section."

Another excellent strategy when starting out is to avoid committing resources to anything until you're sure you've got customers lined up—preferably paying in advance. In some cases, this will be easy—for example, customers who sign up for a class, workshop, or tour usually understand, or can be warned, that the event is subject to cancellation for low attendance. (Just make sure you're ready to return their deposits or payments immediately!) Or, if you take orders for goods, you can tell customers how long they'll have to wait before delivery and use that time to create the goods. (This is another advantage to not opening a store, where you'd have to have a full supply of the goods on hand.) In other cases—particularly for large or expensive orders—you may need to negotiate with customers and sign a contract, asking them to pay in full in advance but to wait several weeks for delivery.

The one catch to this strategy is that small steps into business likely won't gain you large returns in the long run. At some point, you'll need to either invest or risk some real money in order to make money.

Finding Start-Up Money

If you need more start-up cash than you can scare up from existing sources, you'll have to look to major donors, grantmaking foundations or corporations, or bank lenders. Because none of these sources can ordinarily give you overnight returns, be prepared for at least six months' effort in lining up commitments. For some nonprofits, it has taken one to two years.

Starting up a business provides an interesting focus for a major donors campaign. Your pitch to them is that their gifts will go farther than ever, as they'll help to launch a profit-making enterprise. As you'll remember from Chapter 6, launching a campaign requires your leadership and board members to devote several weeks to meeting with various donor prospects and asking for their financial support. You'll want to show the prospects your plans and forecasts, and demonstrate that your organization is ready to launch into this new venture. With the right presentation, this can give you a chance to approach existing donors in a new way, with a new message, to reinvigorate their support. Also consider asking major donors to support you with low-interest loans.

Some foundations will make grants to assist in starting a small business, or at least loans or technical assistance. As with the major donors, you're in the happy position of offering them something new to support. At the same time, your track record of good communication with funders and measurable outcomes on past grants will be an important way of demonstrating your chances of business success.

As a last resort (given the risks that come with carrying a debt burden), you could also approach banks for small business loans. Bank loans are certainly one of the primary methods used by for-profit entrepreneurs. You're at a bit of a disadvantage here, however, if this is your first business effort. The bank will want to see not only a formal business plan, but also evidence that you're capable of getting a small business off the ground and repaying the loan. Enlist the help of any board members and other volunteers who will be participating in this effort, and emphasize their experience, business knowledge, and ongoing roles.

Licensing, Sponsorships, and Other Relationships With Existing Businesses

Rather than developing and implementing your own business idea, you may be able to generate revenue in cooperation with, or through sponsorship by, an existing business. For example, universities can make significant sums by licensing their names and logos for clothing and all sorts of other products. In return for its sponsorship or other payments, a business would normally expect one of the following from your organization:

- **use of your organization's name or logo,** by which the business could give its products a stamp of socially conscious approval. (You've no doubt seen coffee and other companies advertise their commitment to fair trade.)

- **use of your organization's name or logo on a product again, but with a different fee arrangement,** where a percentage of the profits goes to support your organization. This is known as "cause-related marketing." It's similar to the licensing arrangement, but takes it one step farther, not only because of the percentage payment, but because you might also be asked to encourage your organization's supporters to buy the product. (Note: Because of the quid pro quo arrangement, the business cannot deduct from its taxes the amounts it gives your nonprofit.)

- **your display of the business's logo**—for example, in your publications, on your website, on team shirts, or on banners—in return for the business's sponsoring an event or activity. (Also see Chapter 8, on special events, and Chapter 11, on media, for more on the most likely uses of corporate sponsorships.)

- **your assistance with a joint business venture,** in which both you and the business provide a portion of the expertise or services, and share in the profits.

As a practical matter, larger, established nonprofits—with recognizable names and logos—are the ones in the best position to enter into licensing, marketing, or sponsorship arrangements with major companies. For a smaller group, set your sights on businesses that match the size and reach of your organization. For example, a local sports bar might sponsor your little league team, or a local print or photo shop might be happy to say in its catalog, "We're the choice of environmentally conscious organizations such as [*your organization*]," in return for either a fee or a discount on their services.

The arrangement that will require the most creativity is that of a joint venture, in which both you and the business take some role in business activities. Perhaps a local grocery store might partner with you in a catering venture. Or, your bonsai club might arrange to give classes at a local nursery—the nursery would do the advertising through its mailing list, and you would both reap the profits. Or a cancer-care organization might arrange for a local hat store to come offer advice and discounts on attractive headwear to people undergoing chemotherapy—and give a share of any profits from sales in return.

Approaching a business or corporation has some important things in common with approaching an individual—there are no preset rules, and you'll need to do your research first. By learning about the business's values, how it's doing financially, and who the right person to approach is, you'll vastly improve your chances of success. Be open with the business about what it will gain—perhaps an increase in its numbers of customers, access to a new customer base, or a boost to its public reputation.

Before embarking on any plan, make sure your arrangement is written up as an agreement signed by a representative of both parties. This doesn't have to be in legalese—the important thing is to use words and phrases that both sides understand and feel comfortable with.

With all of these business arrangements, there are ethical issues that your organization will need to discuss and consider before the deal is signed. You're not tainted by mere association with businesses—after all, many of them are no more or less moral than your average nonprofit.

However, your reputation may start to suffer if you've got corporate logos plastered all over your website and publications. And, of course, if it's a company that creates harmful products, you'll need to think hard before helping it try to save its reputation. (The Susan P. Komen Foundation, for example, created a PR nightmare by partnering with KFC to provide "Pink Buckets for the Cure.") There's something to be said for letting it atone for its errors through your organization, but make sure your organization gains more than it loses by the association.

The Next Steps

Hopefully, this chapter has guided you toward the front door of your new business, but you'll have to walk through it on your own. A book of this size couldn't possibly advise you on all the aspects of running your small business—obtaining permits, choosing a business name, avoiding trademark disputes, leasing space, managing employees, dealing with customers, paying business taxes, marketing and advertising, riding out hard times, and more.

For a compact guide to all these issues and more, see *Legal Guide for Starting & Running a Small Business,* by Fred S. Steingold (Nolo). It's perfectly appropriate for you to be reading books that aren't geared only for nonprofits at this point—you'll need to play by the same rules as other businesses do, with only a few exceptions. Still, I recommend developing relationships with other nonprofits pursuing business activities, and with organizations that support them, to keep up with new knowledge and developments in this quickly changing area of endeavor.

Seeking Grants From Foundations, Corporations, and Government

t's not terribly hard to write a grant proposal—no magic set of talents, other than solid research, writing, and organizational skills, are required. Experienced insiders realize, however, that there's a lot more to getting a grant than writing a compelling proposal. As this chapter explains, you'll need to:

- understand who gives out grants in your field
- narrow the list by researching your grant prospects
- understand the entire proposal process, from initial inquiry forward, including how to write a targeted grant proposal
- follow up with the funder, and
- apply for grant renewals.

Understand the Funders

There are two primary sources of grants to nonprofit organizations: foundations (private and public) and the government (local, state, and federal). Each source has unique purposes and requirements for granting funds. For example, a large, corporate-run foundation may seek to have its name associated with a certain positive image; a private family foundation may be primarily motivated to carry out the very personal interests of the family that founded it; and a government grantor may be fulfilling legislative requirements.

To improve your chances of winning support, you'll need to know a lot about any funder you approach—particularly when it comes to private foundations, whose organizational personalities can be, and often are, as distinct and quirky as those of any individual donor.

Characteristics of Private and Public Foundations

Most nonprofits find that public and private foundations are their best bets for obtaining grants. A foundation is essentially another form of charity—in fact, its tax status, like yours, is covered by Section 501(c)(3) of the Internal Revenue Code. Over 86,000 grantmaking foundations are active in the United States today. Collectively, they've granted between about $30 billion and $63 billion in funds annually for most of the last ten years.

One of the best things about foundations is that they don't just give out money because they want to; many of them give it out because they have to! Depending on their particular tax status, "private" foundations must spend at least 5% of their investment assets on philanthropy every year; this includes money spent on reasonable administrative expenses, such as salaries, facilities, and travel.

Tax laws also affect the foundation's essential character and way of working with you. Private foundations are usually in the hands of a single source of money, such as a wealthy family or a corporation. (The Bill & Melinda Gates Foundation is a well-known example.) Many private foundations are funded by wealthy philanthropists, seeking to change the world to fit their visions. Some of these organizations are quite small or narrowly focused. For example, the Rauch Family Foundation (#1) supports programs and activities that serve the citizens of Rock Island, Illinois—specifically because during the Great Depression, according to its website, "the Rauch brothers remembered how the community, especially the American Federation of Labor Construction Workers, came to the aid of the Rauch family whose husband and father was a paraplegic."

Some family-based foundations are so private that you might think that they want you to just go away and leave them alone. A few do want just that—as evidenced by the fact that they don't even publish websites. Others are long-established, high-profile players in the foundation world. Whatever their size or provenance, most family foundations tend to focus on one major substantive interest area and two or three other minor ones. This makes it hard for most groups to get in the door, but relatively easy to stay inside once you cross the threshold.

Corporate-sponsored foundations also normally fall into the private foundation category. Although they account for a small percentage of the foundation money granted every year, that's because most corporate giving isn't channeled through foundations alone, but instead is given out directly by the parent corporations. (See "Nonfoundation Corporate Giving," below.)

Any consumer would probably recognize the names of corporate foundations—the Levi Strauss Foundation, the Ford Foundation, and the Merck Company Foundation, to name a few. Some of these make grants that explicitly tie to each of their company's product or philosophy. For example, the Aetna Foundation lists its first giving priority as health—a fitting choice given that its creator company, Aetna Inc., is one of America's largest sellers of health insurance. Other corporate foundations simply try to promote the interests of the communities in which their customers live.

Nonfoundation Corporate Giving

Corporations don't grant money through foundations alone—not all companies that make charitable gifts are organized as corporations—sole proprietorships, partnerships, and limited liability companies (LLCs) can also be generous with their profits.

If yours is a small, local nonprofit, the majority of business giving available to you will be through nonfoundation avenues, such as employee volunteer or matching gift programs, in-kind donations of services, goods, or facilities, event sponsorship, cause-related marketing (where a business's advertising mentions your nonprofit and cause), or cash gifts.

Because most businesses prefer to keep their giving local (sometimes even at the neighborhood level), and because companies can set their own rules for their gift programs, you should research the companies operating in your area to see what they have to offer.

Here are some tips for tailoring your approach to a business that doesn't operate a foundation:

- **View this as another relationship to be built.** Look for existing contacts between your staff and volunteers and the company's employees. For example, if several people from a local company have adopted animals from your shelter, that's a good entry to ask the business for support.
- **Ask yourself what's in it for the company.** Unlike at corporate foundations, your contact person at a local business will quite possibly be in the marketing department. This means you must focus squarely on how you can improve or advertise the company's image or enhance quality of life for its customers or employees. For example, if you want businesses to contribute a gift of attractive products for your silent auction, be ready to tell them how you'll publicize their donations.
- **Think creatively.** Few rules for business giving are written in stone. Thus, you might approach a small food producer that has never given anything to charity before by proposing an exciting way to partner— for example, featuring its rice-based desserts at an event directed at people with gluten intolerance.

Nonfoundation Corporate Giving (continued)

- **Be prepared to sign a contract.** Particularly with event sponsorship, you'll need to sign an agreement with the company, specifying such things as where you'll mention its name and feature its logo.
- **Don't approach a company in financial trouble.** Do your homework —read the business pages and do some online research. You want to catch them when they're feeling generous.

Public foundations are slightly different animals than the private ones —hungrier ones, to be precise. Unlike private foundations, which are usually funded by one or a few families or corporations, public foundations must beat the bushes for funds, typically trying to aggregate lots of small donations. The United Way and the Red Cross are examples of public foundations, as are local community foundations.

Many public foundations also pursue those not-quite-super-rich philanthropists who would like to give away a little of their largesse, but don't have enough to form their own foundations. In this regard, community foundations position themselves as liaisons between such philanthropists and nonprofits, helping the philanthropists learn more about community needs, and efficiently taking care of the administrative aspects of giving.

For your organization, this means that working with public foundations can help you get around the narrow grant guidelines that otherwise plague the foundation world. Public foundations need you to feed them exciting new ideas that they can use to stimulate their donors' interests. In fact, some grant decisions won't be made by the foundation itself, but will be based purely on the donors' choices.

Of course, you're at a particular advantage if your nonprofit works in "fun" or "popular" fields like education, health, or the environment. Even if you don't, however, it's well worth courting your local community foundations' favor, because those that lack immediate grant opportunities may be intrigued enough to link you up with an interested donor later.

People Who Staff Private and Public Foundations

After learning how foundations work, your next task is to understand who works for them. Obviously, you won't expect to find the person after whom the foundation was named sitting behind a desk (although this sometimes happens). The main people you'll interact with are a foundation's "program officers." They typically are responsible for reading and evaluating proposals and presenting the ones they like to their boards of directors—who usually make the final call (although program officers may have discretion to approve small grants on their own).

Many program officers cut their teeth in nonprofit jobs, including fundraising, so you can expect them to be fairly savvy about who you are and what you can reasonably expect to achieve. Above all, most are extremely interested in seeing that their money is invested well. So, it will always be important to present your organization as solid, well organized, and able to produce results.

Government Grantmakers

Government grants are made by local, state, and federal agencies. Statistics are hard to come by, but it's a good guess that nonprofits nationwide get about 10% of their revenues from the government. However, the distribution is uneven, with some nonprofits in certain fields, such as health services or education, relying almost completely on government funds, and others receiving none at all.

If you are one of the lucky ones that gets funded, the amount granted is likely to be quite substantial—the feds, in particular, rarely mess around with pocket-change grants. Although the purposes of government grants have traditionally been fairly narrow, they are now turning toward outsourcing and privatization, which means that grants will increasingly be available for a broader range of purposes. But before you leap clapping from your chair, know that the government tends to be very risk averse, so new organizations and untested projects will have a tougher time getting funded.

Government grants can also be affected by the political goals of the current administration or party in power. For example, the Trump administration has sought to cut funding for arts, food banks, rural development, and foreign assistance.

TIP

The more reproducible your project, the more likely it is to be funded.
The federal government loves to see evidence that your program will serve as a pilot
and model for others to follow. After all, in a huge country, there is little to be gained
from pouring huge funds into creating one local success story.

A big downside to any government grant is the overwhelming amount
of red tape involved. The application alone can be more than some
nonprofits can handle. Although you'll likely need to submit it digitally,
the hard copy version of your federal grant application would likely stack
up to two inches or more once you've completed all the forms, narrative,
statistical information, lists of collaborators and advisory committees,
and so on.

Worse yet, federal grant opportunities are often announced a mere six
weeks before applications are due. State and local grant applications are less
onerous when it comes to paperwork, but often include other requirements,
such as mandatory attendance at dull meetings with large groups of other
applicants or grantees.

People Who Staff Government Grantmaking Offices

The administrators with whom you'll interact on a government grant may
be far away geographically and may not seem attuned to the nonprofit
world. Their background is likely to be more state university than Ivy
League. They may have worked their way into their current job from
another branch of government—and, as a gross generalization, tend
to be highly attuned to rules, requirements, and obedience to orders
from higher up. So don't expect your prospective grant administrator
to overlook deficiencies in your application based on its wonderfully
creative concept.

None of this is meant to say, however, that you shouldn't try to establish
human contact with government grant administrators—their very
remoteness means that you can set yourself apart from the pack by picking
up the phone and trying to get to know them, as well as keeping in regular
contact after you receive your grant.

Research Grant Prospects

Researching your most promising funders, and the grants that they offer, is a critical part of the grantseeking process—and sadly, one that too many people zoom through. While different funders report very different success/rejection ratios, all agree that they receive scads of applications proposing programs that are 180 degrees away from their stated purposes or guidelines—in other words, that are completely unfundable.

The common wisdom is that a mere one of each ten submitted grant proposals gets funded, with a significant portion of rejections attributable to the applicants' failure to understand the guidelines. Knowing this, you'll understand why, before you can even begin entering an online application for a grant at some foundations, they make you take an eligibility quiz. You'll need to affirm that you're with a registered nonprofit, that it's located in the United States, that you're not asking for money for something outside the foundation's guidelines (such as religion or scholarships), and so forth.

CAUTION

Don't get too excited if a funder notifies you that it's accepting grant applications. Especially once your nonprofit is established, funders may mail you grant proposal requests out of the blue, as a courtesy. However, this doesn't mean that your application is any more likely to be accepted. Unless your application is both competitive and relevant to the funder's mission, you'll just be joining the ranks of all the other nonprofits who submit grant applications cold.

To get your application to the top of a grantmaker's pile, do some basic research. Your object is to make sure your proposal is a likely match for the funder's stated—and in some cases, unstated—interests and priorities. Begin with some library or online work, but also be ready to act like an investigative reporter, determined to sniff out the real-deal grant opportunities. Your research progression should typically go something like this:

1. Decide what you're looking for.
2. Research public information.
3. Make personal contacts with funders.
4. Create files to track funders.

Choose a Goal for Each Research Project

Seeking grant money is probably the area where the "plan first, act second" approach gets violated the most. If you get a request for proposals (RFP) from your local city government inviting you to apply for funding, you shouldn't start by writing a proposal, but by first figuring out whether your group is any more likely to be funded than the multitude of other groups in town who received the same solicitation. (If a can't-pass-it-up RFP comes along, you can, of course, alter your fundraising plan—but be realistic about the costs that come with every grant you pursue.)

> ### Sticking to Your Mission
>
> During her time as development and communications coordinator with the World Institute on Disability (WID), Marisa Lianggamphai became all too familiar with the temptation to apply for grants that don't quite fit. "WID focuses primarily on issues affecting adults with disabilities, at the policy level. Although several of its programs have components that serve youth with disabilities, they are not the main focus of the organization. Unfortunately, there are a lot more funding opportunities for youth with disabilities than for adults with disabilities. I often thought it would be great if WID could change its programs to go where the funding is, but that really isn't WID's purpose. Every possible funding opportunity must be run through the question of 'Is this within our mission?' Otherwise, an organization's strength and purpose gets watered down."

Once you're clear on your funding goals, break them into categories and fill out Worksheet 8 below (available online, see the appendix for the link) for each grant-seeking effort.

Most of the chart's criteria should be fairly self-explanatory. Your **clients or issue** depends on how you've defined your fundraising goal. Your answer could be as broad as the entire populace served by your agency, such as the homeless, the blind, or wild birds, or as narrow as the purchase of a new drinking fountain for your dance studio. The **greater goal** would be all or part of your agency's mission, such as "reducing maternal mortality" or "ending youth violence." This goal is important because it should dovetail neatly with goals set out by a funder.

Set yourself a **minimum grant amount**, or at least have an idea of how many grant proposals you're able to write in order to reach your funding goal. You don't want to stretch too far and end up preparing 15 small grant proposals to raise $30,000, when two larger ones would have done the same job. **Geographic area** is a common limitation placed by funders, so you'll need to know exactly what area your agency plans to cover, bearing in mind any future plans for expansion. The funding source will no doubt define other **restrictions** on what you can do with the money, so be clear about which ones your organization can't accept. Prohibitions on legislative advocacy or on working with certain populations are common. For example, in the immigrant services field, certain governmental funding sources will not give support to agencies whose clients include undocumented ("illegal") immigrants, which makes it virtually impossible for agencies serving immigrants to accept this money.

Some organizations also struggle with whether it's moral to accept money from a **funding source** like a drug or tobacco company. You certainly don't want to help one of the sources of society's troubles clean up its reputation at the expense of your own. But it doesn't mean you're crass or ruthless if you don't set such limitations—plenty of nonprofits figure that it's time these corporations gave a little back, and that it's nearly impossible to find money that wasn't raised through someone's exploitation in the not-too-distant past.

With your Grant Priorities Summary Chart in hand, start researching individual foundations and other grantmakers. Although you could just use the chart as a general checklist to identify good matches, it's better to go one step farther and assemble detailed information on the most promising-looking funders. To do this, use the following Grant Prospect Summary worksheet (available online; see the appendix for the link); you can, of course, add to and customize the worksheet to fit your organization's needs and interests. The information on this worksheet will help you decide whether the possible grant is a good fit for your organization and what your next steps should be.

Fundraising Worksheet 8: Grant Priorities Summary Chart

Clients or issue to be served: _____

_____

_____

_____

_____

Greater goal being pursued: _____

_____

_____

_____

_____

_____

Minimum useful grant amount: $_____

Geographic area served or covered: _____

_____

_____

_____

Any unacceptable restrictions: _____

_____

_____

_____

_____

Any unacceptable sources of funds: _____

_____

_____

_____

_____

TIP

Don't hide what your nonprofit is really doing. Occasionally, you may be able to get around funders' limitations by casting what you're doing in a different light. However, if you have to resort to hiding part of your activities or mission to get a grant, it will backfire. Even if you get the grant, the grantmaking community is a tight one—and if your transgression is discovered, word will spread quickly.

Most of the information on this worksheet is self-explanatory. Taking a look at the funder's application deadlines and schedule for answers will also help you decide whether the grant prospect fits into your annual fundraising plan. You're likely to wait three or four months for an answer to your proposal, but some funders can take up to a year—which is a problem if you were counting on this grant to fill a particular, more immediate need. Also, not all funders set specific application deadlines—some accept applications on a rolling basis. However, they're likely to make decisions at one of their board meetings. Therefore, if you can find out when their upcoming board meetings are, you can put yourself in the best position by submitting your proposal two to three months in advance of that date.

The entry regarding similar grants given to other organizations is there as a reality check. No matter what the grantor says it wants to fund, the grants it has actually made tell the real story, helping you interpret what it means by generalized phrases like "vocational training" or "leadership development." For example, a foundation that says it funds environmental projects may really be interested only in water issues or forests. Part of your job is to find out the funder's unspoken, internal guidelines.

Public Information About Grants and Funders

Researching grant opportunities isn't difficult. A number of nonprofit-support organizations and public libraries are dedicated to assisting nonprofits, and the Internet holds a wealth of helpful information.

The Foundation Center (www.fdncenter.org, and in the process of merging with Guidestar and changing its name to "Candid") offers lots of helpful funder information. It has branches offering classes and resources in Atlanta, Cleveland, New York, San Francisco, and Washington, DC, and affiliate relationships with hundreds of "cooperating collections," so chances are that information is available near you. Many of these centers offer personal or group orientation sessions to help you best use their research materials. Or, here's some of the best of what's on the Internet, for free or by subscription:

- **The Chronicle of Philanthropy,** at www.philanthropy.com. A limited number of articles are posted for free, but you must subscribe to the print or online version to see the remaining articles and access its grants database.
- **The Foundation Center,** (by Candid), at www.fdncenter.org. This website pulls together much of what you'll need—substantive advice, research studies, and, by subscription, the *Foundation Directory Online.*
- **Grants.gov,** at www.grants.gov. This U.S. government website lists available federal grants.
- **Guidestar,** (by Candid), at www.guidestar.org. This offers information on all kinds of nonprofits, foundations included. You'll need to register and pay for the advanced search capabilities.
- **The Grantsmanship Center,** at www.tgci.com. By subscribing to Grant Domain you can access a database of foundation, corporate, and federal grantmakers.
- *The Philanthropy Journal* at www.philanthropyjournal.org contains news about foundation grand awards, and recent tips about fundraising trends and other nonprofit issues.
- The *Federal Register's* **Notices of Funding Availability** (federal grants only). The *Federal Register,* which is printed daily and is available at many main larger public libraries, is available online at www.federal register.gov. Unfortunately, reading it every day is hardly practical— you're more likely to find out about good opportunities through other sources, such as a nonprofit-related newsletters, magazines, or listservs.

Information From Funders

Your next research step is to get a look at the foundation or agency's annual reports and grant guidelines. With all but the smallest foundations, you can go online to view and download them.

Fundraising Worksheet 9: Grant Prospect Summary

Basic Information

Foundation/funder's name and address: _____

_____

Foundation's stated mission and purpose: _____

_____

Contact person: _____

Contact person's telephone, email: _____

Names and titles of other staff members: _____

_____

_____

Names of board members and trustees: _____

_____

_____

_____

Total grants made annually: $_____

Eligibility Information

Grant subject matter: _____

_____

Grant eligibility requirements: _____

Geographical limitations: _____

_____

Other limitations: _____

_____

Maximum grant amount: $_____

Funding duration: _____

"Good Fit" Indicators

Other organizations that have received grants for similar work (name the organization(s), list how much received and for what work): _____

_____

_____

_____

Typical grant amount: $_____

Limitations on overhead/administrative costs: _____%

Prospects for grant renewal: _____

Special considerations: _____

Application Process

First steps: ☐ query letter ☐ full proposal

Printed application form or guidelines: ☐ available ☐ obtained

Next application deadline(s) (if any): _____

Board meeting dates: _____

_____

Likely to hear answer by: _____

Research Trail

Have checked:

☐ Website

☐ Directories (name them):

☐ Form 990

☐ Annual report

The annual reports are useful not only to get a sense of the foundation's personality, but also to find out what programs the foundation is proud to have funded in the past. Many reports present useful lists of every group funded, including the amount of the grant and a brief description of its purpose.

The funder's grant guidelines will provide more detail than secondary sources about the foundation or government agency's eligibility requirements, funding priorities, types of projects funded (for example, new or pilot projects, research or direct services only), submission requirements, and timelines for decisions.

> **TIP**
> **Revisit the funder's website regularly.** Requirements and opportunities may change overnight. The funder's website will be your most up-to-date source of information—short of personal conversations with the grantmakers (covered next).

After you've researched funders through the various sources described above, you should have some good information on your most likely grant prospects. For the hottest prospects, create files containing your summary worksheets, notes, and any application materials or other information and instructions.

Make Personal Contact With Funders

As perfect a match as your organization and the funder seem to be on paper, any experienced fundraiser will tell you that there is always more to the story. Your next step is to attempt to make telephone or personal contact with a decision maker within the foundation or other funder's office.

Now is where the real detective work begins. That "Contact person's telephone, email" entry on your summary worksheet is probably still blank. And for good reason: Grants officers could spend all of their days and nights talking to people seeking funds—most of them for proposals that will never get off the ground. While there are exceptions, many foundations are about as accessible as a 14th-century fortified castle.

It may take perseverance and even a little luck to get the needed phone number. First, get a list of the foundation's grant officers and board members, and circulate it among your staff and board. If your people know anyone on the list, that can be your critical link. As you gain experience in the development world, every conference, meeting, or special event will be an opportunity for you to meet people who work for foundations or colleagues who can tell you the right person to call or email. Never think of this as just a preliminary step to your "real" work—making contacts and establishing relationships is your real work. There's no need to be surprised, or worried, if you spend large amounts of time on it.

> **EXAMPLE:** Iris, a development director, is looking for funding for a needle exchange program—never an easy sell. She spends part of one morning reading her email listservs and the *Chronicle of Philanthropy*. Though much of the information doesn't help her, she does notice that Dave, a program officer at an area foundation that has previously funded her organization, has moved to a large foundation—and because it works in health areas, the new foundation is on Iris's prospect list. Unfortunately, Dave is now in charge of grants for children's issues. Iris starts by calling someone she knows at Dave's old job to get his new number. She gives Dave a call, schmoozes a little, and then pops the key question: "Who's the best one to talk to about our needle exchange program?" Dave suggests Iris talk to Radhika, and gives Iris her direct line number. Bingo. And because Dave thinks Iris and her organization do good work, he volunteers to pave the way with Radhika. A couple of days later, Iris has a cordial conversation with Radhika, learns how to structure the grant to meet several explicit and not-so-explicit foundation guidelines, and eventually receives funding.

Sometimes the first person you get on the phone may be an administrative support person or a receptionist. Don't treat this person as a low-level gate-keeper (though gatekeeping might indeed be part of his or her role). Your goal is to develop a long-term relationship with this and every other person in the foundation. Support staffers can be invaluable contacts later—for example, if you have a last-minute question, or need to know whether your proposal arrived by the deadline. In addition, if you needlessly alienate these frontline folks, your organization may develop a reputation for rudeness—one you never find out about, but that may come back to haunt you.

As shown in the example above, knowing a friend or colleague of a foundation staff person can often be your password to a constructive conversation. This isn't simple nepotism (although sometimes it can also be that), but a reflection of the fact that all funders operate, at least in part, on trust. They don't want to spend their time—or, further down the line, a chunk of their foundation's money—or anything other than a legitimate, responsible organization.

Look Solid, But Needy

In any interaction with funders, consider what kind of impression you want to make. First and foremost, you want them to realize that you're a solid operation—not one that will take their money and patch up a few holes in your circus tent before folding it up and leaving town. On the other hand, you want them to know that you genuinely need the grant.

The first requirement is the harder to prove, because it depends partly on intangibles and things beyond your control, like your organization's reputation both on the street and behind the closed doors of the funding community. However, some things that will help bolster your professional and dependable appearance include:

- communications materials (such as an annual report and a brochure)
- audited financial statements
- newspaper articles quoting or describing your organization
- a relatively up-to-date, engaging website (see Chapter 11), and
- letters of recommendation from past funders.

In your narrative, refer to evidence of your organization's good reputation, steady income, and staying power, such as "Our core funders, who include [*name*] and [*name*], have been supporting us for [*number*] years."

Demonstrating that you need the money is the easier part. What nonprofit couldn't use three or four times the amount it has? To distinguish your group, focus not on your abject need, but on how the foundation's funding will help your group meet a documented community need. If possible, also try to show how the grant will fill a particular project gap—something along the lines of "We have everything in place to make this a go except $_____ ." The bottom line is, you want to appear to be the most effective program to accomplish a goal that the funder strongly supports.

💡 TIP

What if foundation guidelines prohibit phone calls? In most cases, this rule really means that the foundation doesn't want unsolicited phone calls from strangers. If you've already done your detective work, preferably have been referred by a trusted intermediary, and have some real questions to ask, by all means give it a try—or at least send an email. If the person hangs up on you, it won't set your group back (as long as you take the rejection graciously). In the case of some large or institutional foundations, however, they may really mean "No phone calls." Jennifer Castner, director of The Altai Project, says, "As head of a small nonprofit, I try to think of this as a way they put grantseekers on an equal footing with one another. I may have no more access to such foundations than the head of a charity that's a household word!"

If one of your staff or board members knows someone at a funder's office, he or she may be the best person to make the initial call. Your ED is the next best bet. The development director is a reasonable choice too, but some grantmaking officers will take the ED more seriously.

The initial conversation should be brief and to the point: "Hello, my name is [*your name*]. Your colleague [*name*] suggested that I call you. I'm the [*your position*] with [*name of your organization*], and I'd like to talk with you a bit about our [*name of your program*]." Your opener shouldn't last longer than a minute. If the officer seems harassed or perhaps even hostile, ask if there is a better time for you to call. Assuming your initial verbal sally is well received, give a very brief overview of your program's purpose and goal—making sure to convey your enthusiasm about it. Then ask your specific questions. This should break the ice with all but the stuffiest grants officers.

If you can get the grants officer chatting, you have done your job. Remember, you're not applying for a grant on the spot. You'll rarely get an outright "no" to funding over the phone, unless your program doesn't fall within the foundation's guidelines, in which case now is the best time to find out. One of the good things about starting with a telephone call is that the person you're talking to probably doesn't have enough information to justify telling you that funding is impossible. By the same token, because a written proposal (or even a query letter, discussed under "The Proposal Process, From Query Letter Onward," below) is very easy to reject, calling first is a great way to introduce your request—and help ensure that it will receive some consideration once you submit it more formally.

If the conversation goes well, you and the officer might agree to meet, or you might be asked to submit a query letter. Meetings are usually held at the foundation offices, though in rarer cases the officer might start with a site visit. If you've got an exciting chance for the officer to come view what your organization is doing—such as Save The Bay's canoe outings, discussed in Chapter 6—this may even be a good time to extend the invitation (depending on the tenor of your conversation, of course). If you are invited to the foundation's offices, it's best for two people to go—a funding person, such as the ED, development director, or a board member, and a program person, who can describe how the funding will be used. This isn't much different from meeting with an individual supporter, as discussed in Chapter 6. You'll want to bring along written materials, such as your organization's brochure, annual report, project description, and budget.

At any meeting, whether at lunch, your program site, or the funder's office, you'll want to spend a fair amount of time listening. Try to find out what the grants officer's interests are, where he or she sees the greatest community needs, what types of program successes the officer gets particularly excited about, and the like.

Also, remember that the officer probably doesn't have the last word on funding your organization (unless he or she is a senior officer and your grant application is small). If you submit a proposal and the officer likes it, he or she will probably have to present it to the foundation board or at least to a director for approval. This isn't entirely a bad thing; a foundation staff person who agrees to support your proposal will likely coach you on how to present it to the board.

At the end of your meeting with foundation staff, you may be invited to submit a proposal. By now, you understand that this is not your first step, but a milestone on your way to your goal. Even if you're told, "This isn't quite right for us," ask whether you can get in touch in a year or so to see whether your program needs have become a better match for their funding opportunities.

Keep Records on Prospective Funders

Your research process should be ongoing. Starting with the information you gather to submit your first proposals, you'll want to build a system that not only tracks the foundations that fund you, but also profiles those most likely to do so in the future.

Any time you read something of interest in the *Chronicle of Philanthropy* or your email listservs—such as a new grants officer, a new program focus, or a particular grant made to another organization—create a record whether on paper or digitally. Similarly, if you attend a social event and meet someone from a foundation on your A-list or someone who has relevant information about it, promptly enter all relevant facts in your database.

Over time, this attention to detail will help you develop an insider's view of your funding prospects and put you in a better position to plan and execute a targeted fundraising strategy.

As part of this process of keeping current, do your best to maintain cordial relationships with grants officers—even those who haven't yet funded you! Jim Lynch of TechSoup Global tells the following story: "I had developed a phone contact with an officer at the Crocker Foundation. Every year, I called to ask what they had going, and every year, the officer told me that it wasn't a good fit. Finally, one year I called, and something did fit—and we got the grant! I think the officer was partly relieved to be able to give me some good news for once. All this had happened without the two of us having met. But when we finally did meet, we fell on each other like long-lost friends."

The Proposal Process, From Query Letter Onward

Lest you get overwhelmed by all the details of the grant application process, this section leads you through it step by step. Depending on the foundation's guidelines and preferences, your path to funding will probably include some combination of the following:

- a query letter
- a written grant proposal

- a site visit
- a presentation or meeting with the funder, and
- grant approval.

Query Letters

A query letter is often the first written communication between you and the funder (particularly if you're dealing with a foundation rather than the government). Other names for a query letter are "letter of interest" or "letter of inquiry." The letter's purpose is to give the recipient foundation a quick sense of who you are and what you're seeking, and to find out whether you should take the next step in the proposal process. A sample query from a fictional organization is provided below.

Many foundations require you to submit a query (often online) as the first step in the funding process. In some instances, as discussed earlier in this chapter, the grants officer may have asked you to submit a query. And, of course, there may be times when you have tried but failed to make personal contact and decide to send a query as your next-best alternative.

Find out whether the foundation publishes guidelines for the query letter (on its website or in its printed guidelines) or has already created an online submission format. If not, don't worry: Query letters are short (one to three pages) and follow a fairly standard format.

But even within the expected or required format, you can and should write a letter that inspires the foundation and grants officer to ask for more information. Don't hold back good material to include as a "surprise" in the full grant proposal. Unless you highlight your best points in your query, you probably won't be invited to submit a full proposal.

The key elements of a query are:

- **Your purpose.** In the opening paragraph, give your organization's name and an overview of the reason for your letter: namely, to seek a particular amount of funding for a purpose or project that you briefly describe. Don't be coy—they are funders, and they expect people to ask for money. And don't beat around the bush when explaining why your proposal fits within the funder's mission and guidelines—explain directly how your project will help the funder further its own goals. You will also briefly want to establish that your organization will be able to accomplish the proposed project. To do this, it's helpful to mention the names and qualifications of key project staff. If someone in the foundation knows your organization and thinks well of it, this is also worth mentioning.

- **Who you are.** In the next paragraph, briefly describe your organization's mission, history, and current programs. Your focus should be on establishing your organization's credentials, in particular its ability to identify and meet community needs. If prominent board members have helped drive your efforts, mention their names.

- **Who or what needs your help.** Here you get to the heart of the matter: the community need that your organization seeks to address. Find the most powerful way to establish that a need exists, whether by statistical data, vivid examples, or both. Be precise about the who, what, and where of those you'll be serving, always looking for ways to tie your project to the foundation's purposes and the people it hopes to serve.

- **How you'll help.** Present a detailed and convincing account of what you'll be doing and how it will meet the stated community need. Explain how you'll measure the project's success. If you haven't already done so, this is a good place to include names and titles of the main project staff, who will bring your project to fruition.

- **Other supporters.** If you've gotten commitments from other grantors or donors, mention them here. You might also mention who else you'll be approaching for support.

- **A wrap-up.** Briefly recapitulate the goal of the project. If possible, mention a few new facts, such as planned future steps or mutual contacts, and thank the potential funder for considering your request.

The letter should preferably be signed by your organization's executive director or board chairperson. Don't include attachments unless the foundation's guidelines request them.

Sample Query Letter

Oakland African-American History Project
123 1st Street, Oakland, California

March 18, 20xx

The California Historical Foundation
321 6th St.
San Francisco, California 95123

Dear Ms. Officer:

I'm writing to you at the suggestion of your colleague Bob Everbuddy, who is familiar with our work at the Oakland African-American History Project. Our organization has, since 1995, taken the lead in collecting and cataloging the personal histories and documents of Oakland's African-American community. We are particularly interested in African-American migration to California during the late 1800s, when many came to work for the railroads. Our organization is currently seeking $65,000 to support a new project—interviewing the children of this migratory generation to preserve their oral histories, before their generation also passes into history. Given your foundation's special interest in collecting histories of California's diverse communities, we ask you to consider a full proposal for support of this project.

Our organization's mission is to preserve Oakland's African-American history, for the education of future generations as well as the inspiration of its existing African-American community. The enthusiasm and commitment of our board members, including such community luminaries as [names], helps drive all our efforts.

We pay special attention to getting young people involved in our projects. In fact, a component of this new project will be to work with schools, churches, and youth groups to locate and train high-school-age volunteers to help out. With the historical information we collect, our staff and volunteers regularly prepare photo brochures and catalogs and maintain an educational website. However, we do not keep the collected materials at our offices, but rather place them with Oakland's public libraries and museums to ensure that they are preserved and made widely accessible to the public.

Without oral history projects such as the one we propose, personal perspectives on historical events are often lost forever. In fact, as earlier mentioned, we must act quickly to preserve the memories of the remaining members of this aging population. Our research specialist, Stella Amanuensis, Ph.D., has collected the names of over 30 potential interviewees, and believes there are at least as many

Sample Query Letter (continued)

more out there. However, the average age of these interviewees is 78 years, and some have significant health problems. In addition, the project will serve a secondary community need—to excite African-American high-school-student volunteers about their community's history, and train them in historical research methods. Studies have shown that Oakland's high school students perform poorly in history as compared to other courses and seldom study history in college.

Our plan is to have our staff and volunteers visit each interviewee at least three times, spending 90 minutes per visit. They will ask the interviewees questions about their early home life, stories their parents told them about where the family came from and why they left, family traditions and recreation, basic household economic issues, such as what they ate, when and how they bought or made clothes, how many people shared living space, and more. We'll also focus on the steps migrants took to forge new community ties within the Oakland area and how these ties have developed or changed over the years.

By the end of the project, we intend to have trained at least ten volunteers, met with at least 35 interviewees, recorded the interviews digitally, and transcribed the interviews into hardcopy for public reading. We also plan to publish a paperback book containing photos and excerpts from the various interviews.

The $65,000 we intend to request from The California Historical Foundation will cover staff salaries, recording equipment, and promotion and incidental expenses associated with finding and visiting interviewees. In addition, we have a commitment of $5,000 from a board member to allow our ten most committed volunteers to attend a special oral history training seminar at a local college. A local printer has also agreed to produce the final publication at no cost.

Our proposed project has both present and future benefits. In the short term, it will teach the student volunteers important research skills, help them understand and take pride in their place in history, and bring them in touch with an older generation. In the long term, it will gather important information about a critical time in African-American history and make it available for this and future generations. Thank you for your interest in our project. We look forward to hearing from you.

Very truly yours,

Carter Pastime

Carter Pastime
Executive Director

Grant Proposals

The next step in the process—or, in rare cases, the first step—is to submit a full grant proposal. A proposal usually contains a written narrative explaining who your organization is, the project for which it seeks funds, and the reasons why the project is important and will succeed. This narrative will be backed up by a budget, proof of your 501(c)(3) status, and other relevant attachments.

By this time, you should have checked (and rechecked) the funder's guidelines. These will specify the format, length, content, and documentation required.

Unless the foundation in which you're interested wants (old-fashioned) paper proposal submissions, you may not be able to see the full application form yet. Most foundations (especially the larger ones) require that proposals be submitted online. But as Susan Messina, Deputy Director at Iona Senior Services in Washington, DC (www.iona.org) has found, "Some online submission portals are intuitive and easy to use, while others still pose barriers, such as not being able to save as you go, or to see the whole application before starting to fill it in. In the former case, you'll need to get everything ready in advance to submit it at one go. In the latter, you might have to put in placeholder answers in order to advance to the next section."

 TIP

Does that maximum character count include spaces? For online, "fill-in-the-box" proposal submissions, you'll obviously want to prepare the text separately, ahead of time. But don't make the mistake that some proposal writers have, and count only the number of word characters, not realizing that the system may count spaces as characters, too. (Some funders will make this clear in advance, others won't; and some systems don't count spaces anyway.) And whatever you do, don't use the old typewriter convention of putting two spaces between sentences—one is fine and normal.

Use the information that follows to help:
- Use the right tone and style.
- Respond to all requests for information.
- Polish your final draft and compose a cover letter.

Writing Style

Clear, communicative writing is important in almost every fundraising endeavor, but it's especially crucial when drafting grant proposals. Here are some tips to keep in mind:

- **Know what you want to say before you begin.** A surprising number of organizations whip out grant proposals without any sense of the program or project they're proposing. But, as Susan Messina puts it, drawing on her consulting experiences, "People forget that it's a two-step process; first you plan, then you write. Often, I've been handed a proposal project where I had to go back to the organization and work with them on the details of program planning."

- **Remember that there's a human being at the other end.** In your effort to respond to the foundation's guidelines and to set a professional tone, it's easy to write a proposal that reads like a master's thesis and is just as turgid. Your audience is a real person who will surely appreciate it if you convey the passion and conviction you feel about your organization's work. This person wants, above all, to be inspired and moved—something that's easiest to accomplish if you are able to write directly and clearly (but still within the guidelines).

- **Convey authority.** In addition to writing convincing and moving prose, you must also demonstrate that your organization can handle a seemingly overwhelming task. Try drawing the reader deep into the world your organization understands best. For example, if your work consists of assisting people in administrative hearings to claim disability benefits, make sure that the reader understands the expertise you've developed in analyzing doctors' reports, interpreting Social Security regulations, and coaching the applicants in preparation for their hearings. Also show your organization's business acumen—even using some business vocabulary may help show that your organization has a well-thought-out plan for success, understands how it stacks up against the competition, and is prepared to make good and efficient use of the funder's investment.

- **Use their jargon.** Every funder has its favorite words—ones like "authentic," "outcomes," or "personal empowerment"—chosen because the meanings resonate for it. No need to confuse the issue by substituting your own words. It's a good idea to identify the funder's key words and echo them back within your proposal—just don't overdo it, and always use the words in their proper context.

These tips may at times seem contradictory. But the beauty of writing is that you can, with a little practice, weave many strands of thought together into a cohesive and convincing whole. In the words of Marisa Lianggamphai, formerly of WID, "The more personal, yet professionally conversational I can make the proposal, the more likely I am to reach someone."

TIP

Find a good editor. There's not a writer in the world whose words can't use improving or who will catch every last typo, ambiguity, or other glitch. Leave time for a talented writer within your organization, or even a freelancer, to review and edit your draft proposal.

Responding to the Standard Application Questions

A grant proposal may remind you of a college application, with questions that require you to write mini essays. Fortunately, as you gain experience, you'll see that most funders ask for similar information, which allows you to reuse good material you've written in the past. In fact, some funders use a so-called "common grant application," the format of which may have been developed on a statewide or local basis.

Funders usually ask for:
- a title page and table of contents
- an executive summary
- a background statement and/or list of your organization's qualifications
- a statement of community need
- a description of your project's grand goals or purposes
- a description of the project's more immediate objectives
- an action plan or project description
- a timeline
- an explanation of the methods by which you'll evaluate the project's success

- a budget (sometimes with line item explanations)
- an explanation of where future funding will come from, and
- various attachments containing the facts necessary to convincingly back up your assertions.

CAUTION

Don't get bogged down on the introductory sections. According to Susan Messina, "The Number One mistake I've seen my nonprofit clients make is spending way too much time writing the perfect statement of who they are and what they've done. These issues are important, but what you really need is a program plan that makes sense, an evaluation plan that's rigorous, and a budget that's detailed and complete. These can be much harder than describing how fabulous you are as an organization."

Title Page and Table of Contents

The title page normally lists basic information like your organization's contact information and the project title. Give your project a name that's short and catchy, but still descriptive. The table of contents simply lists the various headings and page numbers.

Executive Summary

The executive summary should outline all the key segments of your proposal, from background about your organization and a clear statement of the good work you hope to do, to your proposed solution. The summary shouldn't be more than two paragraphs long. You may even be able to use language from your query letter.

Background and Qualifications

Here's where you show that your organization is the best one for the job. Your mission, history, major programs, reputation, receipt of awards, and particular strengths may all be worthy of mention. If your organization has been around for a long time, emphasize its experience and ability to weather the tests of time. If your group is relatively new, emphasize how innovative, exciting, and responsive to current needs it is. Also name the key players in your organization and describe their qualifications, interests, and experience. For example, if your new ED just came on board after running a similar and noteworthy program in another part of the country, be sure to mention it. Even your physical facilities may be worth a mention—a state-of-the-art research boat, learning lab, or health clinic, for example.

This can also be a good place to mention where you fit in with the "competition"—that is, with other organizations doing similar work. Funders will be most interested if you don't present your competition as groups to be elbowed out, but as worthy organizations working in slightly different niches.

CAUTION

Never badmouth another nonprofit. Even if some of your competitors don't produce high-quality results, you have little to gain by pointing this out—except perhaps a reputation as a backstabber. If a competitor really is doing poor work, funders will figure it out fast enough on their own.

Statement of Community Need

The section on community need provides an excellent opportunity to establish your organization's professionalism. Though the community need may seem very real and obvious to you, it's probably much less so to a busy foundation officer inundated by other "crucially needed" funding proposals. In short, you'll want to describe exactly what the need is—and what the consequences are of not acting promptly to meet it.

One way to do this is to run all your statements through the "so what?" test. For example, "There are no suicide prevention hotlines in our city" may seem like an important need to you—but a "so what?" skeptic might ask whether such hotlines actually make a difference or whether callers can simply use national hotlines instead. So, to really rivet the funding officer's attention, take your explanation one step deeper, and express the need like this: "Citizens of River City who might call the suicide hotline we hope to establish have absolutely no other 24-hour access to this highly effective method of suicide prevention. As a result, many deaths will occur that our program could help avoid."

Statistics, results of reliable studies, other information from neutral sources, and your own organization's surveys should all be assembled and presented concisely and coherently to support your assertion of need. Depending on the funder's guidelines, you may want to add charts or graphs within the text or as attachments at the end.

Especially if yours is a local or regional organization, finding recent and appropriate statistics can be a challenge. But with a little imagination, you can usually patch together credible numbers. For example, if you're working to straighten out drug-involved youth, it may be impossible to say how many kids abuse drugs in your area. But you can find out the number of teenagers in your area and the percentage who didn't complete high school, which is a significant indicator of drug-related problems. To this, you might add the percentage of kids in the country as a whole (and possibly in your state) who regularly use drugs and perhaps a quote from a local high school principal pointing out that local teenage drug use is a serious problem.

If no numerical or statistical information is available, you'll have to fill this section in with more anecdotal material—but make a note to ask your program leadership to put more effort into finding ways to quantify the need for your services for future proposals.

RESOURCE

The U.S. Census is still one of the best sources of statistical information. Check it out at www.census.gov.

Project Goals or Purposes

The purpose or goal of your project should be presented broadly and optimistically. To do so, answer this question—if all goes well, what will our organization have achieved? For example, "reduce teen drug addiction" is a goal or purpose; "provide counseling" is not. Don't get too lofty, however. While working to save Riverfront County's historical buildings is a measurable and realizable goal, "saving the world" is neither. Also make sure your goals are consistent with your mission statement.

Objectives

In your "objective" statement, you tell the funder exactly what you plan to use its grant money to accomplish. Objectives should be tangible and should include numerical targets and other signs of success. An example might be "provide job training and counseling that helps 40 developmentally disabled youth develop and market their skills."

In picking hard numbers, it's well to follow the old adage "underpromise and overperform." For example, if you were to say, "provide job training and counseling that results in 40 developmentally disabled youth's finding jobs," you may have given your program staff an impossible task, especially if the job market turns sour. Ask your program staff to carefully review the objectives section of your proposal to make sure you have chosen realistic milestones that will also satisfy the funder.

Another reason to beware of choosing overly optimistic numerical goals is that they can actually result in your organization's taking on only the "easy" cases, because the tougher ones are less likely to show measurable results. I know this trap all too well, from my experience working at a nonprofit that helped immigrants. Our clients included people who'd fled persecution in many of the world's most violent regions. To stay alive, they needed to obtain political asylum in the United States. We could never predict how many cases would be granted—that depended on multiple factors, such as how talkative and convincing an often traumatized client was, whether a doctor could confirm the client's experience of torture and other mistreatment, and the attitudes and prejudices of the immigration officer who decided the case. Yet, until we got wise to dealing with objectives, our promises to some funders included "political asylum gained for ten clients," and the like. If we had succeeded in only seven cases as we neared the end of the funding year, the pressure was on to find at least three more likely winners.

Some funders will accept outcome measurements based simply on your organization's carrying out the steps in its action plan—for example, giving five workshops or meeting with 50 clients. Others will insist that your outcomes relate to your overall goals, such as protecting a natural resource, establishing a cultural center, or opening a recreational facility for elderly veterans. Even in these latter cases, however, a little creativity may yield a way to style your outcomes conservatively. In the job training for developmentally challenged youth example, you might promise to serve 40 youth, but predict job placement for only 20 of them. Incidentally, we eventually followed a similar approach with our immigrant services project, by explaining to one funder that our goal was to take on a certain number of the most challenging cases requiring such a high level and investment of legal expertise that the clients probably would likely be rejected elsewhere. By first establishing the difficulty of our task, we were then able to show that the number of people served and the number of cases won were impressive.

TIP

You can promise more results than the funder's money will cover.
Many projects have multiple funders, or include money or in-kind contributions from individuals. If you're in this situation, never hesitate to set projected outcome at the total project level, not just for the donor's portion. Funders will be pleased to see that you plan to enhance the bang for their buck.

Action Plan or Methods

The action plan (also called the "methods" section) is the most fun part of the proposal. Here, you get to bring your organization's work to life. Explain what activities your organization has chosen, and why and when it plans to meet its goals and objectives. Don't forget to mention behind-the-scenes aspects of the work, like staff training or client selection.

The "what" and "when" of your work are the easiest, because these will summarize your daily activities, such as establishing curricula, planning field trips, mounting events, and explaining how staff will interact with clients or the public. If you aren't asked to include a project timeline elsewhere, you'll also want to fit that in here.

For the "why" of your activity, avoid repeating the old "need plus your project equals success" equation. Instead, explain why your chosen approach was elected over other possibilities. For example, if you've found that your antibullying project works best if you arrange group sessions with the children away from the school campus, explain this. This helps show your organization's expertise and thoughtful approach. Also, be sure to give the project staff credit for any challenges they've learned to overcome—past failures can be advertised as important learning experiences! Make your plan sound effective without making it sound easy.

Timeline

You'll no doubt be asked for a project timeline, whether in a separate section or as part of the action plan. This is fairly self-explanatory. Don't feel that you have to wrap the project up by the end of the funding cycle, but be prepared to say what you will have achieved by that time and what milestones you expect to reach along the way.

Outcome Evaluation Methods

Providing a solid explanation of how you'll evaluate the results of your project affords you another chance to set your organization apart from the rest. Foundations are used to a certain "flake factor" in this area—a mushiness about accounting for results. They also know that many nonprofits regard data collection as a bothersome task that's imposed upon them by foundations. This means that if you can propose a serious and effective system of project evaluation and outcome reporting, you are likely to really impress your readers.

Unfortunately, it's not easy to achieve tight, accurate evaluation and reporting. Nonprofits tackle some of the toughest, most intractable problems in society. They're not like businesses that can tell their shareholders, "We sold 400,000 wombits, hired 200 new workers, and increased profits by 200%!" So how do you shine in this tough endeavor? If you've been realistic in establishing objectives, your task of evaluating the project as a success will be easier—but may at the same time be labor intensive, because you'll likely have to do more than just present raw numbers of people fed, books read, or acres of land preserved.

Creating methods for evaluating your projects will require input and cooperation from program staff. It's not something that you, as the proposal writer, can simply dream up. But working together, and depending to some extent on what your organization does, you usually will want to choose from a couple of broad evaluation methods.

One is to keep the focus on what you did, reporting on numbers of people served or tasks accomplished. If you adopt this approach, you shouldn't have too much trouble developing a systematic and reliable method of data gathering.

Your other main evaluation alternative is to focus more subjectively, by trying to answer the question, "How did we do?" This could involve as simple a method as passing out evaluation forms to your clients, trainees, or participants in activities. If, for example, you go to high schools and show an antismoking videotape, the funder may be less interested in how many kids sat (or slept) in a darkened classroom than in how they reacted to your message.

Of course, you can, and often should, mix and match numerical and judgmental evaluation methods, as appropriate. For example, the funder would certainly be interested in knowing that you showed the videotape in more than one classroom, to more than one student.

Budget and Budget Narrative

The person reading your proposal is likely to turn to the budget section first. Never mind all your fancy explanations: It's the raw numbers that many of them feel tell the real story. Though you'll probably be asking for a nice round number, you'll have to show more precisely how you arrived at this figure and how this money will be spent.

Often the funder will provide a budget format. Usually, the breakdown will include salaries, office and other project supplies, and a miniscule amount for administrative overhead (often no more than 15%). Your project budget should reflect not only new expenses, but also existing costs for staff (at full time or a percentage of their time), supervision, office space, and so on.

If the funder to whom you're applying isn't going to be the project's only source of funds, list other prospective or actual grantors, as well as in-kind donations, such as volunteer time. Funders are always delighted to see that their financial input will be leveraged in these ways, especially if your individual donors will cover administrative expenses so that all foundation money can go directly to programs.

> **TIP**
>
> **Think big.** I asked the former head of one of America's most prestigious foundations what he considered to be a grant applicant's biggest mistake. "Asking for too little," he immediately responded. "Once you sell a foundation on the worthiness of your proposal and your ability to carry it out, it's only logical that most will want it to be bigger, not smaller."

I'm assuming that you are not your office's chief budgeteer, and that someone in the accounting department will actually run the numbers, after consultation with you and with program staff. Just be sure to give this person plenty of advance warning! And remember to consult with both your program staff and your accountant to arrive at a consensus about how much money is realistically required and what the numbers mean.

Many funders will ask not only for columns of numbers, but for a narrative explanation as well. Having consulted with program staff, you should be ready to do this in a way that brings your numbers to life for the potential funder. Along the way, be sure to explain any expenses that might seem unusual, and highlight any ways that you've managed to keep costs down. Keep it short: You don't need to rehash issues like the overall need for the project.

Future Funding Sources

Many funders want to make sure that they're not just going to create a bubble project—one that will burst as soon as its funding stops, without having achieved anything. And, given that renewals are anything but guaranteed (especially because foundations tend to favor new, innovative, start-up, or pilot projects), this should be a real concern for your organization as well. (The exception, of course, would be if you truly are proposing a project with a limited time span, such as restoring a community fountain.)

Hopefully your leadership has thought ahead about the sustainability of the project you're proposing and how it fits into your overall strategic plan.

Of course, you can hardly guarantee where this year's funding will come from, much less next year's. Your best bet when writing the proposal is to describe your carefully constructed development plan (see Chapter 3). You might also mention the development office's record of success—for example, that you've increased individual contributions in the past year or years and can project continued success in this area. If you can name particular funders that you believe are likely to fund the proposed project in the future, great—but don't just toss names around. More likely, you'll simply want to describe the types of funding, whether from foundations, individuals, or others, that you'll be trying to obtain.

Supporting Documents

Most funders will require supporting documents to accompany your grant proposal—at a minimum, a copy of the IRS letter proving your 501(c)(3) status. (For online submissions, be ready to make a lot of PDFs.) Don't wait until the last minute to look at the funder's requirements. For example, you may be surprised to find a requirement that you assemble names of influential people willing to serve on a project advisory committee, which can take weeks or months to accomplish. And, if you're applying to the federal government, the attachments will dwarf the narrative part of the grant proposal and require input from program staff and others.

You may also be permitted to attach documents of your own choosing. Your brochure and latest annual report may be relevant and helpful. Strong and convincing letters of support from funders, city officials, or other influential people can be particularly helpful. Such letters should describe your track record on past projects and express the letter writer's great confidence in your ability to carry out future projects. Depending on your field of work, you could also get letters of support from other figures of authority, such as someone in the administration of a hospital or school with which you're affiliated. Such letters won't arrive on your doorstep spontaneously—you'll have to ask for them. This is an accepted and traditional practice, however, so your friends and funders should not be surprised to hear from you. In fact, many of them will be pleased that you are applying for additional money to expand your programs.

Final Preparation and Cover Letter

The last few steps in preparing your grant proposal are too easily forgotten. First, run your final draft past the executive director and anyone else who needs to approve it (you certainly don't want to have to amend it after it's submitted). You'll also want to prepare a short, optimistic cover letter addressed to the appropriate program officer or other contact person, and typically signed by your ED. Refer to any past grants or positive history with the funder. Make sure that the letter indicates who in your organization the funder should contact for questions, follow-up, and its response. Provide that person's direct-line phone number and email address.

Though I could tell you to plan ahead so you won't be working on the proposal until the last possible minute, that's the sort of advice that rarely changes anyone's behavior (including my own). If you are able to get things in before the deadline, however, you've got an advantage—foundations think of the deadline as the "last possible day," not as a simple due date, and are delighted to have an opportunity to read a submission that comes in before the flood.

> CAUTION
>
> **Snail mail can be tough on lateniks.** If your proposal cannot be submitted online, find out the addresses and hours of all U.S. post offices, Federal Express locations, or other delivery offices well in advance.

Site Visits

A site visit is just what it sounds like—one or more people from the prospective funder's office schedule a visit to your program site to see for themselves what's going on. Usually this happens after your proposal has been received by the funder and gone through one or more layers of review. This is one of those "picture is worth a thousand words" opportunities— and it indicates that your proposal is under serious consideration.

Grant Din can testify to the great opportunity a site visit gives your organization: "Back when I worked as a grants officer at a foundation that had very limited funds, I well remember how heart-wrenching it was to say no to a good project after a site visit. Perhaps we weren't cutthroat enough, but we sometimes ended up giving out many small grants just to avoid rejecting a group outright. Do everything you can think of to get funders to visit!"

The site visit will be scheduled in advance. So don't worry that a black limo will pull up full of people wearing white gloves—you'll have time to plan. If possible, try to schedule the visit for a time when your organization is at its most active, seeing clients or engaging in field work. You want to give the visitor a hands-on experience, to the extent possible. Your chances of success go up if they can meet your clients, handle an art project, savor a tomato in your community garden, or do anything else that involves something other than talking to the ED and meeting board members. Remember, you've already engaged their minds with the grant proposal— now is the time to more fully engage their hearts.

If the most interesting work of your organization isn't at its central office, then take the visitors where the action is (unless it's a wilderness trek, a toxic dump site, or some other dangerous or messy spot).

Advise all program staff and any relevant clients of who's coming, and ask staff to tidy up their workspaces. Also ask staff members or clients to be ready to talk to the visitors about their activities and, if appropriate, to do a "show and tell" presentation—with the emphasis on "show."

But keep things low-key. The visitors want to see your site as it really functions, not turned into a theater. Foundation officers say that one of the biggest mistakes nonprofits make during site visits is putting on a big to-do rather than engaging in business as usual. Ron Rowell, retired program officer with the Common Counsel Foundation, once told me, "Having worked in the nonprofit sector myself, I understand the urge to stage things for the funders' benefit. But now that I'm in the foundation world, the most important thing to me at a site visit is honesty. If all I hear is that everything is just peachy, one success after another, I start to worry about what's really going on."

On the other hand, foundation officers tend to like it when the organization doesn't passively wait to be judged, but actively asks foundation officers what they're interested in, how their proposal can be improved, and so on. (In fact, if the site visit is conducted before your written proposal goes in, this is an ideal chance to pick up some tips on how to present the relevant information most effectively.)

When the visitors arrive, the executive director should take the lead in showing them around. Be ready to offer coffee or tea. Depending on how long they'll be staying, snacks or a light lunch might also be appropriate. Most site visits last from two to three hours.

> ### TIP
> **Out-of-town site visitors need extra attention.** Though they'll probably book airplane and hotel reservations on their own, prepare recommendations, plus tips on good restaurants and entertainment. There is usually no need to be a tour guide, but you might suggest or join in on dinner plans, if appropriate. Also, give any needed tips on transportation or getting to your facility.

Meetings With the Funder

Some funders will ask members of your organization to come to their offices for a formal presentation or question-and-answer session. Again, this is a good sign and a grand opportunity to put a human face on your work. Find out exactly who will be at the meeting—it may or may not be your main contact person. The United Way, for example, brings in "allocation volunteers" who help decide what gets funded. Though the volunteers are briefed beforehand, they'll require a lot more background and introductory information than a foundation staff person with whom you've been in contact for years.

Be careful in choosing who will represent your group at this meeting—the proposal will be judged, in part, by the personality of the person or persons attending. A foundation officer once told me that he was quicker to grant money to an average project with good leadership than to a great-sounding project with leaders who didn't inspire confidence.

Ironically, the development person who wrote the proposal may not be the best one to go along to this event, because foundations often regard development staff as hired-gun salespeople. A program person is usually the best choice—someone who is actually doing the work and can articulate, passionately and in colorful detail, what it involves.

If your program person isn't used to such activities, work together on organizing a short presentation, if one is required or expected. Often the program person takes the lead here, relating events from his or her own working experience: how a client was helped, how an arts project was received by the public, how a research project was undertaken, and so forth.

The Funding Decision

After more time than you'd probably like—usually from three months to a year after you submitted your proposal—you'll receive an answer. If months have passed and you haven't heard anything, it's okay to call your contact person to check in.

If the funding decision is negative, your ED may want to call and politely ask why. Not all foundations will be candid about why you were turned down, but if they are, it's important to listen carefully to the answers and not argue. Remember, a "no" doesn't mean you'll never be funded by a funder. It may be that your proposal didn't quite fit the mix of grants the foundation was trying to achieve or that it misinterpreted some element of your proposal for some reason that would never occur to you. Either way, be alert for information that will help you approach the funder next time.

If the decision is positive, congratulations! This is one of those moments that makes the stress and long nights of fundraising worthwhile. Be loud about your joy. Board members and staff can always use some good news and will be especially gratified if they had any hand in preparing the proposal. If it's a truly substantial grant or will fund something that's story-worthy, mention it on your website, Facebook page, and Twitter feed and consider trying to get local media coverage (see Chapter 11). The funder may be willing to help in this effort.

TIP

How about an independent review of your rejected proposal? That's what the Unfunded List will do for your organization for $100 if you're willing to see it featured publicly. See http://unfundedlist.com.

Don't forget to thank the funder! Many development pros make it a habit to send out a thank-you letter before even cashing the check. In addition, having your ED or board chair call the funder to say "thanks" offers a good opportunity to get feedback that may help you craft your follow-up reports. Try to solicit information about which part of your proposal was most persuasive and what could have been done to make it even better. There's no better time to get constructive feedback than when everyone is in a good mood.

TIP

If your overall funding falls short, try to renegotiate the terms of the grants. Nonprofits will often approach more than one foundation simultaneously, asking each to pitch in enough to reach the total needed for the project. However, if some foundations say "yes" and others "no" to your grant request, what do you do? It's rare that a nonprofit would have to decline the grant money in such circumstances. Your first choice is to ask the foundation or foundations who approved your request to grant a bit more to cover the shortfall. If that doesn't work, ask them to accept a scaled-down version of the project, or reduced outcomes.

Follow Up With the Funder

As you surely know, your grant work doesn't end when you deposit the check. All funders follow up to find out how their money has been spent and what results it has achieved. As soon as you've got the grant paperwork in hand, make sure that the people in your organization understand their role in this process.

Program people will typically need to track their activities and outcomes for progress reports or presentations. Your accounting department may need to track expenses, particularly if the funder operates on a reimbursement basis. Someone will have to set aside time on the calendar for drafting a progress report. Though these reports won't be as time-consuming as the initial grant proposal, they often ask for similar information.

If progress reports are to be drafted by a program person, make sure that a development staff person or the ED gives it a thorough review before it goes out. The object is to make sure that promises made in the grant proposal are being kept, or at least that there's an explanation for any changes to the action plan. It's also important that your organization speak with a consistent voice.

This required follow-up should not be pushed to the back burner. Maintaining strong and cordial relationships with funders is crucial. Not only are you more likely to get a grant renewal if your reports are well organized and timely, but demonstrating your ability to perform may also result in other benefits. For example, the foundation may feature your organization on its website or in its annual report. In addition, a foundation that sponsors donor-advised funds may recommend your organization to individual donors looking for a group that fits their philanthropical inclinations. And, last but not least, because funders talk to each other, your reputation can be burnished or tarnished on the basis of your follow-through.

Beyond just complying with the funder's reporting requirements, think of ways you can use your reports to increase its interest and involvement. Start by treating the contact person at the foundation as you would an important individual donor—who appreciates receiving the occasional update, positive news clipping about your work, or even an invitation to participate. For example, the Zen Hospice Project has invited foundation representatives to monthly donor lunches, informal events at which volunteer caregivers share their experiences before they tour the residential house. Also see "Women's Studio Workshop Uses Regular Letters to Reach Funders," below.

Women's Studio Workshop Uses Regular Letters to Reach Funders

The Women's Studio Workshop (WSW) is an artist's residency and educational program located in idyllic Rosendale, New York (in the Mid-Hudson River Valley). While WSW already provides visiting women artists with studio and living space in which to explore their voices and visions, its ambitions go beyond this—they'd like to routinely pay women a reasonable wage to come to WSW and do art. To this end, foundation funding has been an important resource. In particular, the Andy Warhol Foundation for the Visual Arts has offered WSW significant support.

As Anita Wetzel, development director, describes the course of WSW's relationship with the Warhol Foundation, "WSW had received a good-sized grant from Warhol in 1992. In 1998, a two-year award from the foundation helped us make a big leap forward, increasing the number of funded opportunities we could offer artists. In 2002, WSW received another two-year grant to fund artists working at WSW.

"Part of the reason we got the 2002 grant may have been that I'd been sending the Warhol Foundation and our other major funders regular letters—about once every three months—telling them what had been happening. For example, my letters might talk about an international artist spending time with us, or describe a session of the Arts-In-Education program, where kids from Kingston City Schools come and develop their art skills. In fact, the program officer remarked on the letters when she came to visit.

"It's funny, because no one ever told me to start writing these letters. Like many people, I happened into fundraising because I wanted to make our project happen. But I had come to realize that you need to reach out to anyone giving you a significant amount of money. And, I enjoy writing the letters—it's a chance to tell people what we think is interesting and important, instead of always just answering the questions on their required reports. Also, by writing regularly, I can highlight colorful information before we've moved on to the next project and forgotten the details."

TIP

While things are going well, ask for a letter of recommendation from your funder. It can be useful when you apply for other funding. The best time to ask for this is after you have submitted several progress reports detailing how you are successfully spending the funder's money.

Grant Renewals

Putting "renewals" in the title of this section is a bit misleading, because only a minority of foundation grants come with any expectation of renewal (or in nonprofit lingo, "re-upping" the grant). Many funders specifically prefer that after your one-, two-, or even five-year grant period is completed, you go elsewhere for subsequent funding. Nevertheless, having invested time and effort in educating the funder about your work, it's worth inquiring whether a new grant is a possibility.

Even though re-upping may be difficult to accomplish with a particular funder, it may nevertheless be easier than finding a new funding source. By now, you have the advantage of personal contact with someone in the funder's office. For a one-year grant, the time to bring this up is no longer than nine months into your grant, when things are hopefully going well but you're not yet desperate about how you'll continue. Have a frank talk with your contact person about whether the foundation might be interested in funding continuation of your program or another part of your activities.

The funder may require that your next proposal contain something new and different. (Be ready with some ideas before holding any conversations.) Finding or creating something new to propose can be tricky, especially if you provide ongoing services that don't culminate in anything. This is one of those times when you need to be especially wary of letting the funding stream determine the program—altering or expanding your services just to get a grant can lead to trouble down the line. But realize that not everything about your proposed activities needs to be new. The funder may be happy to support a new phase of your program, an increased focus on the needs of certain members of your clientele, a collaborative effort encompassing existing services, or a heightened need for your services due to new legislation or social or environmental pressures.

If the funder truly can't support your organization any longer, ask for recommendations to other funders. Don't forget to take down the names and telephone numbers of the contact people!

Integrating Nonprofit Communications Into Fundraising Efforts

Nonprofit supporters have come to expect (or dread) more communication from various organizations than ever. Email and social media have, after all, made regular sharing of images and information easy. Any nonprofit that isn't active in these spaces will find its voice drowned out by the many that are.

Strictly speaking, this isn't pure "fundraising." It's about keeping the public apprised of what your group is up to and getting people excited or outraged about the latest developments relevant to it. But regular communications definitely maintain supporters' receptivity to direct asks for funds. That's why as soon as a nonprofit gets beyond bare-bones staffing levels, it often hires people dedicated to managing communications and outreach.

Even if you have separate staff members handling communications, it's important that development office staffers are aware of their plans and activities. Coordination will help avoid conflicting or badly scheduled messages.

This chapter will take a look at the various forms of nonprofit communications and where they fit into the fundraising picture.

Printed Communication Materials

Every organization can use printed materials to educate the public about its mission and activities. Because these materials are not designed primarily as fundraising tools, they can have great credibility with current and potential supporters.

For starters, producing a high-quality brochure should be within the reach of virtually every nonprofit. Creating printed newsletters and annual reports can be useful as well, though far more time-consuming and costly. That's why many grassroots nonprofits create digital-only versions of such publications.

How a Newsletter Paid for Itself

Kate McNulty, then with Sacred Heart Cathedral Preparatory School, described this "happy ending" to the school's production of its newsletter. "We'd been putting out a newsletter to our donors reporting on how our capital campaign to fund the new Student Life Center was going. The newsletter itself cost a couple of thousand dollars to produce, and contained investor profiles, a construction report with photographs, and a fundraising update. After we sent a newsletter out, one of our major supporters took an interest in one of the naming opportunities we listed. He pledged $15,000, and in recognition the school put his name on one of its Campus Ministry Offices. He had been cultivated and asked earlier in the campaign for a gift, but it was the newsletter that clearly tipped the scales—and thereby paid for itself."

Brochures and Fundraising

If a prominent visitor or potential supporter asks for more information about your organization, will you be ready? A good brochure can explain:

- why your organization was founded and continues to exist (your basic mission, but spelled out in compelling language)
- what activities your organization currently carries out to address your mission
- your organization's hopes and plans for the near future
- how your organization is funded, and
- how readers can become involved or make contributions.

The classic brochure is an 8½" by 11" piece of paper folded into thirds, which gives you six panels to fill with text and graphics. It's even smarter to use an 8½" by 14" sheet of legal-sized paper folded into fourths, which creates eight panels. Either size allows you to turn the right-most panel into a tear-off reply or donation card. With the larger version, a professional can also attach a tear-off reply envelope.

Because you want your brochure to have a reasonably long shelf life, include only general information about your group. Avoid dates or detailed descriptions of time-specific projects that will soon be in your rear-view mirror. Instead, focus on continuing programs and long-term results.

Keep the text short and snappy—bold headings and bullet points will make your points far better than long-winded explanations. Photos are also an excellent way of giving readers an instant understanding and appreciation of your work.

The brochure is also a good place to provide key information for people who might need to contact or make use of your organization—perhaps your address and phone number, Web address, hours of operation, a map to your facilities, fees for services or admission, and the like.

 TIP

Hiring a freelance designer can be a bargain. A visually pleasing brochure will be far more attractive and effective than one that's thrown together without much thought or skill. In just a few hours, a freelance design professional can turn an amateurish effort into something you can be proud of.

Newsletters and Fundraising

Many nonprofits send out regular newsletters as a way to communicate with dues-paying members and, in some cases, potential members. (And many others have given up, convinced that no one reads the newsletters— which may be true, given how many nonprofit newsletters are utterly boring—unlike what yours will be, of course.) Downloadable, digital-only newsletters are becoming common, especially since the nonprofit's main cost is for design help. A well-crafted one can provide a series of ongoing tugs designed to pull donors toward deeper engagement with your organization.

Some organizations send their newsletter by both print and email and ask willing supporters to accept only emailed copies. But not everyone is necessarily ready for email-only newsletters. As JoLynn Taylor, former

Membership and Publications Manager at WildCare in San Rafael, California (www.wildcarebayarea.org), explained, "Many of our members don't want all the email! Besides, many of the people who receive our printed newsletter haven't yet shared their email addresses with us. Another advantage to the printed newsletter is that we can drop off free copies at various places around the county, which serves not only fundraising but educational purposes."

A printed newsletter can take many forms, but probably the most common consists of four or eight double-sided 8½" x 11" pages, sent out four times per year, containing photos and one to four substantive stories about your organization and its work. Wealthier organizations might produce a magazine, complete with a glossy cover.

> **TIP**
>
> **Your social media efforts need not undercut your newsletter.** Many nonprofits happily report that the ability to broadcast time-sensitive material via social networks serves as a handy pressure release valve. It means they no longer need to either sit on hot news until the newsletter goes out or try to hurry up the publication date before the news gets stale. Of course, you should still try to put newsy material into the newsletter, but you can go deeper, such as with opinion pieces or discussions of the impact of your group's work. Your social media postings are actually a great way to test what topics are of interest to your readership and might deserve a full newsletter article.

"The quality of your newsletter's content is more important than the frequency with which you send it," advises fundraising expert Eric Talbert. "Too many organizations make it all about the organization itself; 'We are great, our mission is fantastic.' I find that what works better are three or four short pieces addressed to 'you,' the reader, and containing stories of transformation or positive outcomes. These can then link to a longer article or blog on the organization's website. It helps to cover the same three general topics in each issue, so that readers learn what to expect. A university, for example, could include a message from its president, an alumni-related story, and an update on campus facilities."

While one person in your organization—or, if you can afford it, a cost-efficient freelancer—should edit your newsletter, writing the articles can be a fun and educational project for board members and other volunteers with the necessary skills.

If there are plans, projects, or emergencies that you've described in mailed appeals, a newsletter can be a good place to follow up. For example, if your donors were sent an emergency appeal for funds to deal with the aftermath of a flood, and your subsequent newsletter doesn't mention what happened next, your donors might lose interest in your stories, or even become suspicious that you exaggerated the emergency.

From a direct fundraising standpoint, your newsletter is also a good place to advise readers of upcoming special events and other opportunities to get involved. If warranted, you can include a tear-out or cut-out slip of paper to facilitate donations, and enclose a reply envelope.

Annual Reports and Fundraising

You don't have to produce an annual report, but even a short digital one can be effective for purposes of fundraising, educating others about who you are, and helping satisfy various nonprofit watchdog organizations that your group is on the up-and-up. (See "BBB Wise Giving Alliance Recommendations Regarding Annual Reports," below.)

Somewhat like a corporation's annual report, yours should concentrate on a one-year period—usually your fiscal year—and include a summary of any reports from your auditors. Also like a corporate report, your annual report will play a role in marketing your organization by giving a big-picture view of what you've been up to.

No need for a multipage, glossy report. Online-only versions are fine. Some organizations have reduced their print report to a postcard.

BBB Wise Giving Alliance Recommendations Regarding Annual Reports

The BBB Wise Giving Alliance is an industry standard-setter when it comes to nonprofit fundraising practices, disclosure, and more. Although its standards are voluntary, their widespread use as a tool by which to judge your work makes them worth heeding. The group includes the following recommendation among its standards for charitable accountability:

"[The organization shall] [h]ave an annual report available to all, on request, that includes:

- the organization's mission statement
- a summary of the past year's program service accomplishments
- a roster of the officers and members of the board of directors
- financial information that includes (i) total income in the past fiscal year, (ii) expenses in the same program, fundraising and administrative categories as in the financial statements, and (iii) ending net assets."

For the complete list of standards, see www.give.org/standards.

In addition to the BBB's recommendations, the classic annual report includes:

- **An attractive cover.** Your organization's name, as well as the year the report covers, should be clearly displayed. Include a visual image that both conveys your organization's personality and identity and makes people want to read on.
- **Message from the top executive.** A short "letter" from the executive director or chairman of the board (or both) is traditionally included near the beginning. This is the executive's chance to express his or her vision about the core message the report conveys and to remind the donor-reader about his or her key role in bringing it about.
- **Descriptions of, or better yet, stories drawn from the year's major projects or endeavors.** If you began an exciting new initiative, be sure to cover it.

- **Work that remains to be done.** No need to imply that you wrapped up all of your projects by year's end—in fact, such a message works against your ultimate fundraising interests.
- **Photos or illustrations.** Images of your organization's work (with good explanatory captions) as well as a few drawings, graphs, or charts conveying relevant information help reel in the readers.
- **Where the money came from.** Give credit to the various foundations, donors, and others who supported your organization over the past year.
- **Introduction to staff and board members.** If your organization is large, you may want to include only your key staff. In general, however, readers love to see the faces of those involved with the work, even interns or part-timers. So include lots of photos of staff if your people will agree to them.

Website and Fundraising

The checklist below gives you eight simple ways to assess your website's ability to help you raise money. If you are still in the organizational start-up phase, it will obviously be most efficient to address these various issues during the design of your website. But such strategies can help you even if your website is already up and running—particularly if it's running in the wrong direction.

CAUTION

Few websites attract random donors. If only generous people simply surfed the Web, looking for worthy organizations. But this rarely (if ever) happens. Assume that most of your website's visitors have some previous connection to your organization: a member friend, a Facebook link, or they've signed your online petition. Your website should nevertheless be ready for anyone, whether the viewer still needs a basic introduction to your organization or is looking for detailed information.

Fundraising Worksheet 10:
Check Your Website's Fundraising Effectiveness

☐ **Basic identifying information:** Does your website clearly state what your organization does, where it's located, and every possible way to get in touch with development and other staff?

☐ **Your organization's personality:** Does your website convey your organization's personality in a manner that's consistent with your fundraising and other marketing materials?

☐ **Freshness:** Does your website appear current and up to date?

☐ **Content:** Does your website present interesting content about your organization's cause?

☐ **Donation information:** Does your website lead viewers easily to information on how to donate or get involved?

☐ **Information on where the money goes:** Does your website tell donors how their money will be spent?

☐ **Funder and donor information:** Does your website find space to publicly thank funders and donors?

☐ **Tracking users:** Does your website allow you to track where viewers go within the site and how successfully you're leading them to donation or involvement options?

☐ **Optimization for searchability:** Will a Google or another search for your organization's name, or for whatever subject your group provides authoritative information on, actually bring people to your site?

Everything on your website should be easy to find—and, from a fundraising perspective, finding information about donating or otherwise getting involved should be especially easy. Visitors may have landed on your website by chance after searching for content on the Web or clicking a link on a friend's Facebook feed, or they may already have some history with your organization. Perhaps, they are catching up on an issue they care about or checking out a special event. A small but important minority might be one mental step away from donating, given the right opportunity.

At the same time, you don't want to rush people to the payment page, especially without offering them some background information about why, how, and how much to give. Give careful thought to your organization's home page, introductory donation or support page, the nondonation pages of your website, and the mechanism for online donations, all of which will help boost the ease with which viewers can fund your group—and the likelihood that they will do so.

In many of the best websites, if you click on a link called "How You Can Help," "Get Involved," "Ways to Give," or something similar, you're led to an introductory page explaining how different dollar amounts and types of gifts will help the cause, as well as other relevant links, such as "Make a Memorial Gift," "Leave a Legacy," "Events," "Donate While You Shop," and "Volunteer/Intern." Orient donors to their options—and to any premiums or benefits they'll get in return for their support—before proceeding to the bottom line.

The majority of donors worldwide prefer to give online. (The exact percentage varies by generation.) So, you'll need to be ready to receive online, as further described in Chapter 2.

TIP

If you haven't yet arranged an online donation system, tell website visitors how to donate. Whatever you do, don't skirt the issue! You can, for example, offer a downloadable page that contains all the information on your regular reply card, along with information on where to fax or mail the completed form. Such information is also useful for any website visitors who would prefer to fill out a form and send money via U.S. mail.

CAUTION

Online donors expect an immediate thank-you. Without the lag time provided by the U.S. mail, electronic donors expect to hear from you right away. Most ASPs will instantly email a message of thanks, but make sure that this is part of their packages of services. You should then follow up with a mailed thank-you letter, which looks more formal, can be customized to express a more personal message, and guarantees that the donor will have something in print for tax record keeping.

Media Outreach and Fundraising

Many organizations put no energy into media outreach, which gives you a potential edge. Media coverage can provide credibility, which can make fundraising easier. Far more media coverage than you'd imagine is generated by businesses, politicians, authors, and yes, even nonprofits that have learned to place their stories. Here's how to develop and make your own news.

Know What Makes a Good Story

A pitch that you might make to a donor—for example, "For 20 years, our organization has been offering tutoring to homeless children," is likely to fall flat with reporters. They want a story that's newsy, contains drama, is different, or, most often, is closely connected to a current issue or event.

Calling reporters to say, "I'm so-and-so; my organization is doing great work; how about a story?" won't lead to any headlines or airtime.

Most journalists will immediately ask, "What's the hook?" as they evaluate a potential story. You have to know the answer to this yourself before you pitch a story.

Here's how Nick Parker, former communications director at the California School Age Consortium put it: "When I worked in the film industry, we had to condense ideas for a movie into one sentence, like, 'The earth's computers have been taken over by aliens, and humans have 24 hours to get them back before our planet is blown up.' Getting a nonprofit-generated story into the media is not much different: You've got to be able to quickly sum up the central conflict in a way that grabs their attention."

A true hook, for a news story or any other kind, involves a shift in how the audience views the world. Common hooks involve conflict, shock, laughter, something new and different in your community, identification of a trend, a marking of time, such as with an anniversary or holiday, or a "first," such as the first person to be cured of a disease, or the first sighting of a supposedly extinct bird.

Something that just happened in your organization, such as receiving a small grant, may be big news to you. But it's not necessarily interesting enough to hook anyone else's attention. If it was a huge grant, however, with which you will build a new community center, that may warrant at least local coverage. Kids and animals also seem to be perennially interesting to the public.

No matter the current media mood, certain stories are always difficult to pitch and gain coverage for. One is the depiction of the endless train of human suffering: endemic hunger, disease, and injustice all over the world. Compassion fatigue is common.

Also consider how to present your facts or findings in a light that will make others appreciate their significance. The Straphangers Campaign does this well, with its annual "Pokey Award" (a golden snail on a pedestal) given to NYC's slowest bus. (The group advocates for improved public transportation on behalf of subway and bus riders.) In describing the bus that "won" 2018, the M42, the group cleverly noted that "it moved far slower at 3.2 miles per hour than the pace at which a chicken can run (nine miles per hour)." (See www.straphangers.org for more information and links to its press releases.)

How the Traditional Media Categorizes Stories

Though virtually every potential story needs a hook, you also need to recognize the different categories of stories that the media feature. For your purposes, the three most important include:

- breaking news
- feature stories, and
- arts or other events.

Breaking news is what it sounds like—something that's in the headlines. Journalists who work in this area tend to be news junkies who think everything else is mere fluff. A nonprofit can make its own breaking news. For example, your group's successful boycott of a corporation's products resulting in its decision to stop using an endangered type of Southeast Asian hardwood is newsworthy. A demonstration or protest is always news; although whether it's big or interesting enough to cover might be questionable. Releasing a study or report can be news, especially if your conclusions shock or break new ground.

Alternatively, you can tie your work or insights to a story that's already in the news. For example, if one of your elderly nursing home clients attempts suicide, that's probably not news by itself. But if you can legitimately present it as part of a pattern of suicides caused by gaps in public health care benefits and patients' fears of being kicked out of nursing homes, you've got yourself a news story.

Feature stories are a different animal and are usually handled by a different set of journalists. Though feature stories may tie into news of the moment, they usually offer more background and reflection on their subject, and go on at greater length.

Nearly every type of media devotes separate attention to **arts, literary, and social events**. These might include everything from the opening of your nonprofit's fall music or theatre season to a small lecture, dinner, or garden tour—though you'll find that some media outlets report only on events of a certain size or perceived quality, or want to know whether any "big names" will be in attendance. (If anyone famous does attend your event, be sure to get photos for after-the-fact coverage.)

If you ask for coverage of an arts or theatre event, you may have to open yourself up to the world of critics, with their ability to make or break a show's success—but even criticism is a form of publicity. You'll find more about how to invite the press to attend your events later in this chapter.

Who to Approach With Your Story

Let's assume now that you've got a story with a great hook that's just dying to be told. Now you need to decide whom to contact, and understand how the media is organized to accept stories.

Your first step is simply to watch, read, and listen. Observe what types of stories the media serving your area cover, and who's writing or producing them. Don't forget special interest and ethnic papers, free weeklies or monthlies, neighborhood papers, community association newsletters, and magazines and newsletters produced by other nonprofits or public-oriented groups. Take notes or develop a file or document showing how their interests might dovetail with your group's. Also notice what they don't cover, and don't expect to change that.

Print Media Contact Persons

At a newspaper, your contact point is probably either a reporter, for straight news stories, or a columnist, for feature stories. Check the "bylines" on stories that look similar to ones that you'd like to place. The writer may be on staff, a freelancer, or may be from another paper, such as *The Los Angeles Times*, through syndication. (Or you may see no name at all, because the article came from a wire service such as the Associated Press (AP) or Reuters.)

On big-city newspapers, reporters and columnists are assigned a particular topic area or "beat," such as arts, education, environment, food, religion, or city/community issues. If you follow the stories on issues similar to those that your nonprofit would like to weigh in on, you'll see the same names popping up regularly.

> **TIP**
> **Your nonprofit can be covered in the business section.** Business reporters are often hungry to cover something more interesting than the bottom line. For example, an organization that rehabilitates drug addicts by offering training in how to cook for—and run—a restaurant, is likely to attract the attention of the newspaper's business journalists. And, your nonprofit is itself a sort of business, so its creative strategies for success may inspire media interest.

As a non-news alternative, you might offer the newspaper an editorial or op-ed piece, in which case, you would separately contact the editorial page staff. Also look for newspapers that have regular opinion columnists (although many editorials are provided by national news syndicates). They're always looking for something new to opine about—try a quick phone call, followed up by your expert factual materials.

Magazines tend to rely on submissions, often approved in advance, from freelance writers. Many freelancers regularly work for the same publications, however, so if you see a name appearing often, that person is probably your best contact.

Radio Contact Persons

At a radio station, your contact point depends on the type of show. For news shows, reporters or news directors are your best bet. (Listen carefully, though—many stations license news programs from larger outlets, such as National Public Radio (NPR) or the BBC, which means they're less open to locally generated news.) Keep your ears open for the local shows, especially those with a one-hour format.

For public affairs or talk shows, the host is rarely the best one to contact—especially for more popular shows, it's the producer's job to select and schedule guests. Often the producer's name is mentioned briefly at the end of each show or can be found on the station's website. If you can find a producer interested in your line of stories, you're in good shape, because he or she might keep your group's experts' names on file for future shows.

If a leader or an expert from your organization will be visiting another city, think about contacting radio journalists there, as well. Although telephone technology allows you to be interviewed from anywhere in the world, the sound quality and general ambience aren't nearly as good as if you are there in person.

Television Contact Persons

At a television station, whom to contact depends on the type of show and the size of the station. You'll probably have the best luck with local stations. If you're seeking rapid attention to breaking news, such as the birth of an endangered bird in captivity, track down contact information for the "assignment desk"—that's where producers tell their crews, "Go to this location, now."

For news events with more lead time, you'd normally contact the planning desk or assignment editor. Some television programs have less news-oriented formats—for example, focusing on consumer affairs, local events, or travel. If you're interested in placing a story with one of these, get in touch with a producer of that show.

A number of local television stations also offer community event alerts. Call the station or check its website for submission guidelines and eligibility rules.

Educate Know-Nothing Hosts

In both radio and television, many show hosts—often called "talent" by real journalists—aren't personally familiar with the stories they cover. Though they may look good, sound good, and project an aura of celebrity, they won't even have read your press packet. A friend of mine had long respected a San Francisco television talk show host—but when he finally appeared on her show, was dismayed to hear her ask, with just a few minutes to air time, "So, what are we talking about today?"

Fortunately, unprepared hosts are a problem only if you aren't ready for them. Your best bet is to fully cooperate with the producers, to get them excited about the topic, and to help them develop materials and questions that will prepare the host to sound like an informed expert.

 TIP

Alert your supporters and colleagues to your organization's media appearances. If someone from your organization will be appearing on television or radio, it's a perfect time to email your members and post heads-ups on social media. For radio call-in shows, ask them to phone in with questions—to tip the balance against less sympathetic callers!

Online Media Contact Persons

A world of media outlets exists on the Internet, from professional news outlets offering some extras on the side to individual authors or consultants seeking to get their name out. With some noodling around, you should be able to find out the popular websites or bloggers in your area or addressing your issue, and pitch stories to them.

> ### TIP
> **Make your in-house experts available on short notice.** When news breaks, journalists often need to reach experts in minutes or, at most, an hour or two. If you can put your the experts' cell phone and home phone numbers onto local reporters' contact lists, you are far more likely to see their names—and the name of your organization—in the news.

Drafting Press Releases

Anyone can write and send a press release; you need no special credentials or invitations. Simply write up the story you want to convey, preferably in one or two pages, and send it out while it's still fresh and interesting. If you've got some spare minutes, tweak your basic wording to fit the interests of your different news targets.

Craft your release to grab the reader's attention within a few seconds. All journalists receive more press releases than they can read or cover, and they leave many unopened.

> ### TIP
> **Your press releases can do double duty.** Publish them on your website, within the "Press" or "About Us" section. You'll give Web viewers a sense that your organization is a happening place. The press release's long-term availability there will also help educate the broader public and any journalists later doing research.

Formatting and Drafting Your Press Release

For the format for a printed press release, see the template below (also online; see the appendix for the link) and the sample following that, an actual press release from Save the Redwoods League (www.savetheredwoods.org) announcing a kid's art contest. Notice how the release presents key facts, the organization's mission, and a quotable quote, all within a page.

View From the Radio Newsroom

Harry Lin, former news anchor at KQED, an NPR affiliate station in San Francisco, tells the following about the many press releases he received from nonprofit organizations: "Since we covered local news on a daily basis, we received press releases from nonprofits all the time. Much of my daily routine, in fact, was sifting through releases ... deciding which ones to toss, which ones to file as 'just background info,' which ones to give reporters to follow up on, and which ones got tacked to our communal bulletin board so that we could all laugh at them. All of which is to say that news organizations are swamped every day with releases, so to cut through the clutter and stand out is not easy. However: No matter how flashy or elaborate one's release, you can bet that someone else sent in something even flashier. So, the trick to getting noticed isn't to send in the wackiest, weirdest, loudest, most unorthodox release.

"For example, I can still remember the freshly baked icing-covered chocolate cake that was messengered to our newsroom one morning accompanied by a press release about ... well, I can't remember what the press release was about, but we ate the cake in two seconds flat, and no, we didn't attend the event the release was touting.

"The most important factor is actually the most basic: The headline must be relevant, intriguing, timely, and newsworthy. News organizations aren't interested in anything that smells old, already-happened, or historical."

As mentioned in "View From the Radio Newsroom," above, you should spend some time on the title of the release. This doesn't mean being so clever that you obfuscate the meaning—but it also doesn't mean a tired-sounding scholarly title.

Journalists love to lift words straight from press releases, to help them meet their ever-looming deadlines. To increase your chances of publication, write the body of your release in the same style you see in newspaper articles. It's best to start with a colorful story or set of facts, move to the background information, and wrap it up quickly with a snappy closing line.

Press Release Template

[Your organization's name; preferably with logo]
FOR IMMEDIATE RELEASE

Contact: *[Name of one or preferably two persons they can call]*

[Date]

[Phone number of contacts]

[Email address of contacts]

[Centered title of press release, in larger font]

[Your state, in capital letters, such as "OKLAHOMA"]

[Text of press release, in short paragraphs, ending with a brief description of your organization and where to obtain more information, such as on your website.]

[traditional signal of end of text]

Save the Redwoods League Press Release

PRESS RELEASE

Contact: Jennifer Benito, Outreach Director, (415) 820-5814 or jbenito@SaveTheRedwoods.org

Save the Redwoods League Launches National Art Contest to Encourage Kids to Protect Redwoods

SAN FRANCISCO (September 7, 2012) – Save the Redwoods League, the only nonprofit organization dedicated to protecting redwood forests throughout their natural range, **today announced its third annual redwoods art contest for kids**. The League's **Find Me in the Redwoods art contest** is a simple way to encourage America's students to have fun, connect with nature and help protect one of our country's most iconic natural wonders.

Beginning September 10, K–12 students across the nation are invited to create a work of art that features them **playing, learning or exploring** redwoods. Their art will help Save the Redwoods League raise awareness of redwood forests. Students can draw, paint or sketch their way toward a chance to win fabulous redwoods prizes while learning about the tallest and some of the oldest and largest living things on Earth.

"Save the Redwoods League's **Find Me in the Redwoods** art contest uniquely combines art, science and civic participation, while encouraging students to protect redwood forestlands," said Jennifer Benito, outreach director for Save the Redwoods League, "This contest is a wonderful way to encourage children to have fun, be creative, connect with nature and help protect a natural wonder."

Contestants compete in the following three grade categories: K–3, 4–8 and 9–12. **Winners will be announced on November 15** via email and on the League's website. Winning entries will also be showcased in League publications. **All artwork will be mailed to Ken Salazar, Secretary of the U.S. Department of Interior.** Salazar is in charge of protecting America's great outdoors. **Teachers also win.** Educators associated with the first-place winners will win fabulous redwood prizes. The hope is to inspire teachers to educate students about the wonders of the redwood forests.

All entries must be mailed or hand-delivered to Save the Redwoods League, 114 Sansome Street, 12th floor, San Francisco, California, 94104, Attn: Redwoods Art Contest by **October 19, 2012, 5 p.m. US Pacific Time.** No late submissions will be accepted. No fee is required to enter the contest. Spanish and English entry forms will be available online on **Monday, September 10**.

Prizes generously donated by Balloons Above the Valley; Cavallo Point, The Lodge at the Golden Gate; FolkManis Puppets; Mount Hermon Redwood Canopy Tours; Redwoods & Rivers Rafting; REI; Sequoia Park Zoo; and Skunk Train. Media sponsored by the Bay Area News Group

About Save the Redwoods League
Walk through a redwood forest—home of the tallest, largest, and some of the oldest living beings on Earth—and you can't help but feel an overwhelming sense of awe and peace among these magnificent giants. Since 1918, Save the Redwoods League has led the effort to protect the coast redwoods and giant sequoias for all to experience and enjoy. To date the League has completed the purchase of more than 190,000 acres of redwood forest and associated land. For more information, please visit SaveTheRedwoods.org, or to receive monthly email updates, sign up at SaveTheRedwoods.org/signup.

###

114 Sansome Street, Suite 1200, San Francisco, California 94104-3823
Telephone (415) 362-2352 I Facsimile (415) 362-7017 I website SaveTheRedwoods.org

WALK AMONG GIANTSSM

Don't forget to include the "five W's" early on—what, when, where, who, and why. Don't use long sentences or ponderous words—the person reading your release may be skimming it amid the noise and bustle of a newsroom. Most news sources figure that their audience members haven't finished high school, so eloquent literary language is not what they're looking for.

> **TIP**
> **Line up colorful interviews in advance.** Because reporters know that people like to read about people, most feature stories rely on anecdotes about— and quotes from—real folks. Thus, if your press release is about a summer program that teaches wilderness skills to inner-city kids, you'll want to include some names, photos, and contact information about your star pupils. And don't forget to prep them so they say something appropriate should a reporter call.

Sending Out Your Press Release

Once you've prepared a catchy press release, don't just send it out scattershot. The evening news doesn't want to hear about your upcoming garage sale fundraiser, unless it's of a truly staggering size. Your community newspaper, however, might be willing to give it a mention. You'll preserve your credibility with the press by demonstrating that you send only stories that fit their areas of interest. (You'd be amazed at how many people don't follow this rule, so journalists tend to get swamped and stop reading the releases of the serial senders.)

Different outlets have different schedules, and it can be just as bad to send something too early as too late. If you're targeting daily news outlets, they work a day or three ahead, tops. If you send a release about something you want covered two or three weeks from now, you'll be long forgotten once that time rolls around.

On the other hand, feature stories and talk-radio interviews often need a week or two of advance notice. Monthly magazines often need a lead time of three months, and they sometimes want high-quality photos to go with your story, so plan and send accordingly. As you establish contact with members of the media, ask about their schedules.

Sending not only a press release but a whole "press packet" can convince the journalist to pursue the story. You might add:

- photos (high-resolution and available for reprinting)
- a pamphlet about your organization
- the text of an interview with or a speech by one of your leaders or experts, and
- copies of previous articles about your organization.

If you have hard-to-send materials, such as podcasts or videos, add a tip sheet explaining where to find these online.

There are several ways to send your press release. The traditional printed, mailed copy is still used by some, and still effective. Email is good for getting the word out quickly, but it is also easy for journalists to delete or ignore. You may want to combine snail mail with email. One journalist told me that he always opened press release packages sent via Federal Express or another courier first, even though he knew that the extra expense didn't necessarily translate into a better story.

Because you never know what's getting read and what's getting tossed, it's a good idea to follow up on your press release with a phone call, particularly to journalists whom you know should be interested in the story. Ask whether they saw your release, take a few seconds to pitch the story and make it sound exciting, and be ready to send another copy right away.

TIP

There are times when a full press release isn't appropriate. For example, maybe you've got a simple tidbit of colorful information or gossip—such as a tip regarding a natural event or a local politician—to pass on to an interested journalist. Or perhaps you're watching an event that merits immediate media attention—a beached whale, or a face-off between demonstrators at your family planning clinic, for example. Don't waste time writing a press release—just call, text, Tweet, or send an urgent email.

Publicity and Press Invitations for Special Events

An event that your organization sponsors or participates in is, by its very nature, "news." Whether it's interesting news is another matter—a theater piece will probably attract wider attention than your annual spring car wash. If you think your event is sufficiently colorful, will attract enough people, or fits an existing media outlet's area of interest, then by all means send out press releases and get in touch with your favorite media professionals to get the word out.

Many media outlets also collect information on events for their entertainment or community calendars. Find out who carries these, their criteria for submission, and—perhaps most important—how far in advance you need to advise them of the event.

The best way to get journalists to pay attention to your event is to invite some of them to attend—for free, of course. If your group or event is large enough, you might even set up a separate press night, prescreening, or the like (they'll love it if you include free food). Don't just send press members a stack of tickets, or you won't know how many to expect. Instead, contact selected journalists and ask them to contact you for free tickets or a press pass. Offer two tickets to each journalist, so that he or she can bring a companion—few people like to attend an event alone.

Will a journalist who attends your event necessarily do a story about it? No. Many consider freebie invites to be a perk of their no-doubt low-paying job. But even if no story is forthcoming, this is a valuable way to build relationships.

TIP

Hosting a benefit concert or another musical event? Invite radio DJs. Local stations may be interested in playing music by the group you're featuring, along with mentioning the upcoming event on the air. If you offer the DJ free tickets and CDs for audience giveaways, your odds of coverage go up even higher.

Hosting Members of the Press at Events

When inviting members of the press to theater, musical, or other major events, it's customary to ask them to pick up their ticket at "will call" or, if enough journalists will be attending, at a special "press table," usually in the lobby. When they arrive, you can give them not only a ticket and program, but also a "press packet"—a folder with additional background information, and copies of any other media coverage. Having a press table also gives you an opportunity to make personal contact and gently nudge the journalists about when and whether they're planning to feature your event or the artists or other participants—with the emphasis on gently. Mostly, you should just be welcoming. If it's a sit-down event, and seats aren't otherwise assigned, be sure to reserve seats for the journalists. They don't have to be in the very front row, but seat them close enough to appreciate what's going on.

Drafting Letters to the Editor and Op-Ed Pieces

Letters to newspaper and magazine editors and op-ed (opinion-editorial) pieces are great ways to demonstrate your organization's expertise and to affect public opinion (or perhaps correct the public record) on issues of importance. And, the piece will be all in your own words (probably minus a few after it goes past an editor), unmediated by the bias or boredom of a reporter.

Letters to the editor are shots in the dark—you'll have to prepare and send them with little or no guarantee that they'll get printed. To increase your odds, carefully follow the publication's guidelines, particularly the word count. The upper limit is often 200 words. It also helps to send a letter when your topic is in the news. And whether or not it's printed, you can put it on your website or Facebook page.

Op-ed pieces are slightly different—they run to around 700 words and are usually given a special spot on a newspaper's editorial page, essentially as a guest editorial. For this reason, it's best to contact the editor of the relevant page in advance. Your chances of acceptance are best if you're willing to take a reasonably controversial (but not totally wacky) stand on an issue.

Protecting Your Nonprofit in Media Interactions

Here are the primary sources of difficulty you might encounter in working with the media:

- **You may spend a lot of time for little reward.** For example, never agree to write large portions of text for a print journalist without a mention of your organization's name. Also, be wary of freelance journalists who are shopping an article to publications without a firm commitment. Either way, you can spend many hours with no payoff.

- **The article or piece may be careless, wrong, or unflattering.** Print journalists are famous for talking to you by phone, scribbling down notes, then putting quotation marks around something that you don't remember saying. In any personal interviews, try to speak slowly and carefully, avoid sarcasm or parodies that could be quoted out of context, and never, ever, say anything "off the record" if you don't want to see it in print.

- **You won't be sent a copy.** People commonly ask journalists for copies or tapes of the final piece, but unless you're famous or the journalist owes you a favor, you'll likely find that both the journalist and the media outlet are too busy to provide it. Try to find out when the piece will be run, and then follow the news yourself, (an ongoing Google alert for your name should help). Some larger television and radio stations allow you to buy copies of shows.

- **You may be surprised at whose side the journalist was really on.** Especially if your organization does controversial work, you can be sure that some of the reporters who call will be taking the other side. They may try to bait you with innocent-sounding questions like, "Wouldn't you like to tell your side of the story," or "I'm very interested in why you believe such and such."

With good planning and care about who you agree to speak with, you should be able to develop relationships with a select list of media professionals who are accessible, interested in your work, and can be counted on not to misuse your time and trust.

TIP

Track and save any favorable articles. Good media coverage is worth its weight in gold for establishing your credibility with funders and prospective donors. You can send these pieces out with mailings, reprint them in your newsletters (after getting permission of course, to avoid copyright violations), mention and link to them on your website, and attach copies to grant proposals.

Making Your Own News: Social Media

Nonprofits that successfully participate in social media (such as Facebook, Twitter, and Instagram) raise their profiles and public awareness. This leads to interest and engagement (such as volunteer participation) and perhaps to one-time donations from people spurred on by a friend. Some experts describe social media postings as a sort of bait, which nonprofits drop in order to encourage potential donors to self-identify, allowing your organization to send them more personalized messages.

All of this may eventually lead to some long-term support from donors who wouldn't have found or maintained interest in the group otherwise. Establishing a voice and developing an audience takes time, however.

TIP

Say goodbye to your inner control freak. As Jennifer Gennari, consultant and former Communications Director at Greenbelt Alliance explains, "The casual nature of Facebook and Twitter is a shift for communications and development professionals, who are used to very carefully monitoring every word and every image when talking about our work. In my case, I started out thinking, 'How much oversight will I need to have about what gets posted?' And then I realized I should stop worrying. The social network scene is by definition casual, and within 24 hours, most everyone has moved on to the next hot tweet."

Your nonprofit will also need to be systematic in its postings, ideally developing a policy that covers:

- **Who will post content.** Although you'll want to gather suggestions from a wide range of people, it can be wise to choose only one or two to handle actual postings. That avoids overlaps or long hiatuses between postings. Choose an experienced member of your organization, not an intern who is "young, and gets how to use this stuff."

- **What voice and tone your nonprofit wants to convey.** Not stiff and boring, obviously. But look at other organizations' posts to see what you admire and what sounds strident, inappropriate, or immature. Use these insights to create guidance for your in-house social networkers.

- **An annual content calendar—with room for shifts based on current events.** This should show all the important events happening both within your nonprofit (such as appeal mailings and special events) and outside (such as holidays or commemorative days, which often provide tie-ins for thematic postings). Plan ahead for posts to issue (or hold back on) at specific times. Also plan to be flexible, however. In the event of a disaster or other major news occurrence, you don't want to be the only organization obliviously posting cute kitten photos.

- **How and when other staff will report on specific topics.** Your networkers might want to hear, for example, about volunteer activities, progress on advocacy, rescue, or other work, funding, and so forth. Formalizing this information exchange will provide a regular feed of potentially good material. (Also see Chapter 2 for advice on fostering communication and storytelling within the organization.) Some nonprofits offer personal insights into the lives of their staff, for example posting fun photos about how they decorate their workspace, or photos of their pets.

- **Encourage picture taking by staff and volunteers (if appropriate).** Photos and videos tend to pick up more "likes" than plain text. For example, the Berkeley East Bay Humane Society once sent a message asking its volunteers to send in photos and videos to be used on social media: "Everything from dog play groups, to cat cuddling, to snuggling with recovering surgery patients, to you all being your awesome selves…."
- **Plan to post regularly.** At least once a week is optimal and will keep your existence in readers' minds. More is even better!

As your audience responds, you'll start to get a sense of what works and what doesn't, and can refine your strategy accordingly. Susan Messina notes that when she was with the National Hospice Foundation, "We often got the greatest Facebook response to questions of all types, whether open-ended, true/false, or a quiz. For example, I've asked, 'If you've been with someone when they died, what would you say to others who haven't yet had that experience?' It was an intense question, but it brought in amazing answers, such as, 'I wouldn't miss it…. There is a quiet and a peace that fills the room' and 'I was there when my dad died, and I know the last thing he heard was my voice.' In fact, we got multichannel use from this question because I wrote it up, with a sampling of the answers, for our next newsletter."

CAUTION
For staff, create guidelines (but not outright mandates) on the amount of time that's appropriate to spend on personal social networking sites while at work. Add other appropriate cautions, like "Be aware of the damage you could do to our nonprofit's reputation by complaining about your boss or long work hours on the same site where you ask people to attend a fundraising event."

Two-way communication does not end the day you publish the post. Someone needs to go back to the site regularly to see what responses have come in, and then possibly respond to them. Sometimes all you need to do is to say thank you to someone who openly admires your work.

Other times you'll face more difficult conversations. Treatment organizations, for example, sometimes become aware of a person in need of services via a social network comment. They may then post a response inviting the person to contact them.

You may also receive comments from critics or people who've come a bit unhinged. The same rules here apply as in personal communications—take a deep breath, remember that whatever you write will live on the Web for years, and don't press "send" when mad. Fortunately, many nonprofits report that they find they don't need to do a thing about "haters"—their supporters step in to defend them.

CAUTION

Avoid copyright violations. Contrary to popular belief, photos and other content found online are not free for the taking. You can link to other people's work, and share photos circulating on Facebook and the like, but uploading a photo for your nonprofit's use is a no-no unless you've either gotten permission or ascertained that it's already in the public domain. For more information, see the free articles on the "Patent, Copyright & Trademark" section of Nolo.com.

How to Use the Downloadable Forms on the Nolo Website

This book comes with downloadable files that you can access online at:

www.nolo.com/back-of-book/EFFN.html

To use the files, your computer must have specific software programs installed. Here is a list of the types of files provided by this book, as well as the software programs you'll need to access them.

You can open, edit, save, and print the RTF files provided by this book using most word processing programs such as Microsoft *Word*, Windows *WordPad*, and recent versions of *WordPerfect*.

Editing RTFs

Here are some general instructions about editing RTF forms in your word processing program. Refer to the book's instructions and sample agreements for help about what should go in each blank.

Underlines. Underlines indicate where to enter information. After filling in the needed text, delete the underline. In most word processing programs you can do this by highlighting the underlined portion and typing CTRL-U.

Bracketed and italicized text. Bracketed and italicized text indicates instructions. Be sure to remove all instructional text before you finalize your document.

Optional text. Optional text gives you the choice to include or exclude text. Delete any optional text you don't want to use. Renumber numbered items, if necessary.

Signature lines. Signature lines should appear on a page with at least some text from the document itself.

Every word processing program uses different commands to open, format, save, and print documents, so refer to your software's help documents for help using your program. Nolo cannot provide technical support for questions about how to use your computer or your software.

CAUTION

In accordance with U.S. copyright laws, the forms provided by this book are for your personal use only.

List of Forms Available on the Nolo Website

To download any of the files listed on the following pages go to:

www.nolo.com/back-of-book/EFFN.html

Form Title	File Name
Sample Cost Analysis	SampleCost.rtf
Fundraising Assets	FundAssets.rtf
Fundraising Strategy Chart	FundStrat.rtf
Mailing Evaluation	MailEvaluation.rtf
Meeting Checklist	MtgChecklist.rtf
Projected Special Event Expenses	SpEventExp.rtf
Projected Special Event Income	SpEventIncome.rtf
Grant Priorities Summary Chart	GrantPrior.rtf
Grant Prospect Summary	ProspectsSum.rtf
Check Your Website's Fundraising Effectiveness	WebsiteFund.rtf
Press Release Template	PressRelease.rtf

Index

Nolo.com offers a large library of legal solutions and forms, created by Nolo's in-house legal editors. These reliable documents can be prepared in minutes.

Create a Document Online

Incorporation. Incorporate your business in any state.

LLC Formation. Gain asset protection and pass-through tax status in any state.

Will. Nolo has helped people make over 2 million wills. Is it time to make or revise yours?

Living Trust (avoid probate). Plan now to save your family the cost, delays, and hassle of probate.

Provisional Patent. Preserve your right to obtain a patent by claiming "patent pending" status.

Download Useful Legal Forms

Nolo.com has hundreds of top quality legal forms available for download:

- bill of sale
- promissory note
- nondisclosure agreement
- LLC operating agreement
- corporate minutes
- commercial lease and sublease
- motor vehicle bill of sale
- consignment agreement
- and many more.

www.nolo.com

△△ NOLO   *Save 15%* *off your next order*

Register your Nolo purchase, and we'll send you a **coupon for 15% off** your next Nolo.com order!

Nolo.com/customer-support/productregistration

On Nolo.com you'll also find:

Books & Software

Nolo publishes hundreds of great books and software programs for consumers and business owners. Order a copy, or download an ebook version instantly, at Nolo.com.

Online Forms

You can quickly and easily make a will or living trust, form an LLC or corporation, apply for a provisional patent, or make hundreds of other forms—online.

Free Legal Information

Thousands of articles answer common questions about everyday legal issues, including wills, bankruptcy, small business formation, divorce, patents, employment, and much more.

Plain-English Legal Dictionary

Stumped by jargon? Look it up in America's most up-to-date source for definitions of legal terms, free at Nolo.com.

Lawyer Directory

Nolo's consumer-friendly lawyer directory provides in-depth profiles of lawyers all over America. You'll find information you need to choose the right lawyer.

EFFN6